You Have
the Words *of*
Eternal Life

*Reflections on the
weekday readings for the
liturgical year 2020~2021*

MARTIN HOGAN

Designed by Messenger Publications Design Department
Typeset in Times New Roman & DIN Condensed
Cover image: ESB Professional / Shutterstock
Printed by Hussar Books

Messenger Publications,
37 Leeson Place, Dublin D02 E5V0
www.messenger.ie

INTRODUCTION

This book contains a short reflection on the readings for each of the weekdays of the liturgical year which begins with the first Sunday of Advent 2020, and concludes with the feast of Christ the King 2021. The reflections relate primarily to the gospel readings but they also embrace the first reading at times. On the weekdays of any liturgical year, we read from a large proportion of all four gospels, with the Gospels of Matthew, Mark and Luke featuring especially in Ordinary Time, and John's Gospel featuring more prominently in the seasons of Lent and, especially, Easter. I hope that these reflections will be of help to priests who like to share a short reflection on the weekday readings at Mass and that they will also be a resource to parishioners who like to base their daily prayer on the weekday readings of the liturgy. I have been told that in parishes where a Liturgy of the Word occasionally replaces the daily celebration of the Eucharist, the Minister of the Word reads aloud the corresponding reflection after the readings.

The apostolic exhortation issued by Pope Benedict XVI after the Synod on the Word of God in 2010 states that 'the liturgy is the privileged setting in which God speaks to us in the midst of our lives; he speaks today to his people, who hear and respond' (*Verbum Domini*,52), and it goes on to state that 'Christ, truly present under the species of bread and wine, is analogously present in the word proclaimed in the liturgy' (VD, 56). At every Mass we are fed both from the table of the word and the table of the Eucharist. Prayerful reflection on the readings to be proclaimed at Mass disposes us to receive the word as bread of life more fruitfully when it is offered to us in the liturgy. In this regard, the post-synodal exhortation states, 'prayerful reading, personal and communal, prepares for, accompanies and deepens what the Church celebrates when she proclaims the word in a liturgical setting' (VD, 86).

The title for this book of reflections is taken from what is often referred to as 'the Bread of Life discourse' in chapter 6 of John's Gospel. As that discourse progresses, it is clear that the language of 'bread' acquires clear Eucharistic overtones, as when Jesus says, 'The bread that I will give for the life of the world is my flesh' (John 6:51), and then goes on to declare that 'those who eat my flesh and drink my blood have eternal life' (John 6:55). However, earlier in the discourse Jesus' way of speaking of himself as the bread of life evokes the figure of Woman Wisdom in the Wisdom Literature of the Jewish Scriptures, which is also the background to the portrayal of Jesus as the Word of God become flesh in John's Gospel. It is as the Wisdom or Word of God that Jesus says 'I am the bread of life. Whoever comes to me will never be hungry, and whoever believes in me will never be thirsty' (John 6:35). The words of Jesus, including those words that are explicitly Eucharistic, are truly life-giving, satisfying the deepest hunger and thirst of the human heart. As Jesus goes on to declare, 'the words that I have spoken to you are spirit and life' (John 6:63). At the very moment when some of Jesus' disciples 'turned back and no longer went about with him' (John 6:66), Peter, as the spokesperson for the Twelve, acknowledges the life-giving power of Jesus' words, 'Lord, to whom can we go? You have the words of eternal life' (John 6:68).

As so often in the gospels, Peter speaks for us all here. It is my hope that these reflections will help you, in some small way, to appreciate the Word of the Lord as words of eternal life.

30 November, Feast of Saint Andrew

Matthew 4:18–22

In the list of the twelve apostles, Andrew always comes second, after his brother Peter. He is overshadowed somewhat by his more prominent brother, who became the leading member of the church that was formed after Jesus' death and resurrection. The gospel reading refers to Simon, who was called Peter, and his brother, Andrew. The siblings of well-known people can easily become defined by their relationship to the better-known member of the family, 'the brother or the sister of … '. Yet, in the Gospel of John, it was Andrew who brought Peter to Jesus. According to the first chapter of that gospel, Andrew was a disciple of John the Baptist, and he and one other disciple of John the Baptist were the first to spend time in Jesus' company. Having spent a day with Jesus, Andrew found his brother Simon Peter and declared excitedly to him, 'We have found the Messiah'. He then brought Simon Peter to Jesus who, looking upon Simon, said to him, 'You are Simon, son of John. You are to be called "Peter".' Even though Peter went on to have a more significant role in the Church than Andrew, it was Andrew who had the more significant role at the beginning. Indeed, without Andrew's role in Peter's life at that time, Peter would not have gone on to become the great pastoral leader he was. The Lord has a role for each one of us and that role is vitally important, even if it seems less prominent than other people's roles. There is something that the Lord wants each of us to do that no one else can do. Sometimes, the role he is calling us to take on is that of the enabler, as in the case of Andrew, who enabled Peter to begin his faith journey, which went on to bear such rich fruit for the Church. Even though Andrew lived in the shadow of Peter somewhat, without Andrew the Church would not have known Peter. The role of enabler is one of those modest, humble roles in the Lord's work that is, nonetheless, hugely significant. If we find ourselves being called to play that role at some point in our lives, we are indeed blessed.

1 December, Tuesday, First Week of Advent

Luke 10:21–24

In the gospel reading, Jesus draws a contrast between 'the learned and the clever' and 'mere children'. He says that children are better than the learned and clever at grasping what he has come to reveal about God. Jesus came to reveal God's hospitable love for all. He is uniquely placed to reveal God, because, as he says in the gospel reading, 'no one knows who the Father is except the Son'. The Son knows God the Father intimately, yet Jesus struggled to make God known to those who thought of themselves as learned and clever in the ways of God, such as the experts in the Jewish Law. In contrast, those who would have been considered ignorant of the law of God, the ways of God, responded to what Jesus had to say about God with delight and excitement. Many of those went on to become his disciples, like Matthew the tax collector, and various fishermen, all of whom would have been thought of as ignorant of God's ways as revealed in God's Law, mere infants in the faith. Addressing these disciples, Jesus says in the gospel reading, 'Happy the eyes that see what you see … to hear what you hear'. These are the people who have seen what Jesus was showing them, and heard what Jesus was saying, in contrast to those regarded by themselves and others as learned and clever in the ways of God. The first beatitude Jesus speaks in Matthew's Gospel is, 'blessed are the poor in spirit, for theirs is the kingdom of heaven'. Elsewhere Jesus says that unless we become like little children we will not enter the kingdom of heaven. There is a poverty of spirit, a childlike quality, that is needed if we are to receive and welcome all that the Lord is offering us. What is the Lord offering us? According to today's gospel reading, he is offering us nothing less than a share in his own intimate relationship with God, 'no one knows … '. We need something of the openness of the child, of the poor in spirit, if the Lord's amazing desire for us is to come to pass.

2 December, Wednesday, First Week of Advent

Matthew 15:29–37

Today's first reading from Isaiah is often chosen as the first reading for a funeral Mass. It is a vision of a great feast on a mountain at which the Lord is host and from which all mourning and death have been banished for ever. It is truly a feast of life. It is a vision that anticipates much of what we find in the gospels. Jesus often spoke of the kingdom of heaven, the kingdom of God's life, as a great feast to which people from north, south, east and west would come. In today's gospel reading Jesus provides a feast of life in the wilderness. It was an unexpected feast because the resources available for the feast were so few, seven loaves and a few small fish. Yet, Jesus worked powerfully through those meagre resources. The evangelist understood that feast as an anticipation of the Eucharist, where again the Lord works powerfully through meagre resources, offering us his body and blood under the simple form of bread and wine. The Church has always understood the Eucharist, in turn, as an anticipation of the great banquet of eternal life to which people from north, south, east and west will come. The Eucharist, like the banquet of the first reading and of the gospel reading, like the final banquet of God's kingdom, is a feast of life, and we are sent from the Eucharist to promote life in all its forms. Sometimes this will mean working with what seem like scant resources. Yet, today's gospel reading reminds us that the Lord can work powerfully through the little we have, if it is given to him with a generous spirit.

3 December, Thursday, First Week of Advent

Matthew 7:21, 24–27

In more recent decades we have become more aware of how houses can easily get built in places where they should never have been built, such as the flood plains of rivers. When houses are built on flood plains, it can often give rise to flooding further down the river. We have also become aware that faulty material has gone into the foundations of houses, resulting eventually in walls cracking and the whole house becoming unstable. It is vital to get the foundations of a house right, both in terms of the materials in the foundations and where the foundations are laid. It was no different in the time of Jesus. Houses were sometimes built in a way that was suited to the dry, hot, summer climate of the Near East, but left them exposed to the winter winds and rains, because their foundations were not laid down with winter conditions in mind. The foundations rested on sand rather than rock. Jesus sees in this shoddy building practice a message for our lives. Not just our houses, but our lives need to be built on firm foundations. Jesus declares his word to be the firmest foundation we can build our lives on, not just listening to his word, but putting his word into practice, living by his word. When we heed Jesus' words and live according to his teaching, we are building the house of our lives on the firmest foundation imaginable. Then, when the storms of life come, as invariably they will come, we will have a firm footing. Our lives will hold together in bad times as well as good.

4 December, Friday, First Week of Advent

Matthew 9:27–31

The image of blindness and light connects all of today's readings. In the first reading, the Lord, speaking through the prophet Isaiah, declares that 'the eyes of the blind will see'. The responsorial psalm proclaims that 'the Lord is my light and my help'. In the gospel reading Jesus restores the sight of two blind men. Most of us have reasonable sight, even if some of us need to wear our glasses all or most of the time. Yet, even when we can see with our eyes, we are probably aware that there are areas of blindness in us as well. Like the two disciples on the road to Emmaus, we can be blind to the Lord's presence to us, especially in times of great loss and pain. We fail to recognise him, even though he is journeying with us. We can be blind to each other too; we can fail to notice each other, to receive one another fully. Jesus received the two blind men fully; he engaged them in conversation; he showed great awareness of them. He saw them, in that attentive sense. He sees each of us in the same way. He is very aware of us; he engages us in conversation; he responds to our cry for help. He is always working in our lives to bring us towards a fuller light, towards himself, who is the Light of Life. Our calling is to grow in our capacity to see the Lord in the same attentive way that he sees us, and to see others as attentively as he sees them.

5 December, Saturday, First Week of Advent

Matthew 9:35–10.1, 6–8

Pope Francis often speaks of the Church as a field hospital. He is thinking of the hospitals that are set up in the vicinity of a war zone where the wounded come to have their wounds tended to. It is an image of the Church that reflects the ministry of Jesus. He tended to the wounded in body, mind and spirit. Today's readings highlight that dimension of Jesus' ministry. The ending of the first reading from the prophet Isaiah looks forward to a day when 'the Lord dresses the wounds of his people'. In the gospel reading, Jesus proclaims the presence of the kingdom of God by curing all kinds of diseases and sickness. He has compassion on the crowd, whom he sees as harassed and dejected like sheep without a shepherd. In response, he sends out the twelve as labourers to a rich harvest, with authority to proclaim the closeness of God's kingdom by curing disease and sickness. The ministry of Jesus' disciples, the ministry of the Church, is to be a continuation of Jesus' own healing ministry. The Lord, present in the community of disciples, the Church, calls to us to come before him with our wounds of body, mind or spirit, and to open ourselves to his healing presence. The Lord continues his healing ministry among us today, which is why the image of the Church as a field hospital is so suitable. There will be times when we need the Lord to minister to us in our brokenness, when we come before him in need of his healing presence. There will be other times in our lives when the Lord will send us out, as he sent out the twelve, to bring his healing presence to others who are wounded. We are always wounded healers. We need the Lord to heal our wounds, and he needs us to be channels of his healing presence to others.

7 December, Monday, Second Week of Advent
Luke 5:17–26
There is a striking image of community in today's gospel reading. A paralysed man wanted to get to Jesus. However, he was completely dependent on others if he was to get close to Jesus. On this occasion, his community did not let him down. They went to great lengths to get him as close to Jesus as possible. Having carried him to the house where Jesus was teaching, they saw immediately that they would never be able to get through the crowd to Jesus. Far from being put off by this obstacle, they went around it. Indeed, they literally went over the obstacle, bringing the paralyzed man up onto the roof of the house, removing some tiles and letting him down in front of Jesus. Here was an interruption that could not be ignored! Jesus recognised

the faith not just of the paralysed man but of those who carried him, 'seeing their faith'. The man was not just being physically carried by others, but he was being carried by their faith. We are part of the community of faith that we call the Church. Within that community we are called to carry each other. We can do that in very practical, concrete ways, such as physically taking people where they can't go themselves, as that little group did in the gospel reading. We can also carry each other spiritually, by our faith. Whenever we live out of our faith in the Lord, we carry others spiritually. There are times in our lives when, like the paralysed man, we need to be carried by others, and there are other times when, like the man's helpers, we have the strength and the faith to do the carrying. The gospel reading suggests that whenever we carry others or allow ourselves to be carried by others, we will encounter the Lord. The Lord will be there in all his healing and life-giving presence.

8 December, Tuesday, Solemnity of the Immaculate Conception
Luke 1:26–38

John Henry Newman was canonised last year. After his conversion to Catholicism, one of the people that he received into the Church was the poet, Gerard Manley Hopkins, in 1866. Hopkins became a Jesuit two years later; he went on to teach in the Jesuit-run University College that Newman had started on Saint Stephen's Green in Dublin. (Hopkins died there in 1889.) He wrote a poem on Mary entitled, 'The Blessed Virgin compared to the air we breathe'. He speaks of air as the nursing element of the universe. What he calls 'the world-mothering air' speaks to him of Mary. The poem was composed a couple of decades after Pope Pius IX proclaimed the dogma of Mary's Immaculate Conception. In his poem, Hopkins makes reference to Mary's Immaculate Conception: 'Mary Immaculate, / Merely a woman, yet / Whose presence, power is /

Great as no goddess's / Was deemed, dreamed; who / This one work has to do – / Let all God's glory through'. Today's feast celebrates Mary as one who let all God's glory through. If saints are people through whose lives shines the light of God's glory, this is especially true of Mary. There was nothing in Mary to block the light of God's glorious presence. In his poem, Hopkins, addresses Mary, 'Be thou then, o thou dear / Mother, my atmosphere; / My happier world, wherein / To wend and meet no sin'.

The pope's proclamation of Mary's Immaculate Conception in 1854 articulated what had been the faith of the Church since earliest times. It was understood by the faithful that Mary was preserved by God from sin because of her unique privilege of being the mother of God's son. In the words of today's gospel reading, she was 'highly favoured' by God, because she was chosen to carry God's son in her womb, to give birth to him, to nurture him with a mother's love, and then to let him go as an adult for the doing of God's work in the world. In his poem, Hopkins beautifully expresses this special favour that God gave to Mary. He says that she 'Gave God's infinity / Dwindled to infancy / Welcome in womb and breast, / Birth, milk, and all the rest'. Mary was highly favoured and, yet, she had to respond to God's favour. Today's gospel reading shows that her response to God's favour was complete, 'I am the servant of the Lord. Let what you have said be done to me'. She gave a total 'yes' to the unique grace and call that God gave her. There was no holding back. She was completely open to God's call. Her surrender to God's purpose for her life was total and enduring. Her response to God at the moment of the annunciation anticipated her own son's response to God in the garden of Gethsemane, 'Not my will but yours be done'.

Speaking of Mary in these terms may seem to make her remote from us. Perhaps we can more easily recognise something of ourselves in Adam's story in the first reading. Like him, we go against what God desires for us, reaching for what is out of bounds. Like him, we blame others for our own failings. Like him, having gone against God's desire for our lives, we hide from God, and God has to call after us, 'Where are you?' All of that may be true of us, and, yet, it is never our full story. God's question, 'Where are you?' reveals a God who seeks out the lost. Mary's son, Jesus, shows us that God is constantly seeking us out in his love, working to draw us into a life-giving communion with himself. God has a wonderful purpose for our lives, which he never abandons, no matter how often we turn from him. In today's second reading Saint Paul expresses God's purpose for our lives very eloquently. God 'chose us in Christ, to be holy and spotless, and to live through love in his presence, determining that we should become his adopted sons (and daughters)'. God's purpose for our lives is that his son would be formed in our lives, so that we can live through love in God's presence, living in the same loving way that Jesus did. In Mary, we see this person we are called to be. God's son was formed in her, not just physically, but spiritually. She lived through love in God's presence, giving herself in love to God and to others.

The gospel reading suggests that Mary's becoming the person God was calling her to be did not come easily to her. The path that God was asking her to take was not always clear to her, 'How can this come about?' She needed God's help, the overshadowing of the Holy Spirit. The Holy Spirit who overshadowed her at the annunciation overshadowed us at our baptism and remains with us all through life. She herself can help us to become the person God calls us to be. That is why we ask her to pray for us now, as well as at the hour of our death. Hopkins refers to this role of Mary in our lives in his poem, saying that she 'Mantles the guilty globe, / Since God has let her dispense / Her prayers, his providence'.

9 December, Wednesday, Second Week of Advent

Matthew 11:28–30

We tend to associate advancing years with declining energy. As we get older, we don't always have the energy we once had, and this can a source of frustration for us. Yet today's first reading from Isaiah acknowledges that even 'young men may grow tired and weary', and that even 'youths may stumble'. There is such a thing as a weariness of the spirit, which can affect people at any age. Some young people can seem listless, whereas some older people can be full of vitality. Isaiah declares in that reading that the Lord is the one who alone can address and deal with this kind of weariness of spirit. 'He gives strength to the wearied, he strengthens the powerless'. The Lord does not grow tired or weary. He is the Lord of life who remains vibrant at all times. By turning towards him in our weakness and weariness we can imbibe some of his perennial strength and vitality. In the words of Isaiah, 'those who hope in the Lord renew their strength'. This is the promise that Jesus makes in the gospel reading, 'Come to me, all you who labour and are overburdened, and I will give you rest'. There is much in life that can deaden our spirit, at any age. It is the Lord, and our relationship with him, that can keep us young and vital, even in old age, 'still full of sap, still green', in the words of the psalm. The Lord comes to us as strength in our weakness, as vitality in our weariness, as hope in our despondency. What is asked of us is that we welcome his coming and keep drawing strength from his life-giving presence to us.

10 December, Thursday, Second Week of Advent

Matthew 11:11–15

John the Baptist is the saint who comes into his own in the early part of the Advent season. Mary is the saint who comes into her own in the later part of the Advent season. In today's gospel reading, Jesus gives high praise to John the Baptist, 'of all children born of women, a greater than John the Baptist has never been seen'. That comment certainly gives John the Baptist a unique status among human beings. Jesus goes on to affirm John's unique status by identifying him with Elijah, whom the prophet Malachi declared would return to prepare people for the coming of the Lord. After such praise of John, it is surprising to hear Jesus also say, 'the least in the kingdom of heaven is greater than he is'. John the Baptist was executed early in the public ministry of Jesus. He did not live to experience the coming of the kingdom of heaven through Jesus' words and deeds. He certainly never came to know of the death and resurrection of Jesus, through which the Holy Spirit came and the Church was formed. In that sense, the least of Jesus' disciples is greater than John the Baptist. Jesus is reminding us of how privileged we all are to have seen and heard what John never saw or heard. Unlike John the Baptist, we have received from the fullness of the Word made flesh, in the words of the Fourth Gospel. Our calling is to give generously to the Lord and to each other out of all that we have received from him. In this matter of giving from what we have received, John the Baptist can continue to be our model and inspiration.

11 December, Friday, Second Week of Advent
Matthew 11:16–19
In the gospel reading, Jesus reflects ruefully on his contemporaries. They are as good at finding fault with Jesus' behaviour as they were at finding fault with the behaviour of John the Baptist. Yet, Jesus and John the Baptist were very different. The ministry of John the Baptist was more like the children who sang dirges in the marketplace for other children to mourn over; the ministry of Jesus

was more like the children who played the flute in the marketplace for other children to dance to. If the music of John the Baptist's ministry was reminiscent of the mournful music of a funeral, the music of Jesus' ministry evoked the celebratory music of a wedding feast. However, Jesus' contemporaries were equally unmoved by either kind of music. They found fault with John the Baptist and with Jesus. Their readiness to find fault blinded them to God's activity in the ministry of John the Baptist and much more powerfully in the ministry of Jesus. To say John the Baptist was possessed and that Jesus was a glutton and a drunkard was to miss completely what was significant about the ministry of both men. We can all be prone to the kind of fault-finding that prevents us from seeing the ways in which the Lord may be calling out to us through others. The music of the Spirit can take very different forms in different people's lives, and we need to keep attuning the ears of our hearts to that varied music, and resist the temptation to turn it off too quickly by finding fault.

12 December, Saturday, Second Week of Advent
Matthew 17:10–13

On the mount of transfiguration, the disciples saw Jesus in conversation with Moses and Elijah. In today's gospel reading, the disciples are coming down the mountain and the disciples ask Jesus about Elijah and the tradition that he would come to prepare God's people for the coming of the Messiah, the coming of the Lord. If Jesus is Lord and Messiah, where is Elijah? they wondered. Jesus informs his disciples that, in reality, John the Baptist was the promised Elijah. Furthermore, Jesus declares that the fate that John suffered, execution by Herod Antipas, anticipates the fate that he will suffer: 'the Son of Man will suffer similarly'. It must have been difficult for Jesus' disciples to hear him talk about his coming suffering, having just seen him in glory on the mount of transfiguration. Yet, that vision they had on the mountain assured them that there would be glory for Jesus beyond his suffering and death. What people would do to Jesus would be reversed by God. God the Father would bring his Son through death to a new and glorious life. What God did for Jesus, he can do for us all. God can bring new life out of our own experience of death, whether it is the death at the end of our earthly lives, or the various experiences of death and loss that we have to negotiate in the course of our earthly lives. If we keep entrusting ourselves to God in those dark times of loss, as Jesus did, then we will find God to be trustworthy, as Jesus did. God is always at work bringing new life out of our various deaths, which is why we can always be people of great hope, and hope is the virtue that is associated in a special way with this season of Advent.

14 December, Monday, Third Week of Advent

Matthew 21:23–27

Jesus is asked many questions in the course of the gospels. Most of the time, he gives a clear and discerning answer to the questions he is asked. Occasionally, he seems reluctant to give an answer, especially when the person asking the question is closed or hostile to all he stands for. In today's gospel reading, Jesus does not answer the question of the elders of the people, 'What authority have you for acting like this?' We might ask, 'acting like what?' Jesus had recently driven out all who were selling and buying in the Temple, overturning the tables of the money changers and the seats of those who sold doves, declaring that the guardians of the Temple had turned God's house of prayer into a den of robbers. These were provocative actions and words. The question of the elders was a valid one: 'What authority stands behind such words and deeds?'

The response of Jesus to their questions brings to the surface the elders' refusal to take the ministry of John the Baptist seriously. If they were hostile to John's ministry, they will inevitably be even more hostile to Jesus' ministry. Jesus sees no point in giving a direct answer to their question regarding his authority. However, we know the answer to the elders' question. Jesus was in his Father's house and he was acting there with the authority of God's son. He was declaring by his deeds and words that the Temple was no longer serving God's purpose but was serving the interests of those who ran the Temple. The gospel reading poses a question to us all: 'Whose purposes am I serving by what I do or fail to do, the purposes of God or my own self-interested purposes?' 'Whose kingdom am I working to further, God's kingdom or my own personal kingdom?' We are each temples of the Spirit and we always stand in need of the Lord's renewing and reforming zeal so that our lives serve the coming of God's kingdom.

15 December, Tuesday, Third Week of Advent
Matthew 21:28–32

At the end of today's gospel reading, Jesus says something very provocative. He tells the chief priests and elders of the people that tax collectors and prostitutes are making their way into the kingdom of God before them. He thereby turned on its head the conventional moral and religious sense of who was close to God and who was beyond God's reach. He was forcing people to rethink where the good and holy people are really to be found. Jesus implies that they are not necessarily to be found among those who have leading roles in the Temple and the synagogues, but may well be found among those who were assumed to be breaking God's Law. Jesus continues to challenge all of us to rethink our own assessment of who is close to God and who is not. In Jesus' day, it was the tax collectors and prostitutes who responded to the message of John the Baptist and submitted to his baptism of repentance, whereas the chief priests and elders dismissed him as a religious upstart. The same could be said of the response to Jesus. It was those labelled 'sinners' who welcomed him, whereas those considered religious rejected him. What Jesus looked for was for people to recognise their spiritual poverty and, therefore, their need of what Jesus was offering. 'Blessed are the poor in spirit, for theirs is the kingdom of heaven'. Jesus continues to look today for that same attitude of heart which acknowledges our poverty before him, and our need of the gospel that he brings.

16 December, Wednesday, Third Week of Advent
Luke 7:19–23

In the gospel reading John the Baptist sends his disciples to ask Jesus a question from his prison cell: 'Are you the one who is to come, or must we wait for someone else?' It seems as if John might have been having doubts as to whether or not Jesus was actually the one that he and many others had been waiting for. As Jesus' ministry evolved, it didn't quite fit John's earlier depiction of Jesus' future ministry, 'His winnowing fork is in his hand, to clear his threshing floor and to gather the wheat into his granary, but the chaff he will burn with unquenchable fire'. Even people of very strong faith, like John the Baptist, can go through periods of great doubt. Jesus did not answer John's question directly; he simply pointed to the life-giving ministry in which he had been engaged. All that God was doing through Jesus gave John his answer. Jesus was indeed the one who was to come; the one for whom many had been waiting. Jesus' final words to the messengers of John the Baptist were, 'happy is the one who does not lose faith in me'. Jesus was calling on John to keep alive his faith in Jesus as the coming one, even in his time of doubt. Advent calls on all of us to renew our faith in Jesus as the one whom God promised and for whom we are all waiting. We are not waiting for anyone else. Advent reassures us that the one for whom we are waiting, for whom we long, is the Life-Giver whom God has already sent to us and continues to send us each day.

17 December, Thursday, Third Week of Advent
Matthew 1:1–17

It has been said that the genealogy of Jesus in today's gospel reading is a preacher's nightmare. What is to be said about this list of Hebrew names? There is a great interest in genealogy today. There is a television programme given over to the search for one's ancestors entitled *Who do you think you are?* That question gives us a clue to what Matthew was doing in giving his version of the genealogy of Jesus. He was inviting us to ask the question, 'Who do you think Jesus is?' Matthew is not so much interested in past history as in the present identity of Jesus. The two key names in that list are found together at the beginning of the list, almost as an introduction to it, Abraham and David. When Matthew tells us that Jesus is the son of Abraham, he is stating that Jesus is a Jew and that his story is woven into the larger story of the Jewish people. When Matthew says that Jesus is the son of David he is establishing his credentials as the long-awaited Jewish Messiah. We are being reminded that our own Christian faith emerged from the Jewish faith. As Jesus had Jewish roots, so our spiritual and religious roots are to be found in the Jewish faith, which is why the Jewish Scriptures remain important for us as followers of Jesus. Another feature of the genealogy is that four women are to be found in the otherwise relentlessly male list, and all four women are non-Jewish in origin – Tamar, Rahab, Ruth and Bathsheba. Jesus may be son of Abraham and son of David, but Matthew wants to see that Jesus' ancestry already shows an openness to the non-Jewish, Gentile world. The Saviour may be from the Jews but he is intended for all nations, as is clear from the final words of Jesus to his disciples in this Gospel of Matthew: 'Go, therefore, and make disciples of all nations … '. It is because Jesus's disciples were faithful to that mission that we are here today, reflecting on his word. As Israel was to be a light to the nations, so Jesus, the Jew, was a light to the nations. As his disciples, we continue his light-bearing mission to all we encounter. This role is at the core of our identity and needs to be part of how we would answer the question, 'Who do you think you are?'

18 December, Friday, Third Week of Advent
Matthew 1:18–24

As we are only a week away from the feast of Christmas, the gospel readings at this time focus on the events associated with the birth and childhood of Jesus. Today's gospel reading is Matthew's account of the annunciation of the birth of Jesus. In Luke's Gospel, the annunciation of Jesus' birth is made to Mary; in Matthew's Gospel, it is made to Joseph. Artists have tended to depict Luke's version of the annunciation to Mary much more often than Matthew's version of the annunciation to Joseph. In both accounts, the angel announces that Mary is to conceive her child through the Holy Spirit. In both accounts there is a rich description of the unique identity of the child. Matthew's account of the annunciation highlights two aspects of the identity of Mary's child. He is to be named Jesus, a name that means in Hebrew 'the Lord saves', because he is to save God's people from their sins. He is also to be named Emmanuel, which in Hebrew means 'God is with us'. Combining these names indicates that Jesus is the presence among us of the loving mercy of God. When we look upon this child, we are looking upon God-with-us, or as Saint Paul says, God for us, working to reconcile us to himself. Jesus was born, lived and died to reconcile us to God, to lead us back to God. At the last meal Jesus had with his disciples before his death, the last supper, he said, 'This is my blood of the covenant, which is poured out for many for the forgiveness of sins'. It is because Jesus is the face of God's mercy that we celebrate his birth with such gladness and hope. He has shown us that nothing need come between us and the love of God.

19 December, Saturday, Third Week of Advent
Luke 1:5–25

We have a lot of exposure to bad news. Good news is not considered 'news' by our media to the same extent as bad news. If we are constantly exposed to bad news, it can leave us somewhat dispirited. We can be so used to hearing bad news that when good news comes along it doesn't really register with us. In today's gospel reading, the good news that the angel Gabriel brought to Zechariah did not really register with him. When Gabriel told him that he and his wife Elizabeth would soon have a child, John the Baptist, Zechariah did not believe the words of Gabriel, 'How can I be sure of this?' Zechariah's failure to hear this good news from God had a negative impact on his speech. In fact, he lost his power of speech. In the Scriptures the close relationship between hearing and speaking is often highlighted. Good listening comes before good speaking. Our own inability to really absorb into our hearts and minds the good news of God's visitation to us through Jesus can impact negatively on our speech. If we allow ourselves to be really touched by the good news we celebrate at this time of the year, the way we speak will have something of the quality of that good news. At Christmas we celebrate the wonderful way God has graced and continues to grace all our lives. Like Zechariah, we can find that hard to believe. However, if we make that gospel message our own, our own speech and, indeed, our own presence, will be good news for others.

21 December, Monday, Fourth Week of Advent

Luke 1:39–45

We spend a lot of our lives going on journeys of one kind or another. We set out to go somewhere almost every day. Some of those journeys can be significant for ourselves and for others. We set out to visit someone and they are blessed by our visit and we are blessed by visiting them. That is the kind of journey that is put before us in today's gospel reading. Mary set out on a journey to visit her older cousin Elizabeth. Elizabeth was greatly blessed by Mary's visit. The gospel reading says that when Elizabeth heard Mary's greeting she was filled with the Holy Spirit, and even the child in her womb leapt for joy. Mary herself was blessed by her visit to Elizabeth. According to the gospel reading, Elizabeth declared Mary blessed because of the child she was carrying and also because she believed the promise made to her by the Lord. Mary's setting out on this journey turned out to be good news both for Elizabeth and for Mary. The Lord calls each of us to keep setting out on journeys that bless those we journey towards. We then invariably discover that we ourselves are also blessed in blessing others. Mary brought the Lord to Elizabeth in a very physical sense, and so her visit was a source of blessing to Elizabeth, as Elizabeth exclaimed, 'Why should I be honoured with a visit from the mother of my Lord?' We are each called to bring the Lord to one another. We are to journey towards others in ways that make the Lord in some way present to them. When that happens, we bless and grace those we visit and we ourselves are blessed and graced as well. At Christmas, we celebrate the good news that the Lord set out on a journey towards us and visited us in a way that left us all blessed and graced. Mary's journey to Elizabeth captured something of the spirit of the Lord's journey towards us. Our journeys towards each other can do the same.

22 December, Tuesday, Fourth Week of Advent
Luke 1:46–56

The prayer of Mary in today's gospel reading has become the prayer of the followers of her son. Many of us will have prayed her prayer. It has been incorporated into the evening prayer of the Church. It is a prayer that acknowledges the way that God has worked in her life, 'the Almighty has done great things for me'. Mary's prayer encourages us to reflect on how God may be working in our own lives, and to give thanks to God for that work. At the beginning of his letter to the Philippians, Saint Paul declares, 'I am confident of this, that the one who began a good work among you will bring it to completion by the day of Jesus Christ'. God has begun a good work among us and within us. Like Mary, we are invited to recognise God's good work in our lives and praise God for it. We are sometimes more prone to seeing our failings, what we perceive to be our own not-so-good works. It is true that we need to be realistic about our failings and weaknesses, but not to the point where we become blind to the good things, the good work, that God is doing in our lives. God will continue to do God's good work in our lives if we are open to it and desirous of it. In her prayer, Mary sings of a God who has filled the hungry with good things. If we hunger for the good things that God wants to do in our lives, for the good work God wants to accomplish within us and through us, then God will satisfy our hunger. As Jesus says in one of the Beatitudes, 'Blessed are those who hunger and thirst for what is right, for they will be filled'.

23 December, Wednesday, Fourth Week of Advent
Luke 1:57–66

The birth of a child in a family is always a cause of great joy, not only within the family, but beyond it, among neighbours and friends. We find reference to that joy at the beginning of our gospel reading. The naming of the child after or before the birth, however, can sometimes be a contentious issue. Ultimately it is the choice of the parents, although others can get in on the act. That is what we find happening in the case of Elizabeth and Zechariah's child. The extended family and the neighbours had their own ideas – call him after his father, give him a name that is traditional. However, God was about to do something new, something that took tradition in a whole new direction. The child's name would reflect the new thing that God was doing. When Zechariah said that his name would be John, a completely new name within the family tradition, we are told that the people were filled with awe. They moved from a sense of joy at the birth of the child to a sense of awe before this break with tradition. God is always reshaping the tradition, or, in the words of the first reading, refining and purifying it. The gospel reading invites us to be open to the new thing God is always doing within us and among us, and to be in awe of it.

24 December, Thursday, Fourth Week of Advent
Luke 1:67–79
On 21 December, the shortest day of the year, those who are fortunate enough to get places within the megalithic tomb of Newgrange in County Meath in Ireland gather to witness, weather permitting, the rays of the sun penetrating into the inner chamber of this passage tomb. This only happens on the shortest day of the year. This 4,000-year-old monument witnesses to the conviction of our ancestors that, just as darkness is at its greatest, the light begins to return to our world. Since that day, the nights have been getting imperceptibly shorter and the days imperceptibly longer. The feast of Christmas, the celebration of the birth of Jesus, the light of the world, coincides with the emergence of greater light in nature.

Today's gospel reading is the great song of Zechariah, the husband of Elizabeth and the father of John the Baptist. In his hymn he sings of the tender mercy of God who brings the rising Sun to visit us to give light to those who live in darkness and the shadow of death. Zechariah proclaims Jesus to be the rising Sun who visits us with his light, a reflection of the light of God's mercy. All the lights of Christmas, the Christmas tree lights, the candles that we light, point beyond themselves to the warm and gracious light of that rising Sun whom God is his mercy has sent to visit us and to remain with us until the end of time. Our calling is to welcome the light of the rising Sun into our lives and to walk in that light so that we may witness to his light by the way we live.

26 December, Saturday, Feast of Saint Stephen
Matthew 10:17–22

The Holy Spirit is common to both of today's readings. In today's first reading we are told that 'it was the Spirit that prompted what he [Stephen] said', and later on in that reading it is said of Stephen that, 'filled with the Holy Spirit, he gazed into heaven and saw the glory of God'. At the very moment when some people were doing their worst to Stephen, the Lord was helping him in and through the Holy Spirit. In the gospel reading, Jesus tells his disciples that when people will be doing their worst to them, dragging them before governors and kings, handing them over to persecution, the Spirit of God their Father will be speaking through them. Jesus was very aware that his disciples would need the help of the Holy Spirit if they were to bear witness to him in an often hostile world, and he assures them that he will give them that help. Stephen certainly knew the help of the Holy Spirit when his witness to the Lord left him vulnerable to the deadly hostility of others. The same Holy Spirit is promised to us all who are the Lord's disciples today. We need the Holy Spirit, the Spirit of our Father, if we are to be the Lord's faithful witnesses in our world today. In his letter to the Romans, Saint Paul says that the Spirit helps us in our weakness. Yesterday, we celebrated the birth of the child Jesus. That same Jesus, now risen Lord, can only be born in our lives and in our world today in and through the Holy Spirit. Just as the Holy Spirit overshadowed Mary and she gave birth to Jesus, the same Holy Spirit overshadows us so that we can give birth to Jesus by our lives today. The Advent prayer, 'Come Lord Jesus', is one we can pray in every season. The Pentecost prayer, 'Come Holy Spirit', is also one we need to pray in every season.

28 December, Monday, Feast of the Holy Innocents
Matthew 2:13–18
A few days after celebrating the birth of a child today's feast recalls that passage in Matthew's Gospel that describes the death of children. There is a lot of darkness in today's gospel reading, all of it due to the ruler of the time, Herod the Great. Because of him, innocent children are put to death and the family of Jesus, Mary and Joseph become refugees, fleeing to Egypt for their safety. The story has a contemporary ring to it. We think of situations in today's world where those in power are bringing death to others, including children. We recall the hundreds of thousands of people who have been made refugees because of the cruelty of some. Today's feast reminds us that Jesus was born into a violent world, where those in power were often ruthless in their efforts to protect their own position. The birth of Jesus brought a light into that dark world, the light of God's love. The first reading declares: 'God is light; there is no darkness in him at all'. Jesus' life revealed a different kind of power from the power of those in authority at the time. His life and his death revealed the power of love, a love that was self-

emptying in the service of others. Our calling is to allow this love to take flesh in our own lives. It is in this way that, in the words of the first reading, 'we live our lives in the light, as God is in the light'. The calling to allow Jesus, the light of God's love, to shine in and through our lives, is a noble but challenging one. We will often fail in our living out of this calling. We sin, but as the first reading says, 'if we acknowledge our sins, then God who is faithful and just will forgive our sins'. There is darkness in each one of us but the darkness does not define us because the light of God's mercy is always stronger than the darkness of our sins. God remains faithful to us and keeps on calling us to bring the light of his son into the darkness of our world.

29 December, Tuesday, Fifth Day in the Octave of Christmas
Luke 2:22–35

There are some lovely prayers in the opening two chapters of Luke's Gospel. There is the prayer of Mary, the Magnificat, which is now part of the evening prayer of the Church and the prayer of Zechariah, the father of John the Baptist, which has become part of the morning prayer of the Church. The third great prayer in these chapters is the prayer of Simeon, which we find in today's gospel reading, and which has become part of the night prayer of the Church, 'Now, Master, you can let your servant go in peace...' It is the shortest of the three prayers, but some people find it the most attractive. It is the prayer of someone whose deepest longing has been satisfied and who, as a result, is ready to embrace death. Simeon is described as someone 'who looked forward to Israel's comforting', in other words, to Israel's Messiah. It had been revealed to him that he would not see death until he had set eyes on the Lord's Messiah. When Mary and Joseph came into the Temple carrying their newborn child, he recognised that here indeed was Israel's comforting, the

Lord's Messiah. He now saw what he always longed to see, and he had nothing more to live for. He was ready to leave this world. 'My eyes have seen the salvation which you have prepared for all the nations to see, a light to enlighten the pagans and the glory of your people Israel.' Whatever about the opening of Simeon's prayer, we can certainly make that section of his prayer our own. Our eyes have seen God's salvation. We have seen Jesus, our Saviour, with the eyes of faith. His light has enlightened us, has shone upon us. Like Simeon, we have been greatly graced. Yes, it is the case that, in the words of Saint Paul to the Corinthians, 'now we see as in a mirror, dimly', and it is only 'then', beyond this earthly life, that we 'will see face to face'. Yet, dimly as it may be, we nonetheless see with the eyes of faith. Something of the light of eternity has shone upon us. We are called to live out of that vision, to allow the grace of that light to shine within us and to shine through us upon all whom we meet.

30 December, Wednesday, Sixth Day in the Octave of Christmas
Luke 2:36–40

At the centre of today's gospel reading is an eighty-four-year-old widow, Anna, who was constantly in the Temple fasting and praying. She was probably in the last decade of her long life, and by then she had become something of a contemplative. She was at home in God's house; prayer came naturally to her. She needed and wanted to be in prayerful communion with God. You come across people a little like Anna in our parish churches today. They are a regular and prayerful presence in our churches. They are in prayerful communion with the Lord at all times and that prayerful communion spills over into a gracious and generous way of relating to others. Anna's prayerfulness gave her the spiritual vision to recognise the child of Joseph and Mary as the long-awaited Jewish

Messiah. Having recognised the child for all that he was, she then spoke about him to all who were waiting for God's anointed one. She becomes one of the first preachers of the good news in the Gospel of Luke. This eighty-four-year-old widow is the first real evangelist in Luke's two-volume work, the Gospel and the Acts of the Apostles. She shows us that faithfulness to prayer invariably bears rich fruit. Those who are prayerful become witnesses to the Lord by what they say and do. Our openness to the Lord in prayer enables the Lord to work through us for the spread of the Gospel.

31 December, Thursday, Seventh Day in the Octave of Christmas
John 1:1–18

We are in the last few hours of this year. As each of us looks back over the year just ending, we will all have our own personal feelings and memories. Hopefully, there will be much in the past year for which we can each give thanks to the Lord. For many, the year will have had its dark and difficult moments, and at those times our prayer will have taken the form of the prayer of petition, a prayer for the Lord's help. Every year has its light and shade for us all. As we end one year and are about to begin a new one, today's gospel reading gives us that wonderful statement, 'The Word was made flesh, he lived among us, and we have seen his glory'. God became human in the person of Jesus, his son. God could not get any closer to us than that, and having become human flesh through his son, God has remained in the flesh of our lives, the stuff of our lives, through his son, who is now risen Lord. Wherever the journey of life takes us, God is journeying with us through his son and the Holy Spirit. Even in the darkest moments of our life journey, the light of the Lord's presence is shining, a light that darkness could not overpower, in the words of today's gospel reading. As we head into a new year, we do so in the knowledge that the true light who enlightens all people has come into the world and is constantly coming into our personal world. The gospel reading invites us to keep opening our hearts and our lives to that enduring light of the Lord's loving presence, so that, like John the Baptist, we can become witnesses to the light before others.

1 January, Friday, Solemnity of Mary, Mother of God
Luke 2:16–21

In both today's first reading and responsorial psalm there is a reference to the Lord's face. In the first reading, we find that wonderful blessing, 'May the Lord bless you and keep you. May the Lord let his face shine upon you and be gracious to you'. In the psalm, we pray, 'God, be gracious and bless us and let your face shed its light upon us'. In each of those references, the face of God is associated with a shining light; the light of the Lord's gracious presence shines from his face. Both the first reading and the psalm express the longing of the people of Israel to see the face of God, a face they knew to be a gracious source of healing and saving light. At this Christmas time, we, as Christians, celebrate the good news that the child Jesus, the son of Mary and Joseph, reveals the face of God to us. To look upon the face of this child is to look upon the face of God. God has let his face shine upon us through this child. The child Jesus is God-with-us, the Word who is God made flesh, and Mary, as the mother of this child, is the mother of God. In the year 431, the Church at the Council of Ephesus declared Mary to be the God-bearer, the mother of God. It is perhaps the most exalted of all Mary's titles. Yet, the portrayal of Mary in today's gospel reading could not be described as exalted. There she is, with Joseph, probably in one of the caves just outside Bethlehem, with her child in a manger, a feeding trough for animals, listening to the humble shepherds tell their story of what they had just seen and heard while watching over their sheep in the nearby hills. The gospel reading says of Mary that she was astonished at what the shepherds had to say, and that she treasured and pondered it in her heart. Four hundred years later, the Church would proclaim Mary to be the mother of God, but that night in Bethlehem she is portrayed as struggling to come to terms with the mysterious way God was working in her life. Mary's exalted title does not remove her from us. Like her, we are invited to be astonished at the gifts and graces that God sends us and to treasure them. We are also called, like Mary, to ponder over the sometimes mysterious ways that God may be working in our lives. It is because the Lord's ways, his call to us, are not always crystal clear that we need to keep praying with today's psalm, 'God, be gracious and bless us, and let your face shed its light upon us', upon each of us, this coming year.

2 January, Saturday before Epiphany

John 1:19–28

It is evident from the opening verses of today's gospel reading that John the Baptist is very aware of who he was not. He says clearly and publicly that he is not the Messiah, he is not Elijah returned, and he is not the long-awaited end-time prophet. He is clear who he is not, because he is clear as to who he is. He is the voice that cries in the wilderness, preparing people for the coming of the Lord. In the Fourth Gospel, Jesus is the Word who was with God in the beginning and became flesh. John is the voice who publicly proclaims the Word. In the Fourth Gospel, Jesus is the light of the world, whereas John the Baptist is spoken of as a 'burning and shining lamp'; he reflects the light of Jesus to others, as the moon reflects the light of the sun. In the Fourth Gospel, Jesus is the bridegroom, the revelation in human form of the divine bridegroom who enters into a nuptial relationship not just with Israel but with the whole world. John the

Baptist is spoken of as 'the friend of the bridegroom, who stands and hears him', and who 'rejoices greatly at the bridegroom's voice'. The relationship between John and Baptist and Jesus is very clearly outlined in this gospel. There is a sense in which John's relationship with Jesus is the relationship of all disciples with Jesus. We are all called to be the voice to the Word, the lamp to the Light and the friend to the Bridegroom. Our calling is to point to Jesus with our lives, to proclaim his presence by our way of being present, and to reflect the light of his love in the way we relate to others.

4 January, Monday before Epiphany
John 1:35–42
In today's gospel reading, the disciples of John the Baptist began to follow Jesus in response to the witness of John. It was as they were following him that Jesus turned round, saw them and said to them, 'What do you want?' They had already begun their journey of discipleship and Jesus now wanted them to think more deeply about what they were doing by asking them that question. It was a very personal question. Jesus wasn't asking them, 'What does John the Baptist want?' but 'What do you want?' They had begun to follow Jesus in response to the prompting of John the Baptist, but now Jesus wanted to explore why they themselves wanted to follow him. Most of us began the Christian life, the way of discipleship, because others set us on that journey. Our parents brought us for baptism; our teachers instructed us in the faith; our priests preached the Gospel to us and helped us to celebrate the sacraments. However, there comes a time on our faith journey when we need to explore for ourselves why we are following this particular path. We need to answer Jesus' question, 'What do you want?' What is my deepest desire? Jesus offers himself to us as the one who can satisfy our deepest desire. As he will say a little later in the Fourth Gospel, 'Whoever comes

to me will never be hungry, and whoever believes in me will never be thirsty'. At some point in our lives, we have to make our own personal response to the call of the one who stands before us as our heart's desire. We then have to keep renewing that personal response, because the Lord is always saying to us 'Come and see'. There is always another step we can take and there is always more we can see, when it comes to our relationship with the Lord.

5 January, Tuesday before Epiphany

John 1:43–51

Today's gospel reading describes something of Nathanael's faith journey. He starts from a position of scepticism. When Philip tells him that he has found the Messiah and that he is Jesus, son of Joseph, from Nazareth, Nathanael dismissively asks, 'Can anything good come from Nazareth?' However, when Philip subsequently invites him to 'come and see', Nathanael suspends his scepticism for the moment and responds to Philip's invitation; he comes to Jesus. When Jesus then addresses him in a very personal way, Nathanael goes on to confess Jesus as the Messiah, 'Rabbi, you are the Son of God, you are the King of Israel'. Like Philip, he too has found the Messiah. However, Jesus then tells Nathanael that he has only begun to see, and promises him, 'you will see greater things'. His journey is only beginning. Nathanael began his journey in a very inauspicious place, but he soon made progress, and Jesus assured him that he would make greater progress. We can sometimes feel that our own relationship with the Lord is not all we would like it to be; we can feel ourselves in an inauspicious place with regard to the Lord. However, such a place need not determine our future relationship with the Lord. With the Lord's help, we can make unexpected progress, as Nathanael did, and, like him, we journey onwards sustained by the Lord's promise, 'You will see greater things … you will see heaven opened'. This promise will only come to pass fully in eternity when we will truly see heaven opened, but even now we can begin to see and to experience something of that heavenly destiny that the Lord desires for us all.

6 January, Wednesday, The Epiphany of the Lord
Matthew 2:1–12

Matthew's story of the visit of the magi to the child Jesus has inspired artists, poets, musicians and storytellers down through the ages. It has also inspired children. If you go to a Christmas concert in any of our primary schools, three of the children are sure to be dressed up as the wise men and another is likely to be carrying a very big star. This story is one of those passages in the Scriptures that can speak to both children and adults. It can speak to our experience, in different ways at different times of our lives.

In the time of Jesus, magi were associated with Persia to the east of Israel. They were experts in what we would call astrology. They searched the skies and tried to read the movement of the stars to interpret what was happening on earth. They were the ancient equivalent of men of science, using their intellect to understand the universe. It was this search for understanding that set the magi on their journey westwards towards Israel. They interpreted the rising of a new star as a sign that a new king of the Jews had just been born. Their natural gifts of curiosity and reason directed them towards the birthplace of this king. They remind us that reason and faith need not be in conflict. However, their natural wisdom could only bring them so far. They needed a light other than the light of their reason and the light of a new star to bring them to Bethlehem. They needed the light of the Jewish Scriptures to finally bring them to Emmanuel, God-with-us. When they got to Jerusalem, they had to inquire, 'Where is the infant King of the Jews?' It was those with knowledge of the Jewish Scriptures who told them, through King Herod, that the long-awaited king of the Jews would be born in Bethlehem.

The Lord draws each of us to himself in similar ways. He speaks through our ordinary human experience, as we engage with the world around us, using our gifts of reason and curiosity. He speaks to us in a fuller way through his word in the Scriptures. We can receive a certain light by being true to our own natural gifts, our own human search, just as the magi were given the light of a star in response to their searching. We can then receive a fuller light when we open ourselves to the presence of the Lord in his word. The Lord is always showing us signs of his presence, both in our day-to-day human experience and, especially, in his word, the Scriptures. God gives us enough light to guide us towards Emmanuel, God-with-us. The magi are portrayed as being very responsive to the light that God was giving them in their own human experiences and in the Scriptures. They can be an inspiration to us all.

God gives all of us light, just as he gave light to the magi. The word 'epiphany' means 'showing forth'. Today's feast announces that God is always showing himself forth to us. God is always providing us with a star, a light, and, for us, that light is Jesus himself who declared, 'I am the light of the world'. The light of Jesus, which is the light of God, shines upon us in a great variety of ways. Because all things came into being through Jesus, the Word, the whole created universe can reveal the light of his presence. His light shines upon us in a special way in and through the Church, the Church's Scriptures, the sacraments, especially the Eucharist, and the community of faith. We live in a time when it can be easier to see the darkness of the night than the lights that shine in the darkness. Yet, today's feast invites us to recognise the various ways that the light of the Lord's presence shines upon us, and then to act in response to that light, like the magi in today's gospel reading.

The magi made their way to the Lord in Bethlehem, in response to the lights they were given, the light of the star and the light of God's word. They were unlikely candidates to find the Lord because they had so far to come. They were exotic outsiders who didn't really belong in Bethlehem. They came to the Lord by a strange route. In contrast, the chief priests and Herod, who were only down the road in Jerusalem, and who also had the light of the Scriptures, never came to Bethlehem. It has been said that the magi are symbols of hope for all who struggle to the Lord by strange routes. One of the characters in a novel by Evelyn Waugh addresses the magi as 'patrons of all late comers, of all who have had a tedious journey to make to the truth'. They can continue to speak to us when we find ourselves struggling to the Lord by some strange or tedious route.

7 January, Thursday after Epiphany
Matthew 4:12–17, 23–25

A section of today's gospel reading might be familiar as the first reading of the Christmas night Mass from the prophet Isaiah, 'the people that lived in darkness have seen a great light; on those who dwell in the land and shadow of death a light has shone'. That reading fitted the setting of Christmas night, reminding us that with the birth of Jesus a great light, God's light, was dawning in our world. In the gospel reading, Matthew quotes this text from Isaiah as a commentary not on the birth of Jesus but rather on the beginning of his public ministry. When Jesus began his public ministry after his baptism in the River Jordan, the light of God's presence began to shine through him in earnest. Jesus began to proclaim the good news of the kingdom, of God's reign, which brought forgiveness for sinners, and healing for all who were broken in body, mind or spirit. The gospel reading tells us that the light of God's kingdom, which shone through Jesus' words and actions, drew people to him from a huge area, Syria, Galilee, the Decapolis, Jerusalem, Judea and present-day Jordan. The same Jesus, now risen Lord, continues to draw us to himself today. The light of God's kingdom continues to shine through him upon the darkness of our lives. As we begin a new year, we are invited to allow ourselves to be drawn by this 'kindly light', in the words of Saint John Henry Newman. As we enter this kindly light, we are sent forth as his light-bearers to others. In the chapter of Matthew's Gospel following our gospel reading, Jesus will say to his disciples, who have been drawn to God's light shining through Jesus, 'You are the light of the world'. He continues to say the same to us today, whenever we allow ourselves to be drawn to the light of his presence.

8 January, Friday after Epiphany

Mark 6:34–44

One of the most profound statements ever made about God is to be found in today's first reading, 'God is Love'. The reading also states that God showed he was Love by giving us the most precious gift that he could give us, his only Son. If God is Love, the godly person is the loving person, the holy person is the giving person, the one who gives generously of himself or herself to others. The most God-like person, in that sense, the most loving person, was, of course, Jesus. In the gospel reading Jesus struggles to get his own disciples to become giving people. They asked Jesus to send the crowd away because the crowd were hungry. In response, Jesus said to his disciples, 'Give them something to eat yourselves'. Jesus was saying to them, 'Take some responsibility for these needy people, do not just wish them away'. He pushed his disciples into doing something for the people, no matter how small. They eventually found five loaves and two fish, very small resources indeed. But with those few resources, Jesus fed the crowd. Jesus was teaching his disciples and us that the willingness to do something, no matter how little, the readiness to give something, no matter how small, can bear rich fruit. The Lord can take our giving, even our little giving, and work powerfully through it. The gospel reading encourages us to be giving people, even when we seem to have little to give and the situation we are facing seems beyond us. As Paul reminds us, the Lord's power can be made perfect in weakness.

9 January, Saturday after Epiphany

Mark 6:45–52

Today's first reading and gospel reading are linked by a reference to fear. The first reading declares that 'in love there can be no fear'. We do not fear someone that we know loves us fully and unreservedly. Earlier in that reading, the author had made one of the simplest and yet most profound statements about God ever made, 'God is love'. If God is unconditional love, there is no room for fear in our relationship with God. Rather, the response to God's love for us is to love God in return, and we express our love for God by loving those whom God loves and in the way God loves them. As the author says, 'since God has loved us so much, we too should love one another'. If we loved one another in the way God loves us, there would be no room for fear in the way we relate to one another. In the gospel reading, Jesus approaches the boat of his disciples as they struggle with a strong wind, and when the disciples see him they are terrified. Jesus immediately confronts their fear, 'Courage! It is I! Do not be afraid'. If God is love and Jesus is the face of God, God in human form, then there is no need for his disciples to be afraid of him, as they might be afraid of ghosts. There is nothing sinister about the Lord's coming over the waters. He comes in love to help and support them. The Lord comes to us in the same way. He comes in love to steady our ship, to calm and direct us. There is no place for fear in our relationship with him. As we welcome his coming in love, as we receive him into the boat of our lives, he calls on us to relate to each other as he relates to us, in the same loving way that leaves no place for fear. Just as no one should ever fear the Lord, no one should ever fear any of us, because in the words of the first reading, 'fear is driven out by perfect love'.

11 January, Monday, First Week in Ordinary Time
Mark 1:14–20

In today's gospel reading we find fishermen going about their daily work by the Sea of Galilee, casing their nets into the lake, mending their nets in their boats. They were doing what they did every day. It was in that very ordinary setting that they heard the call and the promise of Jesus, 'follow me and I will make you into fishers of people'. Having heard Jesus' call, they immediately responded to it. Their response meant leaving what they were used to and good at, fishing by the Sea of Galilee, and setting out on a very different road, sharing in Jesus' work of gathering not fish but people, not into physical nets but into the nets of God's loving reign. The Lord's call to follow him comes to us too in the course of our daily lives. It is when we are about our ordinary day-to-day activities that the Lord says to us, 'Follow me'. We won't hear those words of Jesus in the way that these fishermen did. The Lord's call will be more subtle than that. It might take the form of a prompt to do something that we sense would bring some benefit to others. A thought might come into our head, or a feeling might surface within us that moves us in a direction that is life-giving for another. Most likely, it won't involve us leaving one whole way of life for another, as it did for some of Jesus' first followers, but it will always involve some letting go, some reaching out beyond ourselves. Whenever we go with the

Lord's prompting we discover that it is beneficial not only to others but, in some way, to ourselves as well. It is like a dying of some kind that brings new life. As we go about the ordinary matters of the day, we can expect the Lord to call us, to prompt us, to inspire us. Hopefully, we will be as responsive to the Lord's call at the heart of our lives as those first disciples were in our gospel reading.

12 January, Tuesday, First Week in Ordinary Time
Mark 1:21–28

Jesus met with various kinds of responses in the course of his ministry. In today's gospel reading, while he was in the synagogue of Capernaum someone who was very disturbed in spirit responded to Jesus in a very aggressive way, 'What do you want with us, Jesus of Nazareth?' When someone responds to our presence in a similarly aggressive way, we can be very tempted to react in kind. We become aggressive towards them, which in turn can bring out further aggression in them. Jesus, however, did not respond to this man as the man had responded to him. Jesus responded to this disturbed man with a word that proved to be a healing and life-giving word for him, 'Be quiet! Come out of him!' The gospel reading says that the crowd were astonished at the authority of his teaching, his word. His authority was such that he was able to absorb this man's aggression and respond to it with a word that was healing and calming in its impact. This is what divine authority looks like, the authority of the Spirit. It is the kind of authority that the world needs today, an authority that is rooted in our relationship with God, with his Son and the Holy Spirit. It is the authority to retain a loving, life-giving stance towards all, even in the face of great provocation and hostility; it is the authority to bring calm where there is disturbance.

13 January, Wednesday, First Week in Ordinary Time
Mark 1:29–39

Two quite different activities of Jesus are presented in today's gospel reading. The first is the activity of healing. Jesus heals Simon Peter's mother-in-law in the house of Simon and Andrew by taking her by the hand and lifting her up, and then goes on to heal many sick people who were brought to the door of the house. This healing activity of Jesus is very public and is greatly appreciated by everyone; the whole town came crowding around the door, according to Mark. The second activity of Jesus is quite different. It is much more private. In the morning, long before dawn, Jesus goes out by himself to a lonely place to pray. Whereas Jesus' public activity of healing the sick was much appreciated by all, this second activity of going off by himself to pray is not appreciated by others. Even those closest to him didn't think much of it. Peter, the leading disciple, rebukes Jesus: 'Everybody is looking for you', as much as to say, 'Why are you wasting time out here on your own?' Yet, Jesus knew that the source of his life-giving work was his relationship with God, which is nurtured in his prayer. The activity of prayer was even more important to him than his activity of healing. Prayer is as necessary for us as it was for Jesus. We need the Lord if we are to live as he desires us to live and if we are to share in some way in his healing work. In prayer we acknowledge and give expression to our dependence on the Lord; we open ourselves to the Lord's life-giving presence so as to be channels of that presence to others.

14 January, Thursday, First Week in Ordinary Time
Mark 1:40–45

It may strike us as strange that having healed the leper in today's gospel reading, Jesus sternly orders him, 'Mind you say nothing to anyone'. Apart from going to the priest in the Temple in Jerusalem, the healed man was not to tell anyone what Jesus had done for him. Why wouldn't Jesus want everyone to know that he had performed this powerful work? Perhaps he was aware that if people came to hear of his reputation as a healer, they would start to follow him for the wrong reasons. They would follow him not for who he was in himself but for what he could do for them. Jesus was happy for whatever good he might do for someone to remain below the radar. He knew that his healing and life-giving ministry would bear its own good fruit, without it having to be trumpeted abroad. This is how the Lord often continues to work today. He works through someone in the service of others and the good that is done by that person often remains below the radar. So much of the good that is done in the world is like that. It doesn't become widely known. Sometimes it is only after someone dies that people become aware of all the good the person did. Yet, every act of service done out of love for someone bears its own good fruit, in the life of the one serving and the one being served, and, very often, in the lives of many other people who are impacted indirectly by this act of service. We can learn from Jesus in the gospels to be faithful to the good work the Lord may be asking us to do, without using it to promote ourselves in any way.

15 January, Friday, First Week in Ordinary Time
Mark 2:1–12
When it comes to our faith journey we are all very dependent on one another. We are supported on our journey towards the Lord by the faith of others, and our own faith supports others on their journey towards the Lord. Today's gospel reading shows this in a very graphic way. Jesus was in a house in Capernaum, probably Peter's house, preaching the word of God. A paralysed man wanted to get to Jesus but he was completely dependent on others to carry

him to Jesus. Fortunately, he had good friends who were determined to bring him to Jesus, to do for him what he could not do for himself. Such was their determination that they created an opening in the roof of the house where Jesus was preaching so as to lower their friend in front of him. The paralysed man's faith in Jesus was matched by their faith in Jesus. Their struggle to get their friend to Jesus was inspired by their faith in him. The gospel reading shows that Jesus saw their efforts not as an unwelcome disturbance but as a powerful act of faith. 'Seeing their faith, Jesus said to the paralytic, "My child, your sins are forgiven".' It was the faith of his friends that allowed this man to meet Jesus personally and to hear Jesus' very personal and liberating word to him. Even before his physical healing, the paralytic needed reassurance that God loved him unconditionally and had forgiven his sins. It was his friends that made it possible for him to hear this liberating word from God. Each one of us has a role to play in helping others to hear God's loving word, spoken to us through his Son who is with us until the end of time.

16 January, Saturday, First Week in Ordinary Time
Mark 2:13–17

When I read the gospels I am often struck by the questions people ask. Jesus himself asks many questions, as do many of the other characters who appear in the gospels. In today's gospel reading, the scribes and the Pharisees ask the question, 'Why does Jesus eat with tax collectors and sinners?' As far as they were concerned, to eat with tax collectors and sinners was to risk being contaminated by them. They would have argued that it was better to keep yourself separate from such people in order to preserve your moral health. However, Jesus did not share this concern. Rather than fearing that the sin of others might morally infect him, he knew that his goodness, God's goodness in him, would transform others. The Lord is never diminished by our failings; rather, we are always ennobled by his holiness. That is why the Lord does not separate himself from us, even when we might be tempted to separate ourselves from him, because of what we have done or failed to do. The Lord is always ready to sit with us, to share table with us, to enter into communion with us, in order that in our weakness we might draw from his strength and in our many failings we might draw from his goodness and love.

18 January, Monday, Second Week in Ordinary Time
Mark 2:18–22

In the gospel reading, Jesus uses the image of a wedding feast to speak about his own ministry. Weddings are almost always very happy occasions. The couple are starting out on a new life together and everyone present is delighted to share their joy. The image Jesus uses in the gospel reading suggests that his ministry among us was a joyful time. After all, he had come to preach good news, the good news of God's loving and powerful presence in our midst, liberating us from all that diminishes us. Jesus also uses the image of new wine in that gospel reading. Wine always flows at wedding banquets. Again, the image of wine suggests joyful celebration. The gospel reading reminds us that our relationship with the Lord brings us joy, not a superficial kind of joy, but that deeply rooted joy that comes from knowing that we are deeply loved by God and that God has a wonderful purpose in store for all of us. Saint Paul lists joy as one expression of the fruit of the Spirit. Even as he sat in his prison cell, he wrote to the church in Philippi, 'Rejoice in the Lord, always, again I will say, Rejoice'. We too can rejoice in the Lord; our relationship with the Lord is the source of our joy. We have heard good news, and if we allow that good news to seep into us we can become good news for others.

19 January, Tuesday, Second Week in Ordinary Time

Mark 2:23–28

If you ever have the good fortune to go to the Holy Land, you will be struck by how fertile the region of Galilee in the north really is. Crops of various kinds can grow there in abundance. The image of Jesus and his disciples walking through fields of ripe corn in today's gospel reading reflects that fertile landscape. Jesus had no difficulty with them plucking some of the abundant ears of corn, rubbing them in their hands and eating what was edible. However, the Pharisees objected and made their objection known to Jesus. Their difficulty was that the disciples were doing this on the sabbath day. They interpreted the actions of the disciples as a form of reaping, and reaping corn was forbidden by the sabbath law. For them, God's law comes first and such law judges people's actions. However, for Jesus, people come first and all law, including God's law, is at the service of human well-being and flourishing. He considered that his hungry disciples had a right to satisfy their hunger in this way, even on the sabbath day. The sabbath was there to serve people, not the other way around. We can learn from Jesus here that whatever promotes human well-being has to take priority over all other considerations. No set of laws, no institution, no matter how hallowed or sacred, can be promoted at the expense of the fundamental needs and entitlements of people. The question Jesus would always want us to ask is, 'Who is being served here?' For Jesus, and for his followers, it is the service of the hungry, the weak, the most vulnerable, that must take priority over all other considerations.

20 January, Wednesday, Second Week in Ordinary Time

Mark 3:1–6

There are two very contrasting attitudes in today's gospel reading. There is the attitude of Jesus' enemies towards him. They were watching him, hoping for something to use against him. Their only interest was to bring Jesus down regardless of the good he may appear to be doing. They had no interest in the well-being of the man with the withered hand. He was of interest to them only as a kind of bait to allow them to bring Jesus down. The attitude of Jesus stands in contrast. His only concern was to do good to the man with the withered hand, regardless of how that was perceived by others. Jesus was honouring the sabbath, and thereby God, by working to bring greater life to someone in need. Jesus' enemies, for all their protestations in support of the sabbath, were dishonouring the sabbath, and thereby God, by trying to bring down a man in whom God's Spirit was powerfully at work, while ignoring the plight of one of the vulnerable members of God's family. Jesus' desire to build up stood in contrast to their desire to tear down. His passion to give strength was opposed by their passion to undermine. We can all be tempted to tear down and undermine when the call of the moment is to build up and give strength. Jesus inspires us and empowers us to honour God by strengthening the weak and encouraging the good that others are doing.

21 January, Thursday, Second Week in Ordinary Time
Mark 3:7–12

I think we all appreciate it when people say that they will pray for us. We feel a sense of spiritual solidarity with them, which can be very reassuring at vulnerable moments in our lives. In that context, the opening words of today's first reading are very reassuring. According to the author, Jesus 'is living for ever to intercede for all who come to God through him'. The risen Lord himself is praying for us. When we come to God through Jesus we are being assured of his prayerful support. The gospel reading speaks of 'great numbers' coming to God through Jesus, people not just from Galilee and Judea, but from further afield, from Idumaea, Transjordania, and the region of Tyre and Sidon. Jesus is the object of popular attention over a wide area. It is said of this large crowd that they were crowding forward to touch him. One of the ways we touch Jesus today is through prayer. In prayer, we enter into communion with the Lord, touching his presence to us. Whereas the Lord prays *for* us, we pray *to* him. That coming together of the Lord praying for us and of our praying to the Lord can create an opening for the Lord to work in a life-giving way in all our lives, just as in the gospel reading he worked to heal people of their afflictions.

22 January, Friday, Second Week in Ordinary Time
Mark 3:13–19

In today's gospel reading Jesus calls twelve from among the larger group of disciples. There were two elements to the Lord's call. Firstly, he called these twelve to be his companions, to be with him, and, secondly, he called them to be sent out to preach and to heal, to share in his own work. They would first need to be with him before they could go out on his behalf. They needed to get to know the Lord of the work before they could take up the work of the Lord. The pattern that applies to the twelve in our gospel reading applies to all of us, to some degree or another. We too are called to share in the Lord's work, to witness to him, to bring his Gospel into the world by our lives. Yet, prior to that, we are called to become the Lord's companions, to be with him. One of the primary ways we spend time with the Lord is through prayer. In prayer we attune ourselves to the Lord's presence to us, we become present to him as he is to us. That is true of all prayer, whether it is the public prayer of the Church, like the Eucharist, or our own personal and private prayer. Our prayerful presence with the Lord creates space for the Lord to work in and through us. The gospel reading suggests that we need to grow in our relationship with the Lord by spending time with him, before we can go forth in his name, as his ambassadors.

23 January, Saturday, Second Week in Ordinary Time
Mark 3:20–21

Mark suggests strongly in the course of his gospel that a lot of people did not really understand Jesus during his public ministry. One of the questions that keeps coming up in one form or another is, 'Who then is this?' In today's very short gospel reading, it is clear that even Jesus' relatives do not understand who Jesus is or what he is about. When Jesus' workload prevents him from eating properly, Mark tells us that his relatives set out to take charge of him, because many were saying that he was out of his mind. They would go on to learn on that occasion that Jesus was not open to being taken charge of by his relatives. The only one who was in charge of Jesus was God. Jesus was doing God's work, and part of that work was to form a new family, a family of disciples, of brothers and sisters of Jesus, sons and daughters of God. Jesus' own natural family, his relatives, would have to come to terms with that. We are all part of that new family; we are all the fruit of Jesus' work, a work that even Jesus' family struggled hard to understand at the time. For us who are part of this new family, the question, 'Who then is this?' remains a relevant question. We can answer that question to some extent, but we are always struggling to know more fully the Son of God whose brothers and sisters we have become.

25 January, Monday, Feast of the Conversion of Saint Paul
Mark 16:15–18

A certain kind of religious zeal can make us very intolerant of those who do not share our religious beliefs. At its worst, religious zeal can drive people to persecute and even kill those of other faiths.

This was the kind of zeal that drove Paul. He was such a zealous Jew that when he saw some fellow Jews preaching a message that he considered heresy, he launched a campaign of violence against them. He thought he was doing God's work. However, an experience on the road between Jerusalem and Damascus brought home to him that he was actually opposing God. He came to understand that he was persecuting the followers of God's Son. Indeed, in persecuting them, he was persecuting the Lord: 'Why are your persecuting me?' From that moment, the zealous persecutor of the Lord's followers became the Lord's most effective ambassador to others, especially to pagans. It was the Lord who worked this transformation in Paul's life. This was the Lord's doing, not Paul's. The story of Paul reminds us that the Lord can transform all our lives. The Lord never gives up on us, even when we are opposing him by our way of life. He continues to knock on the door of our lives until we admit him. As Paul's story shows us, the Lord is never held prisoner by our past. He is never rendered powerless by our resistance to him. Paul's story assures us that where we have been in our relationship with the Lord does not determine where we can be in that relationship or where we will be, with the Lord's gracious help. As Paul would go on to say in one of his letters, looking back at this experience on the road to Damascus, 'By the grace of God I am what I am, and his grace towards me has not been in vain'.

26 January, Tuesday, Memorial of Saints Timothy and Titus
Luke 10:1–9
Timothy and Titus were two of Paul's closest co-workers. Paul was arguably the most influential member of the early Church. He was hugely influential in his own time, and his letters have shaped the life of the Church down the centuries. Yet, for all his significance, he was keenly aware of himself as dependent on the gifts of others.

He had many co-workers, men and women, on whom he depended. They were as significant for him as he was for them. He didn't simply have a working relationship with people like Timothy and Titus; he had a sense of real communion with them. That comes across with regard to Timothy in today's first reading. Paul writes to him, 'always I remember you in my prayers'. His communion with Timothy found expression in prayerful remembrance. As he remembered his associates in prayer, they must have remembered Paul in prayer. We have an image here in microcosm of what the Church is called to be. As members of the Church, we are in communion with each other, a communion that is the fruit of the Spirit. One of the ways in which we give expression to this communion is by praying for each other. Like Paul, we are aware of our dependence on others within the Church. Within this communion of faith and love, we each have something to give to each other and much to receive from each other. We are members of one body, the body of Christ, and, like the physical members of a human body, we are mutually interdependent. In the gospel reading, Jesus did not send out the seventy-two, one at a time, although that might have been the best way to cover the widest possible area. He sent the seventy-two out two by two, in thirty-six groups of two. Jesus wanted no one to work alone; he knew that each would be dependent on the other. He also encouraged each pair to become dependent on those to whom they preached the Gospel. They were not to bring a haversack of food because they were to rely for hospitality on those to whom they preached. Today's feast of Timothy and Titus reminds us that the Lord can work most powerfully through the many, rather than the one, provided the many are in a communion of faith and love.

27 January, Wednesday, Third Week in Ordinary Time

Mark 4:1–20

Speaking through the prophet Isaiah the Lord says, 'So shall the word be that goes out of my mouth; it shall not return to me empty, but it shall accomplish that which I purpose, and succeed in the thing for which I sent it'. To some extent the parable in today's gospel reading reflects that declaration of the Lord that his word will accomplish God's purpose in the end. Much of the farmer's work in sowing the seed seems like a waste of time. Nature's elements, like the birds of the air, rocky soil and thorns, inhibit the work of the sowing. However, in spite of the loss, some seed falls on good soil and the return from that seed far outweighs the failure of the other seed. If the seed is an image of the word of God, as the interpretation of the parable suggests, then the Lord's word accomplishes the Lord's purposes, in spite of the many resistances in the human heart, be it our failure to allow the word to take root there, or our unwillingness to be faithful in times of trial, or our allowing the attractions of the world to choke the word. Human resistance will not, in the end, undermine the power of the Lord's word. Human failure will not have the last word. In the language of Paul, where sin abounds, grace abounds all the more. This realisation does not make us complacent. However, it does keep us hopeful when we are faced with the various forms that our own failure can take. Our resistance to the Lord's word does not weaken the life-giving power of that word. After failure, the word remains in all its nurturing efficacy. Even after all our various resistances, we can always return to the Lord, saying with Peter, 'Lord, to whom can we go? You have the words of eternal life.'

28 January, Thursday, Third Week in Ordinary Time
Mark 4:21–25

The verses we have just heard come immediately after the parable of the sower and its interpretation. That parable sought to reassure Jesus' disciples that the word Jesus proclaimed would bear fruit in people's lives, in spite of the many obstacles working against that word, such as the cares and pleasures of this life and the persecution that the word can bring. The verses that make up today's gospel reading remind us that we have our part to play in the word bearing fruit. Jesus says, 'If anyone has ears to hear, let him listen', and 'Take notice of what you are hearing'. We need to become good listeners to the word. Jesus goes on to say that the more we invest ourselves in that attentive listening to the word, the more we will be given: 'The amount you measure out is the amount you will be given'. In that sense, 'the one who has will be given more'. As we give of ourselves to the word, we discover that we keep receiving more. On the other hand, 'from the one who has not, even what he has will be taken away'. If we don't make the effort to hear the word and receive from its riches, our spiritual understanding of the word diminishes and our capacity to receive from its riches can be undermined. We can never underestimate the power of the Lord's word, but today's gospel reminds us that its power is rendered less effective if we do not make the effort to hear it.

29 January, Friday, Third Week in Ordinary Time
Mark 4:26–34

The first of the two parables in today's gospel reading, the parable of the seed growing secretly, is only to be found in Mark's Gospel. It is an intriguing parable. Parables are like that; they are meant to make us think. Rather than telling us the message straight, they tease us into reflection. In the parable, once the farmer sows the seed, he has to wait until the harvest. There is very little he can do between sowing and harvesting. He has to stand back and let the seed grow of its own accord. There are times in life when we too will need to stand back; there is a time to act and there is a time to wait, recognising that the real action is happening away from us and without us. In our relationship with the Lord there is also a time to act and a time to step back and allow the Lord to act without any direct involvement from us. There are times when we need the humility to recognise that the Lord can work better in some situations if we do nothing rather than if we do something. What we need, and what we can pray for, is the wisdom to know when to act, when to sow and to reap, and when to refrain from acting so that the Lord can work more effectively through the work we have already done.

30 January, Saturday, Third Week in Ordinary Time
Mark 4:35–41

When a storm breaks over us in life, we often find ourselves in panic mode. At such times, it can be very helpful to have someone who remains calm as the storm rages. Their calmness can help to calm us. We find such a scenario in today's gospel reading. The disciples and Jesus find themselves in a storm at sea. As a gale blew, waves were breaking into the boat, just as waves sometimes break over the sea wall when the wind is especially strong and the tide is high. In the midst of this storm, the disciples are clearly in panic mode. 'Master, do you not care? We are going down!', they exclaim to Jesus. In contrast, Jesus is a centre of calm in the midst of the storm. He is so calm that he sleeps through the storm. The evangelist gives us that graphic little detail of the head of Jesus asleep on a cushion in the stern of the boat. The disciples' panic does not disturb Jesus, rather his calm becalms his disturbed disciples and the raging storm. When the storm has passed, Jesus asks his disciples two questions: 'Why are you so frightened? How is it that you have no faith?' In Mark's Gospel, the opposite of faith is not so much doubt as fear, the failure to trust. The Lord is always present to us as the centre of calm in the midst of the storms of life. Rather than allowing ourselves to be overcome with fear, he keeps calling on us to open ourselves to his calming presence, trusting that he is more powerful than any storm that life can hurl at us and that he will ultimately protect us from all that threatens us.

1 February, Monday, Feast of Saint Brigid

Luke 6:32–38

Saint Brigid is the secondary patron of Ireland, after Saint Patrick. She was born around 454. When she was young her father wished to make a suitable marriage for her but she insisted that she wanted to consecrate herself to God. She received the veil and spiritual formation probably from Saint Mel and she stayed for a while under his direction in Ardagh. Others followed her example and this led to her founding a double monastery in Kildare, with a section for men and a section for women. Through Brigid's reputation as a spiritual teacher, the monastery became a centre of pilgrimage. She died in 524 and is venerated not only throughout Ireland but in several other European countries. She was renowned for her hospitality, almsgiving and care of the sick. All of her service of others flowed from a rich interior spiritual life. The two readings for this feast express both the interior dimension of the Christian life and its outward expression of service. In the first reading, Saint Paul prays for the Church in Ephesus, asking that their hidden self, their inner self, would grow strong, so that Christ may live in their hearts through faith. It is a wonderful way of speaking about the inner dimension of our lives as followers of the Lord. Christ wants to live in our hearts through our faith, so that our hidden self, or inner self, may grow strong. In that reading Paul goes on to identify our inner self growing strong with being filled with the utter fullness of God. When Christ lives deep within us, when we are filled with the fullness of God, then our inner self will grow strong. In the gospel reading, Jesus speaks of the outer life that flows from such an inner self. It is a life of generous self-giving love of others, including those who are hostile to us. It is a compassionate life that is slow to judge, slow to condemn and ready to forgive. As Jesus says, it is a life that befits sons and daughters of the Most High who is kind to ungrateful and the wicked. Saint Brigid embodied both that deep interior life that Paul speaks about in the first reading and the generous outer life that Jesus speaks about in the gospel reading. On this, her feast day, we look to her, asking her help to grow into the fully mature follower of the Lord that she was.

2 February, Tuesday, The Presentation of the Lord
Luke 2:22–40

The feast of the Presentation of the Lord is a day when, traditionally, we bless candles that will be used in the church's liturgy or at home. The blessing and lighting of candles speaks to us of Jesus, the light of the world. When Mary and Joseph brought their child, Jesus, to the Temple in Jerusalem to present him to God, Simeon addressed their child as a 'light to enlighten the pagans and the glory of your people Israel'. We all have a longing for light, especially at this dark time of the year. Occasionally at this time of the year, we have a bright day, when, even though it may be very cold, the sun shines for the few hours of light we have and the sky is blue from sunrise to sunset. We appreciate such days all the more in these dark winter months. When Mary and Joseph brought their newborn child into the Temple, they were presenting him not just to God but, in a sense, to all of humanity as a light to shine in darkness, a 'light to enlighten' all. We can all experience a darkness of spirit at any time of the year, but perhaps especially in the dark months of winter. Today's feast reminds us that no matter how dark our spirit, we always walk in the light of the Lord's presence. The candles we bless today, the candles we light in our church or in our homes, speak to us of that greater light from God, Jesus, our risen Lord. In the words of Saint John's Gospel, 'the light shines in the darkness, and the darkness did not overcome it'. Today's feast invites us to keep opening our minds and our spirits to this light from God, which shines through Jesus. It is the light of love and the light of life. As Mary and Joseph presented Jesus in the Temple, we are invited to keep presenting ourselves to the Lord, the light of whose presence is always shining upon us, especially in those times when we sense a darkness of some kind coming over us.

3 February, Wednesday, Fourth Week in Ordinary Time
Mark 6:1–6
In today's first reading, the preacher of this written homily called 'the letter to the Hebrews' says to his listeners, 'Be careful … that no root of bitterness should begin to grow and make trouble; this can poison a whole community'. The bitterness he warns against seems to have been there among the community present when Jesus was preaching in his home synagogue in Nazareth. According to Mark, when Jesus preached elsewhere in Galilee 'they were all amazed, and they kept on asking one another, "What is this? A new teaching – with authority!"'. When he healed the paralytic, 'they were all amazed and glorified God, saying, "We have never seen anything like this!"'.' The reaction of the people of Jesus' own Galilean village was very different. They recognised the wisdom of his teaching and the powerful deeds that were worked through him, but, far from glorifying God, recognising that God was the source of Jesus'

wisdom and powerful deeds, they would not accept him. Jesus met with a wall of unbelief, with the result, according to Mark, 'he could work no miracle there'. It was as if the resistance of the people of Nazareth disempowered him. The gospel reading suggests that it was the very familiarity of Jesus, one of their own, that prevented the people of Nazareth from appreciating who was standing among them. Sometimes familiarity does breed contempt. Our familiarity with the gospel message can breed, if not contempt, at least a certain indifference and ennui within us. We need to keep on recovering the freshness of this ever new teaching, so that we continue to stand in amazement at all Jesus says and does in the gospels, and, also, at the enduring power of his words and his presence among us today.

4 February, Thursday, Fourth Week in Ordinary Time
Mark 6:7–13

When Jesus chose a group of twelve from among the larger group of disciples, he chose the number twelve very deliberately, as an echo of the twelve tribes of Israel. He seems to have seen the group of twelve as the nucleus of a renewed Israel. They were to have a special role in Jesus' mission of renewing God's people. In today's gospel reading, we have Mark's account of Jesus sending out the twelve for the first time to share in his mission. It is noteworthy that Jesus sends them out in pairs. Rather than twelve individuals going off in twelve different directions, there are six groups of two going off in six different directions. Some might think that it would have been more efficient to send out the twelve individually; in that way twice the area could have been covered. However, Jesus clearly saw a greater value in sending out the twelve in twos. No one was to work alone; each would have someone else to work alongside. As disciples of the Lord today, we still need to work together, rather than as individuals or loners. When we work together we learn to receive from and give to each other and, thereby, the Lord is more fully present to others. He did say that where two or three are gathered he would be there in their midst. Even Paul, the great apostle to the Gentiles, was very aware of the debt he owed to what he called his co-workers, and he understood the Church as the body of Christ in which all the members were interdependent. The Lord needs us to work together if his work is to be done in today's world. In the life of faith, we never go it alone.

5 February, Friday, Fourth Week in Ordinary Time
Mark 6:14–29

At the beginning of today's gospel reading, people express their views as to who Jesus really is. Some say that Jesus is a prophet, like the prophets of old. Others are more specific and say that he is Elijah the prophet, whose return was expected at some time. Herod Antipas, the ruler of Galilee, thought that Jesus might be John the Baptist risen from the dead. If this is what Herod Antipas actually thought, it may have sprung from a sense of guilt over ordering the execution of John the Baptist. The gospel reading goes on to say that Herod knew John to be a good and holy man and that he listened to John, even though he was often perplexed by what he had to say. It seems that Herod had John beheaded against his better judgement. He felt bound by a rather rash public oath he had made to his stepdaughter. Herod's wife, Herodias, took advantage of Herod's very public promise by getting her daughter to ask for the head of John the Baptist. Rather than follow his better instincts, Herod gave in to his wife's request, to protect his honour. He felt honour bound to keep an oath he had made publicly. Preserving his honour was more important than preserving the life of a man whom he knew to be good and holy. The dilemma of Herod is the dilemma of us all, at some time in our lives. We sense a call from deep within us to do what is good, noble and honourable, what is generous and life-giving. At the same time, we feel pressures of various kinds to ignore that call and act in a more self-serving, self-protecting, way. At such moments, we need help from beyond ourselves, the help of the Holy Spirit, so that we can take the path the Lord is calling us to take, even though it is the more difficult path, the one that will demand more of us.

6 February, Saturday, Fourth Week in Ordinary Time
Mark 6:30–34
Today's gospel reading suggests that Jesus knew the value of rest. After the disciples had engaged in a period of mission Jesus took them off to some lonely place so that they could rest for a while. There was plenty of work to be done. Jesus and his disciples could have been busy twenty-four hours a day, yet every so often Jesus stood back from his work, and encouraged his disciples to do the same. Jesus was teaching us that there is more to our lives than work. That value of rest is proclaimed in the very first page of the Bible, the first chapter of the Book of Genesis, according to which God rested on the seventh day having engaged in the work of creation for six days. As people made in God's image, we need to rest as well as work. A time of rest is an opportunity to look around and appreciate what we have been given; it is a time to take in God's work, in our own lives, in the lives of others and in our world. In the gospel reading, Jesus' planned time of rest with his disciples was interrupted by people who sought him out, and Jesus adjusted to that unexpected interruption with great grace. Sometimes our plans for times of rest will be interrupted too and we have to adjust, ideally in the same generous way. Yet we continue to seek out times and places of rest in the course of our lives, times when we hand over the initiative to the Lord.

8 February, Monday, Fifth Week in Ordinary Time
Mark 6:53–56

Today's gospel reading brings home to us the extent to which Jesus drew people to himself, especially those who were sick and broken. We are told that 'people started hurrying all through the countryside' and that they 'brought the sick on stretchers to wherever they heard he was'. It was above all those in need of healing who reached out towards Jesus and sought to touch even the fringe of his cloak. They reached out to him because they recognised him as the source of life and healing. We ourselves very often reach out towards the Lord with greatest energy in those times when we experience our own need of healing, whether it is physical or emotional or spiritual healing. The struggles of life, the brokenness and suffering we experience in the course of our lives, can make us more aware of our need of the Lord and more open to his presence. It is often the cracks in our lives that allow the Lord's light to enter and shine on us. It can sometimes be through our experience of the cross that we grow in our relationship with the risen Lord. The darker times of our lives can leave us more spiritually aware by bringing home to us our need of the Lord. It is in such moments that we truly make our own that prayer that forms part of a well-known hymn 'Help of the helpless, o abide with me'.

9 February, Tuesday, Fifth Week in Ordinary Time
Mark 7:1–13

In the gospel reading Jesus places the commandment of God, the word of God, above what the Pharisees call the tradition of the elders, the various oral and written traditions that had developed over the centuries in an effort to apply the commandment of God, the word of God, to daily life. This body of tradition was a genuine effort to bring the word of God in Scripture to bear on the concrete details of people's lives, such as how and what to eat, which is the issue in today's gospel reading. There is always a danger that such religious traditions can assume an authority equivalent to or even greater than the authority of God's word. Jesus is calling on the guardians of this tradition to return to the source of the tradition, the word of God. Every religion has to keep returning to its sources so as to ensure that the traditions that have grown up over the centuries do not become more important than those sources. For the Church, the sources are the Scriptures, especially the New Testament, and the early tradition that emerged through reflecting upon and living out the Lord's word. The work of the Second Vatican Council was a movement of returning to the sources. The Lord can never be fully contained by the Church's traditions. Those traditions need to be constantly purified by exposure to the word of God, especially as found in the New Testament. As a community of faith, but also as individual believers, we need to keep returning to the source, to the well, the living and active word of the Lord, so that the Lord can continue to renew us and reshape us in his own living image and likeness.

10 February, Wednesday, Fifth Week in Ordinary Time
Mark 7:14–23
Today's first reading is the second of two accounts of the creation of the human person in the opening chapters of Genesis. There are two elements at play in human creation in this account, the dust of the soil and the breath of God. The author is suggesting that the human person is both of the earth and of God. We are not purely spiritual beings, and we are not purely material beings. We are embodied spirits. Because we are of the earth, we are intimately related to the rest of creation. Because we have the breath of God within us, we are intimately related to the Creator God. We don't have to flee our bodies, or flee creation, to encounter God. We come to God in

all our embodied reality. Similarly, we relate to the rest of creation as God's agents, endowed with God's creative Spirit, tasked with giving expression to God's care for creation. As people who have received the breath of God, the Spirit of God, all we say and do in the body is to be shaped by God's Spirit. In the gospel reading, Jesus lists attitudes and actions that are not shaped by God's Spirit, such as theft, murder, adultery, avarice, deceit, envy, pride and folly. 'All these evil things,' Jesus says, 'come from within', from an inner core that is not shaped by God's Spirit. We need God to keep breathing his breath or Spirit of life into our lives, if our lives are to help 'renew the face of the earth' in the words of today's responsorial psalm.

11 February, Thursday, Fifth Week in Ordinary Time
Mark 7:24–30
It is often the way in the Scriptures that those perceived to be closest to the Lord turn from him, whereas those perceived to be beyond the reach of the Lord turn towards him. Both unbelief and faith can be found in unexpected places and people. We can never take our faith for granted, and neither can we take someone's lack of faith for granted. The woman who approaches Jesus in today's gospel reading was a pagan. To a Jew she was an infidel, someone without faith in the one, true God. Jesus gave the woman in the gospel reading a good reason for not believing in him as God's agent. In his mini parable, drawn from the experience of a reasonably well-to-do family, Jesus publicly identified with the children, the people of Israel, rather than with the house dogs, the pagans. Yet, the woman's faith in Jesus was not deflected by this provocative image of Jesus. She accepts her identification as the house dogs, expressing a willingness to eat any crumbs that fall from Jesus' table, just like the house dogs who benefit from children's often untidy eating habits.

Jesus could not but respond to such persistent and unexpected faith. The woman in the gospel reading is an inspirational character. She inspires us to be faithful to Jesus, even when our faith in him is put to the test, when he seems silent and remote before our heartfelt prayer and, perhaps, gives us good reasons for not believing in him or trusting him. Her determined, persistent faith was life-giving for her daughter. If something of her faith is found in us, then our presence will likewise create a space for God to work creatively in the lives of others.

12 February, Friday, Fifth Week in Ordinary Time
Mark 7:31–37

There is a lovely prayer of blessing over the ears and mouth of the child during the liturgy of baptism. It is prayed shortly after the pouring of water on the child's head, 'The Lord made the deaf to hear and the dumb to speak. May he soon touch your ears to receive his word, and your mouth to proclaim his faith, to the praise and glory of God the Father'. The Lord did indeed make the deaf to hear and the dumb to speak. In today's gospel reading, he made someone who was both deaf and dumb to hear and to speak. The prayer over the child at baptism reminds us that we all need the Lord's help to hear and to speak, even if, unlike the man in the gospel reading, we are blessed with the gift of physical hearing and speech. We need the Lord's help truly to listen to his word to us, and to proclaim our faith in him courageously. The fact that it was only after Jesus enabled the man to hear that he began to speak clearly suggests that good speaking presupposes good hearing. In many respects, hearing is more important than speaking. As it has been said, perhaps that is why the Lord gave us two ears and one mouth. We need to listen twice as much as we speak. If we listen well, we are more likely to speak a word that builds up and enlightens. If we listen well to the

Lord's word to us, we are more likely to speak in the way that the Lord would want us to speak.

13 February, Saturday, Fifth Week in Ordinary Time
Mark 8:1–10

At this point in Mark's Gospel, Jesus has journeyed into a region that would have been populated mostly by pagans. A few chapters earlier, Jesus had fed a large crowd by the Sea of Galilee. Now he is faced with another hungry crowd in this mainly pagan region. The pagan woman had told Jesus that she would settle for crumbs that fall from the table of the children of Israel. However, in this scene, there is no question of this crowd having to settle for crumbs. Jesus shows the same compassion for this hungry, predominantly pagan crowd as he showed earlier for the Jewish crowd. The disciples show the same resistance to taking any responsibility for feeding this crowd as they had earlier shown before a Jewish hungry crowd, 'Where could anyone get bread to feed these people in a deserted place like this?' The kind of questions we ask can either open up space for the Lord to work or close it down. The disciples' question was closing down such space; it was devoid of any expectant faith. Jesus' question, 'How many loaves have you?' was his effort to open up the space for God to work powerfully through him. There were some resources among the crowd, even if they seemed hopelessly inadequate, seven loaves and a few small fish. Yet, once these were offered to Jesus, he worked powerfully through them for the feeding of the multitude. As Paul reminds us, the Lord can do immeasurably more than all we ask or imagine, if we are generous with our resources, small as they may seem to us.

15 February, Monday, Sixth Week in Ordinary Time

Mark 8:11–13

In today's gospel reading, Jesus displays a weariness of spirit in response to the Pharisees' demand for a sign from heaven. Surely Jesus had already given them sufficient signs from heaven by healing the sick, communicating God's forgiveness to sinners, proclaiming the presence of God's kingdom in word and deed. They clearly wanted a more spectacular sign from Jesus that would make it impossible for them not to believe in him as God's anointed one. Jesus does not submit to the demand of the Pharisees for such a sign but, rather, leaves them and crosses to the other side of the Sea of Galilee. The demand for some kind of clear sign from God is not unique to the Pharisees. At some time in our lives, we can all find ourselves hoping for such a sign, even if we don't demand one. Especially, if we are trying to discern what the Lord may be asking of us, we often long for some sign that would make the Lord's will for our lives clearer to us. It is a legitimate and understandable longing, yet the response of Jesus to the Pharisees in the gospel reading suggests that the obtaining of clear signs should not be our primary longing. Rather than asking for signs from the Lord, what should we ask for? Wisdom is something we can certainly pray for, in the expectation that our prayer will be heard. We need the wisdom from on high if we are to discern what the Lord may be asking of us. Here is certainly a case of, 'ask and you will receive, seek and you will find', in the words of Jesus elsewhere in the Gospels.

16 February, Tuesday, Sixth Week in Ordinary Time

Mark 8:14–21

Today's gospel reading is unusual for the number of questions that Jesus asks his disciples. They are all asked in desperation. It seems as if Jesus is almost ready to give up on his disciples. He has invested a great deal in them, yet they don't seem to be making any progress. Jesus asks them, 'Do you not yet understand?' His questions suggest that their minds are closed, that they don't see with their eyes or hear with their ears, that they are without perception. He speaks like a frustrated teacher who just can't seem to get through to his pupils. Jesus may have been tempted to give up on his disciples, but he didn't. They would go on to disappoint him in a much more dramatic fashion in the hour of his passion and death, deserting him when he needed them. Yet, it was to these same disciples that Jesus as risen Lord appeared, commissioning them to go forth in his name to preach the Gospel. Today's gospel reading suggests that there is hope for us all. We often get it wrong in our following of the Lord. Like the disciples in the gospel reading we can be slow to perceive and understand what he is showing us. We can be attracted and seduced by our own wrong desires, failing to stand firm when our faith is put to the test, yet the Lord remains faithful to us. As long as we are seeking him, the Lord will not give up on us. In a sense, we are all he has and he needs us. If the Lord does not give up on us, we must resist the temptation to give up on ourselves, especially in those times when we feel we are falling short of where we could be.

17 February, Ash Wednesday
Matthew 6:1–6, 16–18
The opening words of the first reading of Lent, from the prophet Joel, capture the primary message of Lent,: 'Come back to me with all your heart … turn to the Lord your God again, for he is all tenderness and compassion, slow to anger, rich in graciousness.' The call to come back, to turn to the Lord is at the heart of Lent. It is a call to turn towards the one who is always turned towards us in tenderness and compassion. Coming back or turning suggests a change of direction. The word that is translated 'repent' in

English means to have a change of mind or heart. We often think of repentance as a feeling of sorrow for any wrong we have done or good we have failed to do. However, repentance is a more positive movement than that. It is a turning towards the Lord, which will often mean a turning away from other directions we could take. That turning, that change of direction, that change of mind or heart, is supremely life affirming because the one who is turned towards us and who calls out to us to turn towards him more fully is the one who is the source of our joy. In the words of today's responsorial psalm, 'Give me again the joy of your help, with a spirit of fervour sustain me'. The traditional Jewish practices of almsgiving, prayer and fasting that Jesus talks about in the gospel reading are all in the service of that turning towards the Lord as the source of our life and joy. Lent is not intended to be a gloomy season. It is what Paul calls in today's second reading, a 'favourable time'. It is a time when we are invited to taste afresh the favour of God, to draw life from his sustaining presence, so that we can more fully become what Paul calls in that reading, 'the goodness of God'. It is a wonderful way of thinking about the journey of faith, becoming the goodness of God. We can only become the goodness of God if we keep on turning towards the God of all goodness.

18 February, Thursday after Ash Wednesday
Luke 9:22–25

When we hear the language of self-renunciation in today's gospel reading, we can think of it as something negative, a saying 'no' to things. Perhaps that is some people's perception of Christianity. They see it as something negative, yet the call of Jesus is fundamentally positive. He calls us to follow him and in following him to find life. Jesus' call to renounce ourselves is in the service of that positive call to follow him as the source of life. The call to follow Jesus is a call to life. In saying 'choose me', Jesus is saying to us in the words of today's first reading, 'choose life'. Jesus calls us into a personal relationship with himself and he promises us that if we respond to his call we will become fully alive as human beings; we will save our life, in the words of the gospel reading. In the Gospel of John, Peter shows an appreciation of this positive understanding of Jesus' call when he puts this question to Jesus, 'Lord, to whom shall we go? You have the message of eternal life.' It was as if Peter was saying, 'What direction would we take other than following you who came that we may have life and have it to the full?' That question of Peter, 'To whom shall we go?' is one worth sitting with as we begin our Lenten journey. What is to be the basic direction of our lives? Lent is a season when we turn afresh towards the Lord and go in his direction more fully, a time when we renew our response to his call to follow him and, in so doing, experience the life-giving power of his presence and his message.

19 February, Friday after Ash Wednesday
Matthew 9:14–15
In the first reading Isaiah makes a strong connection between fasting, on the one hand, and almsgiving and working for justice, on the other. The kind of fasting that pleases God, according to Isaiah, is one that finds expression in feeding the hungry, sheltering the homeless, letting the oppressed go free. We fast so as to be freer to give ourselves in the service of others. In the gospel reading Jesus affirms the value of fasting for the period after his death and resurrection. He too linked fasting and almsgiving closely together and he linked both with prayer, as was clear from the gospel reading that we read for Ash Wednesday. Within the Christian vision, fasting or abstaining is not about losing weight. Rather it is about becoming free of what is not essential, so as to be able to give ourselves more

fully in love to God in prayer and to our neighbour in loving service. We all have something to fast from; it may not necessarily be food or drink. We all have something to let go of so that we can be more available to the Lord for his work in the world. There may be something that absorbs us too much and that blocks our relationship with God and with others, especially those who need us most. Lent is a time when we ask for the grace to fast and step away from whatever is holding us back, and hindering us from being all that God is calling us to be.

20 February, Saturday after Ash Wednesday

Luke 5:27–32

Jesus clearly saw something in Levi the tax collector that many others didn't. The Pharisees and the scribes categorised him as a 'sinner', asking Jesus, 'Why do you eat and drink with tax collectors and sinners?' Yet, Jesus was not only prepared to eat and drink with tax collectors and sinners but called one tax collector, Levi, to become part of that small group of twelve he gathered around himself to share in his work in a more focused way. The gospel reading raises the question, 'How do we look on people?' Jesus looked on people with a generous and hopeful spirit. Levi may have left a lot to be desired in terms of his compliance with God's Law, as it was understood by the experts in the law at the time. When Jesus looked on Levi, he didn't simply see what was lacking in him, but also, and more importantly, the person he could become. Yes, he was 'sick', but so too were all men and women in different ways, including those who thought of themselves as virtuous. Jesus, as the divine physician, could heal what needed healing in others and empower them to become all that God was calling them to be. The Lord looks upon each one of us with the same generous and hopeful spirit. He is more attuned to the person we can become than to the ways we have failed. The Lord also calls on us to look on each other in the same generous, hopeful way that he looks upon us.

22 February, Monday, Chair of Saint Peter
Matthew 16:13–19

In the Gospel of Matthew, Jesus speaks of 'the scribes and the Pharisees who sit on Moses' seat'. The scribes and Pharisees were teachers and 'Moses' seat' was a symbol of their teaching authority. Such teachers in the time of Jesus usually sat to teach, with their disciples or pupils gathered around them. The chair or seat of Peter is a symbol of the teaching authority of the bishop of Rome, whom we call the pope. This feast commemorates the teaching authority of the vicar of Christ. In the lifetime of many of us, we have witnessed several popes, each of them very different from the preceding one and the following one. In the past fifty years alone we have had popes from Italy, Poland, Germany and Argentina. Yet, as Roman Catholics, we believe that what they have in common is a special teaching authority. They each exercised that teaching role in their own very distinctive way. It is a teaching role that goes back to the teaching role entrusted by Jesus to Peter. In the gospel reading, Jesus says to Peter, 'Whatever you bind on earth shall be considered bound in heaven; whatever you loose on earth shall be considered loosed in heaven'. The language of binding and loosing is a little strange to our ears, but it was a common Jewish term to refer to a teaching role. As teachers, the scribes and Pharisees had the authority to determine what aspects of the Jewish Law were binding and what aspects could be interpreted more loosely. However, Peter is being given authority as teacher not with regard to the Jewish Law but with regard to Jesus' own teaching. He has a special role in interpreting the teaching of Jesus for the Church of Jesus: 'On this rock I will build my church'. We believe that this role given to Peter now resides in a special way with the bishop of Rome. As disciples of Jesus today, we listen to his word as it comes to us in the Scriptures, but we also listen to it as it comes to us through the teaching of our present pope, who seeks to interpret Jesus' word for us today. In that sense, we are all listeners, we are learners, we are pupils, seeking to know and to do the will of God as Jesus has revealed it to us by his teaching, his life, his death and resurrection.

23 February, Tuesday, First Week of Lent

Matthew 6:7–15

Today's gospel reading highlights one of the three great Lenten practices, that of prayer. In the gospel reading, Jesus declares that, when it comes to prayer, many words are not needed. The pagans use many words in prayer hoping that by doing so that they will force the god to act. Jesus insists that his followers concentrate on quality rather than quantity in prayer. The chief quality for the Christian is trust in God the Father's loving providence. It is that quality above all that is expressed in the short prayer that Jesus gives his followers, the Lord's Prayer, as we call it. The Lord's Prayer is not only a prayer but also a lesson in how to pray. The first part of this prayer teaches us to focus on the coming to pass of God the Father's purpose for our world rather than on our personal concerns – 'your name, your kingdom, your will'. God's name will be honoured when God's kingdom comes and God's kingdom will come when God's will is done. In praying that God's will be done we are committing to doing God's will ourselves. It is only after the focus on God's purposes that we are encouraged to focus on ourselves, our basic needs, our daily bread, forgiveness for our sins and deliverance from evil. We are encouraged to focus on ourselves not as individuals but as members of a community; that is why the language of the second part of the prayer is 'our' rather than 'my'.

We petition God not just for ourselves as individuals but for each other. Jesus teaches us that prayer is always a going out of ourselves towards God and towards our neighbours.

24 February, Wednesday, First Week of Lent

Luke 11:29–32

I have often been struck by those sayings of Jesus in today's gospel reading, 'There is something greater than Solomon here … There is something greater than Jonah here'. It was as if Jesus was trying to get his contemporaries to appreciate the full reality of his ministry. They were looking but not really seeing and listening but not really hearing. They were looking for a sign when Jesus was already giving them more signs than they needed, if only they were attentive. The Lord remains present to us in all his 'fullness', in the language of the Fourth Gospel. We can easily fail to appreciate the full reality of his presence and ministry among us. We, too, can look but fail to see, listen but fail to hear. It can happen that people only discover the richness of their faith after many years, often quite late in life. Their relationship with the Lord has been there but somewhat dormant. Then something comes along that makes them appreciate that relationship more fully. They begin to appreciate in a new way the 'something greater' that Jesus talks about in the gospel reading. There is always a 'something greater' to be discovered in our relationship with the Lord. There is always more to our faith than we appreciate at any one time in our lives. We are on a journey of endless discovery when it comes to our relationship with the Lord and all it implies for ourselves and our world. It is an adventure that it always before us to be explored. Every day we can discover 'something greater'.

25 February, Thursday, First Week of Lent
Matthew 7:7–12
The prayer of Queen Esther in today's first reading is a very powerful prayer of someone in mortal peril, especially the final petition of her prayer: 'Come to my help, for I am alone and have no one but you, Lord'. She is a powerful woman, a queen, but at this desperate moment in her life she recognises that she is completely powerless and totally dependent on the Lord alone for help. There can come a time in all of our lives when we recognise that if the Lord does not help me no one will. These are moments when our total dependence on the Lord for our personal survival is crystal clear to us. We come before the Lord in our poverty, our vulnerability, and in desperation we cry for his help. This is the kind of prayer out of the depths of mortal peril that the Lord never fails to answer. This is the backdrop against which we can hear the exhortation of Jesus in today's gospel reading: 'Ask and it will be given to you; search, and you will find; knock, and the door will be opened to you'. He is not saying 'God will give you anything you want', but rather, 'God will never abandon you when you feel completely isolated and truly desperate'. It is then that, in the words of Jesus in the gospel reading, 'your Father in heaven will give good things to those who ask him'. Sometimes we have to be in dire straits, like Queen Esther, to realise how much we need the Lord. It is often moments of greatest weakness that open us up most fully to the Lord's 'faithfulness and love', in the language of today's responsorial psalm.

26 February, Friday, First Week of Lent
Matthew 5:20–26
Jesus was very aware that actions have their roots in something deeper. The awful action of killing someone often has its roots in anger residing deep within the person. That is why Jesus goes

beyond the commandment 'Do not kill' and prohibits the kind of anger that leads to killing, an anger that often finds expression initially in speaking disrespectfully of others, such as calling them 'fool'. Behind a certain way of acting is often to be found a certain way of speaking and behind both can be found dark emotions in the human heart. Jesus wanted to get to the root of actions that inflict harm, sometimes deadly harm, on others. That is what Jesus means in today's gospel reading by a 'virtue that goes deeper than that of the scribes and Pharisees'. Such a deeper virtue is not something we can create from our own efforts or willpower alone. It is the Holy Spirit, the Spirit of the risen Lord, who can transform the deepest roots of our lives. The Jewish Scriptures speak about the Spirit creating a new heart within us, the heart understood as the inner core of the person from which so much else flows. Within our own Christian tradition, there is a prayer that reflects this understanding of the role of the Spirit of God: 'Come Holy Spirit, fill my heart, and kindle in me the fire of your love'. In one of his letters, Paul says, 'It is no longer I who live, but Christ who lives in me'. Through the power of the Holy Spirit, Christ can live deep within us, and that is the source of the deeper virtue that Jesus speaks about in today's gospel reading.

27 February, Saturday, First Week of Lent

Matthew 5:43–48

The call of Jesus at the end of today's gospel reading sounds very daunting: 'You must therefore be perfect just as your heavenly Father is perfect'. We are all very much aware that we are a long way from being perfect. Even the word 'perfect' can be off-putting for us. When we speak of someone as a perfectionist we are not always paying them a compliment. We think of perfectionists as overly demanding and somewhat intolerant of human weakness.

However, when we read back over the whole of today's gospel reading, we can see that when Jesus calls us to be as perfect as God, he is calling on us to be as loving as God. He is talking about the perfection of love. Jesus declares that God loves the good and the not so good equally, just as the sun shines and the rain falls on both alike. God's love does not discriminate. There is no less or more when it comes to God's love. As Saint John says in his first letter, God is Love. To say God's love is perfect is to say that what we do or fail to do has no impact on the quality of God's love for us. God loved the people who crucified Jesus as much as the martyrs who were killed for bearing witness to Jesus. God's love cannot change. What changes is our capacity to receive God's love and to allow ourselves to be transformed by it, so that something of God's perfect love takes flesh in our own lives. We will never be as loving as God is loving in this life, loving others without any regard to how they relate to us. Some few people come very close to loving in such a divine way. When such people come to our attention, we stand amazed by them. Yet, with the help of the Holy Spirit, we can all, at least, keep growing towards that quality of love that is of God. That is the goal of our lives as followers of Jesus. That goal is very beautifully expressed in the prayer, 'May we come to share in the divinity of Christ who humbled himself to share in our humanity'.

1 March, Monday, Second Week of Lent

Luke 6:36–38

Today's first reading from the prophet Daniel is one of the great communal prayers for forgiveness in the Jewish Scriptures. The people as a whole declare, 'we have sinned, we have done, wrong, we have acted wickedly … We, the people of Judah, the citizens of Jerusalem, the whole of Israel, near and far away'. Everyone takes responsibility for the failure of the nation, the people. When something is clearly wrong in society or the Church, it can be tempting to place the blame on some individual or some group. It is somebody else's fault, not mine. The kind of prayer we heard in today's first reading acknowledges that everyone is at fault and each person has to take some responsibility for what has gone wrong. That sense of all of us having failed in some way is a healthy antidote to placing the blame on others. In the gospel reading, Jesus calls on us not to judge or condemn others. He was aware of the tendency of us all to see the problem as residing only in others and not also in ourselves. A realistic sense of our own failings can act as a break on our tendency to condemn others too quickly. That communal act of confession in the first reading doesn't just focus on the sin of the people. It has an even stronger focus on God's loving kindness, 'To the Lord our God mercy and pardon belong'. That conviction of God's mercy and pardon gives the author the confidence to publicly acknowledge the sin of the whole people. Our primary focus too is to be on the God of mercy and pardon, and that focus gives us the confidence and freedom to acknowledge our failings, our sins, before him.

2 March, Tuesday, Second Week of Lent
Matthew 23:1–12

Jesus is critical of the religious leaders of his time because their teaching, their interpretation of the Jewish Law, is unnecessarily burdensome for people, 'They lay up heavy burdens and place them on people's shoulders.' Jesus was aware that many of his contemporaries felt burdened by religious obligations. In contrast to the religious leaders, Jesus calls out to people, 'Come to me, all you that are weary and are carrying heavy burdens, and I will give you rest'. Jesus was saying that his teaching, his interpretation of God's will, far from burdening people will give people rest. What does

Jesus mean by 'rest' here? He is not referring to inactivity or sleep, clearly. There is a line in the psalm, 'The Lord is my shepherd' which might help us to understand what Jesus means by 'rest': 'Near restful waters he leads me to revive my drooping spirit'. The restful waters revive and energise those who are drooping. The teaching of Jesus is rest-giving in the sense that it energises and enlivens us. His word is life-giving, not burden-imposing. Certainly, the teaching of Jesus is demanding, even more demanding than the Jewish Law, but what Jesus asks of us corresponds to the deepest desires of our heart, and in coming to him and submitting to his word, that deepest desire will be satisfied and, as a result, we will be revived and energised. Jesus did not come to burden further an already burdened people; he came that we may have life and have it to the full.

3 March, Wednesday, Second Week of Lent
Matthew 20:17–28

The question, 'What is it you want?' is one that Jesus often asks in the gospels. How people answer that question is an indication of what their priorities are. When Jesus asked the question of the blind man, he answered, 'Let me see again'. When Jesus asked the question of the disciples of John the Baptist at the beginning of John's Gospel, they answered, 'Where are you staying?' In both cases, Jesus could respond to the answer given to his question. When the same question was asked of the mother of two of the twelve, James and John, Jesus could not respond to the answer he got to his question. The answer given by the mother revealed that her priorities were for her sons to have positions of status and honour in Jesus' kingdom. Mark's version of this story suggests these were really the priorities of her sons, as there is no mention of their mother. This was to misunderstand the nature of the kingdom that Jesus came to proclaim. It was at the moment when Jesus was devoid of all status and honour, as he hung from a Roman cross, that he was publicly proclaimed king. This was intended in mockery, but, ironically, it proclaimed a truth. Jesus revealed God's kingdom of love most fully at that moment of greatest shame and humiliation. James and John and the other disciples needed to know that they were signing up to a kingdom that bore no relationship to the kingdoms of this world. Jesus was not to be found among the 'rulers' and 'great men' who 'lord it over' their subjects and 'make their authority felt'. His authority showed itself not in being served but in the self-emptying, loving service of others. The same goes for all who would be his disciples. Jesus' work today remains that of bringing God's kingdom to earth, not building another earthly kingdom.

4 March, Thursday, Second Week of Lent

Luke 16:19–31

Today's first reading from the prophet Jeremiah contrasts two types of people, those who put their trust in things of the flesh, and those who put their trust in the Lord. The prophet is inviting us to ask, 'Where do we put our trust?' 'On what or whom do we rely?' The parable that Jesus speaks in the gospel reading puts this contrast in the form of a story. The rich man put his trust in things of the flesh. He lived for himself; his priority was the satisfying of his own needs. The poor man, Lazarus, put his trust in the Lord; he had no one else on whom he could rely. On the surface, the rich man seemed much more fortunate than Lazarus. In reality, to use the imagery of Jeremiah in the first reading, the poor man was like a tree by the waterside whose foliage stays green even in the heat, whereas the rich man was like a dry shrub in the wastelands. That became clear in the life beyond death. The Lord in whom Lazarus trusted did not let him down, whereas the things of the flesh in which the rich man trusted ultimately failed him. The parable poses the question, 'In what does true riches consist?' It suggests that the truly rich person is the one whose trust is in the Lord, for whom the Lord comes first, whose first love is the Lord. Such a person will have something of the Lord's own awareness of and compassion for those in greatest need, like Lazarus.

5 March, Friday, Second Week of Lent

Matthew 21:33–43, 45–46

Brothers don't always get along very well. It is not unusual for siblings to go their separate ways in the course of their lives. In today's first reading we have a somewhat extreme case of sibling animosity. Jacob had twelve sons, and his favourite was his youngest son, Joseph. Joseph's brothers wanted to kill him and would have done so were it not for the intervention of one of the brothers, Ruben. As a result, Joseph suffered the lesser fate of being thrown into an empty well. It was jealousy that drove the antagonism of Joseph's brothers. They recognised that he was their father's favourite, his coat of many colours being a symbol of that favouritism. In the language of today's gospel, Joseph was the stone rejected by the builders. Yet, that rejected stone went on to become the cornerstone. Joseph was eventually taken captive into Egypt. There, his natural abilities resulted eventually in his gaining a very important position in the Egyptian civil service. When famine struck the land of Israel, Jacob sent his sons to Egypt for food, and the minister for food when the brothers arrived was none other than their brother Joseph. The one they had rejected became their saviour. The early Church saw in the story of Joseph a symbol of the story of Jesus. In today's gospel reading, Jesus clearly identifies with the son of the landowner who was killed by the tenants. He is the stone rejected by the builders. Yet, beyond his rejection, his crucifixion, he became, as risen Lord, the cornerstone of a spiritual building, the Church.

The story of Joseph and Jesus reminds us that God can turn even our worst instincts to a good purpose. God is always working to bring good out of the mess we sometimes create. That realisation can keep us hopeful when we are tempted to get discouraged by the consequences of our own failings.

6 March, Saturday, Second Week of Lent

Luke 15:1–5, 11–32

The younger son in today's parable wants his freedom and the financial resources to exercise his freedom, so he asks for his share of his father's inheritance long before it is due to him. The father indulges his younger son's request; he allowed him to head off on his journey into freedom. Yet the heart of the father goes with his son. When the son's adventure turned to disaster, he experienced a desire for home. This was the small opening that the father needed. He ran out to his broken son to make his journey home shorter. It has been said that the arms and kisses of the father in the parable speak more eloquently of God's love for the lost than all the books of theology. It was at this point that the father discovers his older son is also lost. Whereas the father ran to meet his younger son, the older son kept his distance from his brother. For a second time the father goes out to a lost son. The father showed his love for his younger son above all by his actions; he showed his love for his older son above all by his words, 'My son, you are with me always and all I have is yours'. The older son mistook his relationship with his father as one of slave to master: 'All these years I have slaved for you'. Yet this was not the kind of relationship the father wanted with his son; he desired a relationship of love between equals. One of the messages of this powerful story is that God is always pursuing us in love to offer us what Paul calls the glorious freedom of the children of God, a freedom that is the fruit of a loving relationship with the

God who loves us unconditionally and who is always at work in our lives bringing new life out of death.

8 March, Monday, Third Week of Lent

Luke 4:24–30

In today's first reading, we hear of two people who were asked to do something and initially reacted in a very negative way to what was being asked of them. When the king of Aram asked the king of Israel in a letter to cure his commander Naaman of his leprosy, the king of Israel thought the king of Aram was trying to pick a quarrel with him. When Naaman was asked by Elisha the prophet to bathe in the River Jordan for the healing of his leprosy, Naaman thought Elisha was trying to insult him. However, both the king of Israel and Naaman misinterpreted what was being asked of them. They interpreted something positive in a very negative way. Our first reaction to what is being asked of us is not always the best reaction. Sometimes we need another person to point out to us that there is something good in what we initially see as negative. In the gospel reading, the people of Nazareth heard what Jesus was saying to them as insulting, whereas it was intended to be reassuring. Jesus identifies with two prophets, Elijah and Elisha, who helped two people beyond Israel, showing that the God of Israel was also the God of the pagans. This was good news, but the people of Nazareth heard it as bad news. If God is the God of the pagans then he cannot be the God of Israel as well, they seemed to think. We need the wisdom to hear and see the good in what we can be tempted to dismiss as problematic. The Lord can be speaking to us in and through situations that we initially find disturbing. If we stand back and allow ourselves to reflect and truly listen to what is unfolding, we can be helped to see the Lord in places and in situations where we might never have expected to find him.

9 March, Tuesday, Third Week of Lent

Matthew 18:21–35

It has been said that everyone is in favour of forgiveness until they have someone to forgive. It is easy to talk about the value of forgiveness but not so easy to give expression to that value in our lives when the need arises. It is only when we see forgiveness in action that we realise what a powerful reality it is. I was very struck by an expression of forgiveness some time ago in the aftermath of the killings in Christchurch, New Zealand. A Muslim man in a wheelchair was in one of the mosques at the time of the shooting. His wife was killed trying to protect him. The following day, he was asked by a member of the media what he would say to the mass murderer, if he were to meet him. He said, 'I will tell him that inside him he has great potential to be a generous person, to be a kind person, to be a person who would save people, save humanity, rather than destroy them.' He went on to say, 'I hope and I pray for him he would be a great civilian one day. I don't have any grudge.' Such willingness to forgive in the face of evil leaves us all feeling very humbled. Here was a man who had so little reason to forgive and he freely forgave. In such moments, we catch a glimpse of God's forgiveness. In the parable Jesus told, the master had much to forgive his servant but he forgave him freely. This same servant, having been forgiven so generously, subsequently had very little to forgive someone else but refused to do so. The parable suggests that God's willingness to forgive generously is not in doubt. What can be in doubt is our willingness to pass on the forgiveness we have received to those who sin against us.

10 March, Wednesday, Third Week of Lent
Matthew 5:17–19

In today's first reading, Moses asks the following question of the people of Israel, 'What great nation is there that has its gods so near as the Lord our God is to us whenever we call to him?' The people of Israel had a great sense of the otherness of God, the sense that God is distant from us, and, yet, as Moses' question shows, they also believed that God was near to them and that God heard their call on him when they prayed. As Christians, we can have an even stronger sense of God's nearness to us. We believe that God became flesh in the person of Jesus and that Jesus as risen Lord is with us to the end of time. He is not only with us in some kind of general way, but he is with us in a very personal way. He is close to each one of us. Indeed, through the Holy Spirit, the Lord resides deep within us. It is good to become more aware of the Lord's presence to us and within us at times when, for whatever reason, we find ourselves somewhat cut off from others. In the gospel reading, Jesus says that he came to complete the Law and the Prophets, to bring to fulfilment all that is best in the traditions of his own people, and that includes his people's sense of God's nearness. By his life, his passion and his death, Jesus showed that God is with us in all the details of our lives, including those times when we find ourselves travelling the way of the cross. Many people are suffering in many different ways, from isolation, from sickness, from anxiety, from loss of employment. At such times we need all the more to appreciate that the Lord is very close to us, closer than we are to ourselves. We can draw from him the strength we need. Like Saint Paul in his letter to the Philippians, which he wrote from prison, we can all say, 'I can do all things through him who gives me strength'.

11 March, Thursday, Third Week of Lent

Luke 11:14–23

There is a kind of a mini parable nesting within today's gospel reading. Jesus speaks of a strong man fully armed, guarding his palace, ensuring his goods are undisturbed. Then a stronger man comes along attacks and defeats the strong man, takes away all his weapons on which he had relied, and shares out his spoil. In the context, it is clear that Jesus understands the strong man as Satan and the stronger man as himself. Jesus is responding to his critics who accused him of acting out of Satan's power. He is declaring in no uncertain terms that the power of God, which is at work in his life and ministry, is much stronger than the power of Satan, the power of evil, in its various forms. In his little parable, Jesus does not shy away from using an image that is rooted in the reality of warfare. He is suggesting that he is engaged in a spiritual warfare with the power of Satan, with evil, but that in that warfare, the power of God active in his ministry is much stronger and will ultimately win a decisive victory. The image of spiritual warfare may be a little foreign to our contemporary ears, yet the underlying message of Jesus can continue to speak to us today. Saint Paul expressed this message of Jesus very succinctly in his letter to the Romans: 'Where sin abounds, grace abounds all the more'. No one of us can afford to be blind to sin and evil. It is staring us in the face every day. Yet the gospel reading suggests that there is another power at work in the world, and that is the power of God, the power of the Holy Spirit. This power is stronger and will win out in the end. Our calling is to align ourselves with this power of God, and to allow ourselves to be shaped by this life-giving power which has been released into the world through the life, death and resurrection of Jesus.

12 March, Friday, Third Week of Lent

Mark 12:28–34

In today's first reading from the prophet Hosea, God says to the people of Israel, 'I will love you with all my heart', even though they had repeatedly turned away from God. In the gospel reading Jesus declares that the greatest commandment of the law is to love God with all our heart. Our love of God is always in response to God's love for us. As Saint John reminds us in his letter, 'We love because God first loved us'. The first love is God's love for us. The second love is our love for God, which, as Jesus declares in the gospel reading, is inseparable from our love of our neighbour, understood as our fellow human being. Jesus brings together these two commandments of love of God and love of our neighbour, which were found in different parts of the Bible. Genuine love of God in response to God's love for us will always catch us up into God's own love for humanity. The scribe in the gospel reading who recognised the connection between these two commandments was declared by Jesus to be 'not far from the kingdom of God'. God's kingdom is always present among us whenever we open ourselves to God's love for us and respond to that love by loving God in return and loving all whom God loves. This is what we are asking for whenever we pray, 'Thy kingdom come', in the prayer Jesus gave us to pray.

13 March, Saturday, Third Week of Lent

Luke 18:9–14

The parable in today's gospel reading suggests that how we see ourselves and others is not always how God sees us and others. The Pharisee in today's gospel reading saw himself as virtuous and saw the tax collector as a sinner. The prayer that he prayed reflected this view of himself and of the tax collector. In his prayer he told God his moral achievements, which he believed put him in a different category from the other man praying some distance away, the tax collector. How we pray can be very revealing of who we are. There was a great deal of himself in the prayer of the Pharisee; we can't help but notice the repetition of the little word 'I'. The prayer of the tax collector was quite different. It was much shorter and it consisted not in telling God the good he had done but in asking him for his help, in the form of his mercy. His prayer, 'God, be merciful to me, a sinner', reflects one of the petitions in the prayer that Jesus taught us to pray, 'Forgive us our trespasses'. Without having heard the Lord's Prayer, he prayed in the spirit of that prayer. The prayer of the Pharisee isolated him from God; it kept him closed in on himself. The prayer of the tax collector opened him up to God. His prayer didn't just have the appearance of prayer; it was genuine prayer. Authentic prayer is when we come before God as beggars, recognising our own poverty before God. Both the Pharisee and the tax collector were sinners, in different ways, but it was only the tax collector who recognised himself as a sinner. He recognised his own truth and thereby entered into communion with God, the source of all truth.

15 March, Monday, Fourth Week of Lent
John 4:43–54
In today's first reading, the prophet Isaiah is preaching to a people who have been recently traumatised by the experience of exile. They had returned home to a land and a city that was in ruins. At such a moment, the prophet speaks a message of hope from the Lord: 'I create new heavens and a new earth, and the past will not be remembered … I now create Jerusalem "Joy" and her people "Gladness".' The creator God is creating something new and wonderful out of the ruins of exile and loss. This was a message

of hope that the people needed to hear, if they were to begin the work of rebuilding what had been destroyed. We need messengers of hope when times are bleak. As people of faith we are always people of hope, because we believe in a God who can bring new life out of death, and create new beginnings from losses and endings. It was above all in and through Jesus that God revealed himself to be the Life-Giver. Jesus spoke of himself as the Bread of Life, the Resurrection and the Life, and the Way, the Truth and the Life. He said that he came that we may have life and have it to the full. In today's gospel reading, he brings new life to the seriously ill son of a court official. When Jesus told the court official that his son would live, the gospel reading says that 'the man believed what Jesus had said and started on his way'. He had a hopeful faith as he started back for home. We too need a hopeful faith, especially in troubling and anxious times. Such hopeful faith is more than optimism. It is a hope which springs from our faith in the Lord of life who is always creatively at work in every situation, no matter how unpromising it may be from a human point of view.

16 March, Tuesday, Fourth Week of Lent
John 5:1–3, 5–16

In the gospels, people who are in great need often approach Jesus for help and he responds to their plea. In today's gospel reading, we find a man in great need, suffering with a paralysis for thirty-eight years, which was the best part of a lifetime in that era. He does not approach Jesus for help, but, rather, Jesus takes the initiative towards him. Jesus sees him and, having seen him, engages him in conversation. We often approach the Lord in our need, but the gospel reading reminds us that the Lord also approaches us in our need, without waiting for us to approach him. The Lord doesn't only engage with us in response to our engaging with him. He draws near to us, whether or not we draw near to him. He often takes some particular initiative towards us without our doing anything to make it happen. In the words of the book of Revelation, he stands at the door and knocks. When we pray, especially the prayer of petition, we are knocking on his door. Today's gospel reading suggests that he also comes to knock on our door without waiting for us to knock on his. This calls for a different kind of prayer from the prayer of petition. It is the prayer of listening, the prayer of attentiveness to the Lord, the prayer of waiting on the Lord's coming, the prayer of noticing his noticing of us.

17 March, Wednesday, Feast of Saint Patrick
Mark 16:15–20

Saint Patrick lived at a time and place very different from our own. He was born at the end of the fourth century on the embattled edge of the crumbling Roman Empire, probably somewhere in Britain. This was a time when the Roman legions had been withdrawn from the edges of the empire, and there was a general breakdown in Roman law and order. The way Patrick speaks of his family in his *Confessions* suggests that they were from the rural gentry. His father was a deacon of the church and his grandfather a priest. Yet, their reasonably comfortable background did not prevent them from suffering the effects of the general breakdown of order in Roman society. The protection of Rome was not there to prevent Patrick being captured at the tender age of sixteen. He spent six years as a slave in Ireland, escaping only at the age of twenty-two. Ireland, at the time, was very different from anywhere in the Roman Empire, even the edges of the empire where Patrick was from. He often refers to himself as living among strangers. Coming to Ireland at that tender age must have been a huge culture shock, apart altogether from the hardships of slavery.

Yet he subsequently came to see these six years as a time of great grace. He refers to 'the many great blessings and graces which the Lord chooses to give me in the land of my captivity'. When he was taken captive, he said, 'I did not yet know what I ought to desire and what to avoid'. Although born into a Christian family, he had never taken his faith seriously. He uses a striking image to describe his life at the time he was taken captive: 'I was like a stone lying in the deepest mire.' Yet, in exile as a slave in Ireland, he underwent what can only be called a profound spiritual transformation. He writes, 'I must not hide the gift of God which he gave us bountifully in the land of my captivity, because it was then that I fiercely sought him and there found him'. At one point in his confession he writes, 'When I had arrived in Ireland and was looking after flocks the whole time, I prayed frequently each day. And more and more, the love of God and the fear of him grew in me, and my faith was increased.' This spiritual renewal would form the basis of his extraordinary missionary work in Ireland many years later. This was a time of great loss in Patrick's life, but also a time of deep spiritual and personal growth. It is often the way in our own lives that the most painful experiences can also be the most life–giving, for ourselves and for others. Patrick discovered that when so much was taken from him, the Lord worked powerfully in his life. The Lord is always at work in a life-giving way in all our struggles and losses. At any stage of our lives, we can find ourselves in a kind of exile experience. Our personal landscape changes and we feel estranged, lonely, frightened. We are not alone at such times. The Lord is at our side. He is always close to the broken-hearted, those whose spirit is crushed, working to bringing something new out of what is dying.

After six years of captivity, Patrick made his escape and managed to board a boat. After a long and perilous journey, he finally made his way back to his home. He writes, 'I was again with my parents in Britain who welcomed me home as a son. They begged me in good faith after all my adversities to go nowhere else, or ever leave them again.' It is likely that Patrick believed he would never leave them again. However, God works in mysterious ways. Patrick writes in his *Confessions* that after many long years 'God chose to give me a great grace towards that people [who had held me captive)] but this was something I had never thought of, nor hoped for, in my youth'. He had a vision in which he heard the voice of the Irish call out to him, 'O holy boy, we beg you to come again and walk among us'. After studying for the priesthood, he was eventually sent on mission to Ireland as a bishop. In the course of that difficult mission, he says that he often felt the urge to go back to his homeland, but he resisted it because, as he writes, 'I fear the loss of the work I have begun here, since it is not I but Christ the Lord who ordered me to come here and be with these people for the rest of my life'. If his first visit to Ireland was as a young slave, this second visit was in response to the Lord's call; he came as a slave of the Gospel. As he says right at the end of his Confessions, 'The one and only purpose I had in coming back to that people from whom I had earlier escaped was the gospel and the promises of God'. This second visit of Patrick to Ireland with all its momentous consequences brings home to us the unexpected nature of God's call to all of us. God's call can surprise us. God can be prompting us to take a path we might never have considered if left to ourselves. God's purpose for our lives can be so much greater than our own plans. Patrick teaches us to hold ourselves in readiness for the Lord's surprising call in our lives.

18 March, Thursday, Fourth Week of Lent

John 5:31–47

At the beginning of today's gospel reading, Jesus speaks about John the Baptist as a lamp alight and shining. Later on in this same gospel Jesus will speak of himself as the light of the world. John may be a shining lamp, but Jesus is the true light. Jesus also says that John the Baptist's testimony is valid and that he gave his testimony to the truth. Jesus, however, says that his testimony is greater than John's; his testimony to the truth is fuller because, as he will say later on in this gospel, 'I am the truth'. Jesus is honouring John the Baptist but he is also stating that he is so much greater than John. As Jesus says in that reading, people were content to enjoy the light that John the Baptist gave, but there is a greater light here now. Jesus is calling on his contemporaries and on all of us not to settle for a lesser light, wonderful as that light may be. We can all be tempted to settle for less than what God wants for us and is offering us. We can be content to bathe in a lesser light than the light that comes to us through God's Son. We can settle for a partial truth rather than continuing to seek after the one who is full of God's truth and God's grace. We can place our hopes on one of God's gifts rather than on God's greatest gift, his Word who became flesh and dwelt among us.

19 March, Friday, Feast of Saint Joseph

Luke 2:41–51

Saint Joseph has a somewhat low profile in the Gospel story. He doesn't feature at all during the public ministry of Jesus. He is present in the Gospel story only in the context of the childhood of Jesus. This may suggest that Joseph had died before Jesus began his public ministry at the age of thirty or so. Yet he must have been a hugely significant figure in the early years of Jesus. In the Jewish culture of Jesus' time, it was the father who passed on the religious traditions to the children. It was the father who taught the children how to live in accordance with God's will as revealed in the Scriptures. This role of the father is reflected in the earliest document of the New Testament, the first letter of Paul to the Thessalonians. There Paul compares his role in the church of Thessalonica to that of a father in a family: 'We dealt with each of you like a father with his children, urging and encouraging you and pleading that you lead a life worthy of God.' It was above all from Joseph that Jesus would have received instruction in his Jewish faith. Through Joseph, he came to know the God of Abraham, Isaac and Jacob. Jesus, of course, was no ordinary child. He had a unique relationship with the God of Israel; he understood himself to be the son of Israel's God. This must have complicated Joseph's task of bringing up his son in the practice of the Jewish faith. This is evident in today's gospel reading from Luke.

When his parents eventually find the boy Jesus in the Temple, his mother says to him, 'See how worried your father and I have been, looking for you'. Jesus replied, 'Did you not know that I must be busy with my Father's affairs?' By 'your father' Mary meant Joseph. By 'my Father' Jesus meant God. The gospel reading suggests that from an early age Jesus' heavenly Father had a greater influence on him than his earthly father. This must have left Joseph confused and disturbed at times. According to today's gospel reading, Jesus' parents 'did not understand what he meant' when he spoke about being busy with his Father's affairs. Joseph struggled to discern God's will for his son. He came to see that what he wanted for his son was not necessarily what God wanted for him. He had to learn to let go of his son to God's greater purpose for him. We can all identify with Joseph's struggle in this regard. We, too, sometimes struggle to surrender to God's purpose for our lives and for the lives of those who are close to us. God's way of working in our own lives and in the lives of others can seem a mystery to us and, sometimes, like Joseph, we have to learn to let go to a mystery we do not fully understand.

20 March, Saturday, Fourth Week of Lent

John 7:40–52

Many people today feel that nobody is listening to them; they are not being given a hearing. We may not end up agreeing with people's opinion on something but we can still listen attentively to them and try to understand them. In today's gospel reading, the Temple police who were sent to arrest Jesus found themselves listening to him and, against their expectations, being greatly impressed by what he said, 'There has never been anybody who has spoken like him', they said. However, the chief priests and Pharisees who had sent the police to arrest Jesus were completely closed to what Jesus had to say. They had made up their minds that he was not from God. Yet one of their number separated himself out from his peers and challenged their refusal to listen with the question, 'Surely the Law does not allow us to pass judgement on a man without giving him a hearing and discovering what he is about?' Nicodemus was insisting that Jesus was deserving of being given a hearing before judgement was made on him. It takes courage to stand up to one's peers and express a view that is at odds with the consensus. A kind of herd mentality can easily dismiss someone who is seen as a threat to the position and status of the group. Every group, no matter how small or large, needs at least one person who, from time to time, sees through the prejudice and blindness that may lie buried within the easy consensus. Every group needs someone who is prepared to stand up and say, 'Wait a minute! Let us not rush to judgement. We need to listen to this other point of view. It may have something to teach us. God may be speaking to us through this alien voice'. God was speaking through Jesus of Nazareth in Galilee, even though the informed consensus was, 'prophets do not come from Galilee'. Nicodemus inspires us to be open to the Lord speaking to us in ways we might never have expected.

22 March, Monday, Fifth Week of Lent
John 8:1–11
We all have to deal with human weakness and moral failure both in ourselves and in others. The gospel reading raises the question as to how moral failure is to be dealt with. The religious authorities who bring the woman to Jesus deal in the currency of condemnation when it comes to moral failure. They invoke the authority of the Jewish Law, which condemns the act of adultery. They test Jesus to see whether he will go along with the Jewish Law in this matter, thereby undermining his reputation for mercy, or whether he will reject the Jewish Law, thereby showing himself to be in defiance of God's Law. Jesus' enigmatic response, bending down to write on the ground, shows that he refuses to engage with this situation in the terms put to him by the religious authorities. Jesus' concern is not whether or not the woman is deserving of condemnation, but rather that she be set free for a new life more in keeping with God's desire for her. Jesus' searing proposition to the woman's accusers, 'If there is one of you who has not sinned, let him be the first to throw a stone at her', stops the woman's accusers in their tracks. Jesus is the only one who is without sin, and he is not in the business of condemning the woman. Who are sinners like the woman's accusers to do so? Once the accusing men have slipped away, Jesus looks directly at the woman for the first time and addresses her personally. Jesus' declaration to her that he does not condemn her and his call to her to go away and sin no more show that his entire concern is to rescue her from her plight and set her free for that fullness of life

God desires for her. None of us is without sin, yet the Lord is not in the business of condemning us for our many failings. His primary desire is that we live in a way that is worthy of our dignity as sons and daughters of God. He came to show us the way that will be truly life-giving for ourselves and for others and to empower us to follow that way and to keep returning to it after we have failed.

23 March, Tuesday, Fifth Week of Lent

John 8:21–30

The early Church saw in the lifting up of a bronze serpent on a standard in today's first reading a symbol of the lifting up of Jesus on the cross. According to our first reading, those who looked upon the bronze serpent lived. In the gospel reading, Jesus speaks of the lifting up of the Son of Man, and elsewhere he says that those who look upon the Son of Man lifted up from the earth will live, will share in his own life. We all need to look upon something or someone that will give us hope. The news coming to us through our various media channels tends to be bad news and, after a while, it can easily leave us feeling very helpless and even a little hopeless. In such a scenario we need all the more to look upon what gives us hope and keeps us going. We can look upon the Lord at any time and in any place. We don't have to come to church to look upon him. In the gospel reading, Jesus says, 'He who sent me is with me'. Jesus was very aware that God his Father was always with him. Jesus, our risen Lord, is always with us and, through him, God is always with us. We can each say with Jesus, 'He who sent me is with me'. Some kind of religious image in our home can remind us that the Lord is with us. Looking upon such an image is one way of looking upon the Lord. Such a looking upon the Lord is always life-giving for us, because the Lord is the Lord of life, who is always working to bring new life out of death. The Lord is always looking upon us and he calls out to us to look upon him, so that we may draw strength from the power of his risen presence.

24 March, Wednesday, Fifth Week of Lent

John 8:31–42

Today's first reading from the Book of Daniel is the story of three young men of Israel who remained faithful to the God of Israel, even though threatened with the loss of their lives unless they abandoned their faith. This story emerged from a time at the beginning of the second century before Christ when Jews were being persecuted for refusing to worship the gods of Greece. It was intended to inspire and give courage to the author's contemporaries. Here were young men who had the freedom to remain faithful to God and the ways of God, in spite of the enormous pressure on them to do otherwise. Even while they were imprisoned in the fiery furnace, they remained free, free to live according to God's will as revealed in God's laws or God's word. This is the kind of freedom that Jesus refers to in today's gospel reading. As God's Word in human form, our freedom to live according to God's will is now the freedom to live by Jesus' word. As Jesus says in the gospel reading, 'if you make my word your home you will indeed be my disciples, you will learn the truth and the truth will make you free'. Jesus was the freest human being to ever live, because he was free to do God's will fully, without counting the cost. We are truly free to the extent that we make our home in Jesus' word, in Jesus himself who is God's Word made flesh, God's truth in human form. The truly free person is the one in whom Jesus is fully alive. When his word, his Spirit, shapes our lives we are 'free indeed', free to become all God intended us to be, namely, people conformed to the image of God's Son, in the language of Saint Paul.

25 March, Thursday, Feast of the Annunciation

Luke 1:26–38

The feast of the annunciation celebrates the moment when Mary said 'yes' to God's call to be the mother of God's Son. The gospel reading suggests that her 'yes' did not come without a struggle. When God first approached her through the angel Gabriel, Mary was 'deeply disturbed'. When Gabriel went on to announce God's purpose for Mary's life, Mary was full of questions: 'How can this be?' It was only when Gabriel spoke for the third time that Mary surrendered to what God was asking of her through Gabriel, 'Let what you have said be done to me'. The gospel reading suggests that Mary's 'yes' to God's call was not a foregone conclusion. Yet, because of her 'yes' we have all been greatly blessed, and, so, today, on the feast of her annunciation, we give thanks for her generous response to God's call, which has been a source of grace for us all. The portrayal of Mary in today's gospel reading suggests that our own response to the Lord's call will often involve something of a struggle. The reading also suggests that, as in the case of Mary, our saying 'yes' to the Lord will be a source of blessing for others. My relationship with the Lord may be personal, but it is never private. It always has consequences for others. When I am generous in my response to the Lord's call, as Mary was, others are helped to come to the Lord. Mary has been described as the first and the model disciple of the Lord. We look to her to inspire us as we seek to take to Lord's call to heart. We ask her to pray for us sinners, now and at the hour of our death.

26 March, Friday, Fifth Week of Lent

John 10:31–42

Jeremiah was one of those prophets who really suffered because of his calling from God, and he often gave expression to his suffering in very direct language. He laments before God, complaining to God about what is happening to him, yet trusting that God will somehow take care of him. We have a very good example of Jeremiah's prayer of lament in today's gospel reading. He complains aloud, 'all those who used to be my friends watched for my downfall'. In no uncertain terms he demands that God look out for him by taking his side against his enemies, 'Let me see the vengeance you will take on them'. It is an honest prayer, but a prayer we might be uncomfortable with. Yet Jeremiah shows us that every human emotion can be brought to prayer, even those emotions that incline us towards wishing our enemy ill. Many of the psalms in the Book of Psalms are psalms of lament and they sometimes display that same vindictive spirit that we find in Jeremiah's prayer in today's first reading. Bringing those dark emotions to the Lord in prayer makes us less likely to act them out. In the gospel reading, Jesus has to deal with the same kind of deadly hostility that Jeremiah complains of. People want to stone him and seek to arrest him. We could never imagine Jesus praying aloud to God as Jeremiah did, 'Let me see the vengeance you will take on them'. Yet, the prayer of Jeremiah is venerated as the word of God. It is an acceptable form of prayer in God's eyes, provided we leave vengeance to the Lord and not try to take it on ourselves. Our day-to-day lives can generate many different emotions within us, some of them, perhaps, very dark. Jeremiah shows that we can always bring such emotions to the Lord in prayer. The Lord is comfortable with us coming to him as we are, because in doing so we open ourselves to his transforming presence.

27 March, Saturday, Fifth Week of Lent

John 11:45–56

There is less in the way of real face-to-face working meetings these days. The phenomenon of the virtual meeting, without physically coming together, is growing. We hear mention of a face-to-face meeting in today's gospel reading. A meeting is called by some chief priests and Pharisees in response to the growing popularity of Jesus, which they see as a threat to the status quo. A note of panic is sounded: 'If we let him go on in this way, everybody will believe in him, and the Romans will come and destroy the Holy Place and the nation'. It takes the high priest to gather together this panic into a coldly calculating decision: 'It is better for one man to die for the people, than for the whole nation to be destroyed'. Jesus' fate is now sealed. In the interests of the common good, this man Jesus must be sacrificed. There is a strange irony in the words of the high priest. Jesus would indeed die for the common good, but in a very different sense from how Caiaphas understood. Jesus' whole life was in the service of others, and his death would be in the service of others. It would serve the good of all humanity. As the evangelist says in our gospel reading, Jesus dies 'to gather together in unity the scattered children of God'. Jesus' death would come to be understood, in the light of the resurrection, as a tremendous outpouring of God's love for the world, a love that would gather people together into a new kind of community, shaped by the Spirit. The early Church recognised that God who worked powerfully through the life of Jesus worked even more powerfully through his death. The darkness of Calvary revealed the light of God's unconditional love for humanity. We can be hopeful that God will also be working powerfully in our own experiences of death and loss, and will reveal the light of his loving presence in a whole variety of ways.

29 March, Monday in Holy Week
John 12:1–11
In today's first reading, God, speaking through the prophet Isaiah, identifies his servant as one who brings true justice to the nations

and in doing so does not break the crushed reed nor quench the wavering flame. The early Church recognised in Jesus the fulfilment of this portrayal of God's servant. Jesus came to bring God's justice, the justice of the kingdom of God, to all nations. In doing so he did not break the crushed reed nor quench the wavering flame. He was attentive to the vulnerable, the weak, the lost, the isolated, the rejected, the various crushed reeds and wavering flames of his time and place. The Lord is attentive to all of us who feel vulnerable and weak, lost and isolated. He invites us to be attentive to him who is attentive to us, opening our hearts to his presence with us. During the last week of his life, the week in which he endured his passion and death, Jesus himself became a crushed reed and a wavering flame. The scene in today's gospel reading is placed six days before the Passover, the Jewish feast in the course of which Jesus would be crucified. It is the beginning of the last week of Jesus' life, during which he becomes the crushed reed and the wavering flame. Many people in the course of that week will be intent on breaking this crushed reed and quenching this wavering flame. Some of these are mentioned in our gospel reading – Judas who would betray Jesus, the chief priests who would hand him over to Pilate. Yet the scene is dominated by a woman who displays an outpouring of tender love towards this now vulnerable human being, anointing his feet with ointment and drying them with her hair. At the beginning of a week when Jesus will suffer from the worst instincts of the human spirit, he experiences an outpouring of gratitude and tender loving care from a woman. She serves Jesus, as Jesus would go on to serve his disciples by washing their feet. In her own way, she gives expression to the portrayal of the servant in the first reading. She shows us what it means to love others as Jesus has loved us.

30 March, Tuesday, Tuesday in Holy Week
John 13:21–33, 36–38

In today's gospel reading, Jesus announces his betrayer. Betrayal by a close friend or associate is probably one of the most painful human experiences. If we are betrayed by someone close to us, we have to conclude painfully that the friend was not what he seemed to be. Jesus had to come to terms with the realisation that one of his closest associates, in whom he had invested so much time and energy, whose feet he had just washed, was not the disciple he appeared to be but was intent on betraying him to his enemies. It was one of Jesus' many sufferings in the final hours of his life. It is a different kind of suffering from the physical suffering of the crucifixion he would soon endure. It was a suffering of the heart and spirit. The gospel reading declares that as Jesus announced the presence of his betrayer at the table, 'he was troubled in spirit'. Many people suffer at this level of heart and spirit, because they are anxious about the future, or because of a sense of isolation or because they have to forgo activities that are important to them. This is a different kind of suffering from physical suffering but every bit as real. It is a suffering that Jesus understands because he endured it himself. He knows what it means to be 'troubled in spirit'. Yet Jesus saw his suffering, including this suffering of his heart and spirit, in the light of God's greater purpose for his life and the life of humanity. As Jesus says at the end of the gospel reading, 'Now the Son of Man has been glorified, and in him God has been glorified'. Jesus shows us how to place our own suffering against that broader canvas of God's greater purpose for our lives and the life of humanity, a purpose which always has in view our present and ultimate well-being, our 'glory'.

31 March, Wednesday in Holy Week

Matthew 26:14–25

When Jesus announces at the Last Supper that 'one of you is about to betray me', they all ask Jesus in turn, 'Not I, surely?' Yet, whereas Judas asks, 'Not I, Rabbi, surely?', the other disciples ask, 'Not I, Lord, surely?' All of the disciples, except Judas, speak as people of faith, addressing Jesus as Lord. Judas will betray Jesus, a shocking breaking of communion. Yet, the other disciples, even though they are people of faith, will soon desert Jesus, and Peter will publicly deny him three times. This larger body of disciples shows that faith in Jesus and failure to live up to the demands of following Jesus can go together. Just because we fail in answering the Lord's call to witness to him by our lives and to be faithful to him in good times and in bad does not mean that we have no faith in him. In this Gospel of Matthew, from which our gospel reading is taken, the disciples as a whole are often addressed by Jesus as people of little faith, standing somewhere between no faith and full faith. Perhaps that is where many of us find ourselves, at least at some stage of our faith journey. If that is where we are, then today's gospel reading and the Gospel of Matthew as a whole suggest that we are in good company, because it seems to have been where the first disciples were a lot of the time. When it comes to our relationship with the Lord, our faith, we always have a long way to go. The realisation that our faith is not as strong as it could be need not trouble us but rather it can leave us more open to seeking the Lord's help. We all need to keep turning to the Lord in the prayer of another gospel character, 'Lord, I believe; help my unbelief'. This is a prayer we can be confident the Lord will always answer.

EASTER TRIDUUM, 1 – 3 APRIL

5 April, Easter Monday
Matthew 28:8–15

It has often struck me that in all of the gospels, whereas men are largely to the fore in the story of Jesus' passion and death, it is women who are to the fore in the story of Jesus' resurrection. Nearly all of the men in the story of Jesus' passion and death fare badly, whereas the women in the story of Jesus' resurrection are portrayed in a very positive light. The strong association of women with Jesus' resurrection reminds us that so often it is women who have proven to be the guardians and protectors of life. In Matthew's Gospel, a group of women are the first to hear the good news of Easter from an angel in the tomb of Jesus: 'He is not here, for he has been raised'. It is to these women that the risen Lord first appears, as in our gospel reading. 'The women came up to him and, falling down before him, clasped his feet.' It is these women who are the first to be sent by the risen Lord to proclaim the Easter Gospel: 'Go and tell my brothers that they must leave for Galilee; they will see me there'. All of this is happening against the background of a group of men, chief priests and soldiers, conspiring together to spread a false story about Jesus' disciples stealing his body during the night. Today's gospel reading might prompt us to thank God for all those women who have revealed the risen Lord to us in a whole variety of ways. It is time that women's profile in the Easter story was reflected more clearly by their profile in the structures of the Church. All of us as followers of the Lord, men and women, have a vital role to play in proclaiming the Easter message of the triumph of life over death. We are all called to be life-givers in some way, people who care for and protect life, the life of each other, the life of the vulnerable, the life of our common home, our environment. This mission of proclaiming the Lord of life, the God of the living, by our lives is all the more vital in a world where the taking of life has become more commonplace. The world needs the life-proclaiming ministry of the risen Lord now more than ever.

6 April, Easter Tuesday
John 20:11–18

The Easter garden in our church is looking lovely. Several parishioners have contributed potted plants to transform what was a Lenten garden with a desert look into a flowering Easter garden. Today's gospel reading makes a link between Easter and a garden. John's Gospel, from which we are reading, places the tomb of Jesus in a garden. When the risen Lord appears to Mary Magdalene, she initially mistakes him for the gardener. Because Jesus had been raised into a new and glorious life, into a transformed life, he wasn't initially recognisable by his disciples. He was the same Jesus who had been crucified, yet he had been changed. He could no longer be seen in the way other people are seen. It was only when the risen Jesus called Mary by name that she recognised that the man speaking with her was not the gardener but Jesus himself. We, too, do not see the Lord as we see other people, yet the Lord is present to us even more fully than other people are because he is more alive than anyone else, as he shares in God's glorious life. The risen Lord calls us by name as he called Mary Magdalene by name. He declares to us, as he declared to her, that his Father is our Father and his God is our God. He draws us into a sharing in his own intimate relationship with God, because of which we become his brothers and sisters. These are the graces of Easter. This Easter week is a time when we allow ourselves some space to savour these graces and, also, to hear the call that goes with those graces, the call to witness to the risen Lord before others, as Mary Magdalene did.

7 April, Easter Wednesday

Luke 24:13–35

In today's first reading we find a man crippled from birth who is put down every day by others at the entrance to the Temple so that he could beg. He relies on others completely to put him in the most auspicious place to collect alms. By the end of the reading, as a result of his encounter with Peter, he is walking and jumping and praising God. Peter didn't give him alms, but gave him a more precious gift, enabling him to walk through the power of the risen Lord. The transformation in that man's life has a parallel in the gospel reading in the transformation of the two disciples who were heading from Jerusalem to Emmaus. At the beginning of the gospel reading, they are not crippled, they are walking. However, they are certainly not walking and jumping and praising God. Theirs is a slow, sad walk, with downcast faces. In their own way, they are crippled too. They walk in the shadow of Jesus' death. They are soon joined by a stranger, who, unknown to them, is the risen Lord. His impact on them is akin to Peter's impact on the crippled man. Having told their sad story to the stranger, he in turn tells them a different story, drawn from the Scriptures. It is a story that ends not in death but in glory. Their hearts begin to burn within them; they begin to come alive. They don't want this stranger to leave them and so they invite him to their home where, in the breaking of bread at their table, they finally recognise him as the Lord. Having left Jerusalem, dragging their feet, they return in joy, with a spring in their step. They rejoin the community of disciples to share their Easter story and to hear other Easter stories, a wonderful image of the Church. The risen Lord comes to us all, as he came to the crippled man through Peter, as he came to the two disciples through the stranger, through God's word and through the Eucharist. He comes to renew our life, to recreate us in his love, to fan into a living flame the gift of our faith, to replenish our hopeful spirit. This is the season to open our lives to the many ways that the risen Lord comes to us with his many Easter graces.

8 April, Easter Thursday
Luke 24:35–48

The risen Lord's first words to his disciples in today's gospel reading were, 'Peace be with you'. It is a greeting that has made its way into our own celebration of the Eucharist. We sometimes think of peace as the absence of conflict. However, in the language of Jesus, the word translated 'peace' has a much richer meaning. The word 'shalom', which lies behind the word 'peace' in our gospel reading, means fullness of life. It is that full and rich life that the Lord desires for all of humanity, a life of loving communion with God and with others. It is the life of heaven and will be experienced to the full only beyond this earthly life. Yet, through our relationship with the risen Lord, this fullness of life can begin to become a reality for us in the here and now. When the risen Lord said to his disciples, 'Peace be with you', he was imparting to them a foretaste of the fullness of life that awaits us in eternity. In giving his disciples the gift of his peace, he was also calling on them to bring that peace into the world. We are familiar with the beatitude, 'blessed are the peacemakers, for they shall be called children of God'. The Lord needs us to share in his peacemaking work. He wants to work through us so that others may have life and have it to the full. This mission we receive from the Lord to be his peacemakers is all the more urgent today, when so many people seem intent on bringing the opposite of flourishing life for people. As we wish each other the Lord's peace at this Mass, we commit ourselves afresh to becoming the Lord's peacemakers in our world.

9 April, Easter Friday

John 21:1–14

In the course of the four gospels, Jesus issues many invitations to his disciples and to the people he encountered. The invitation that the risen Lord offers to his disciples at the end of today's gospel reading has a lovely warmth and simplicity: 'Come and have breakfast'. It is the kind of invitation any one of us could make to others. Indeed, early every Easter Sunday morning, the parish hospitality group says to those who pray at the ecumenical prayer gathering at the rising of the sun, 'Come and have breakfast'. Last Easter Sunday morning we had around fifty people in our parish centre for breakfast. The invitation to 'come and have breakfast', or to 'come and eat' or to 'come and have a cup of coffee' or whatever, is an invitation to communion. We are inviting the other or others to be in communion with us. That is what the risen Lord is doing by the Sea of Galilee in today's gospel reading. All of his disciples, apart from the beloved disciple, had broken communion with him with the arrival of the hour of his passion and death. Peter, the leading disciple, had denied him three times. Yet the Lord had not broken communion with his disciples. He appeared to them to call them back into the communion they had broken. Whenever we come to the Eucharist, the Lord is saying to us, 'Come and eat'. He is calling us into communion with himself, even though in various ways we may have broken communion with him. It is very fitting that we sometimes refer to the Eucharist as Holy Communion. At every Eucharist, we celebrate the Lord's communion with us, and we hear again the call to be in communion with him, the same call the disciples heard by the Sea of Galilee.

10 April, Easter Saturday

Mark 16:9–15

There are many examples both in the past and in the present of people in power and authority seeking to silence those whose public utterances are considered a threat. The spoken or written word can often be experienced as dangerous by those who have a vested interest in preserving the status quo. In today's first reading from the Acts of the Apostles, the religious leaders attempt to silence the preaching of Peter and John: 'They gave them a warning on no account to make statements or to teach in the name of Jesus'. The pressure by those in authority to silence those considered dissidents does not always meet with success. Courageous people who know they have truth and right on their side can continue to speak out, in spite of the pressure to do otherwise. In our first reading, Peter and John show such courage. They refuse to be silenced, declaring to those who try to silence them, 'We cannot promise to stop proclaiming what we have seen and heard'. Peter and John recognised that they were subject to a higher authority than the authority of the religious leaders and that was the authority of God, saying to the religious leaders, 'You must judge whether in God's eyes it is right to listen to you and not to God'. They were clear that they must listen to God, and that God was calling them to proclaim the Gospel of Jesus. Peter and John can be an inspiration to us all to be courageous in our own witness to our faith, in spite of pressure to be silent. At the end of the gospel reading, the risen Lord says to his disciples, 'Go out to the whole world; proclaim the good news to all creation'. We have all received that same commission, to proclaim the good news by what we say and above all by the way we live. If we turn towards the Lord, he will give us the courage to be faithful to that commission, just as he gave courage to Peter and John.

12 April, Monday, Second Week of Easter
John 3:1–8

Nicodemus must have been a restless person. He was a Pharisee, yet he was somehow looking for more. He was still searching, so he came to Jesus by night, under cover of darkness, afraid perhaps to show his interest in Jesus publicly. He was drawn to Jesus in some way. We were drawn to Jesus through our parents, through our teachers at school, through our parish community. Having come to know Jesus somewhat, he continues to draw us to himself. He never ceases to draw us to himself. In that sense, we all find ourselves in the situation of Nicodemus. We have made some progress on the road of faith, but we remain searchers; we continue to feel a restlessness within us. The Lord continues to call us to himself, drawing us into an ever deeper relationship with him. Jesus said to Nicodemus that he had to be born from above; he had to be born of water and the Spirit. We have all been born of water and the Spirit through baptism but we need to keep opening ourselves ever more completely to the presence of the Spirit within us. The last we see of Nicodemus in John's Gospel is at the foot of the cross, helping to arrange a dignified burial for Jesus; he had allowed himself to be drawn to Jesus more fully; he had opened himself to the Spirit a little more. That is our calling too.

13 April, Tuesday, Second Week of Easter
John 3:7–15

Jesus often speaks about spiritual realities with reference to various aspects of human experience. When he seeks to give an understanding of the kingdom of God, he tells parables, stories that are deeply rooted in everyday life. We find something similar happening in today's gospel reading. He speaks about the mysterious reality of the Spirit, the Holy Spirit, with reference to the everyday reality of the wind. There is a mysterious quality to the wind. As Jesus says, 'it blows where it pleases'. Nowadays we can harness the wind to generate electricity, but there is so much about the wind that is beyond our control and understanding. In the words of the gospel reading, we certainly cannot control where it comes from or where it goes to. Nor can we control the strength of the wind. If the wind is beyond our control and understanding, this is true to an even greater extent of the Spirit of God, the Holy Spirit. We cannot manage the Holy Spirit. If we are not masters of the wind, we are even less masters of the Spirit. Yet, whereas the wind is an impersonal force, the Spirit is a personal force. We speak of the Spirit as the third person of the Trinity. The Spirit is the Spirit of God's personal love for the world. Whereas the wind can be destructive, the Spirit is always life-giving. Our calling is to surrender to the movement of the Spirit in our lives, to allow the Spirit to shape and mould us. When that happens, our lives will give expression to God's personal love for the world.

14 April, Wednesday, Second Week of Easter
John 3:16–21

According to today's first reading, Peter and the message he preaches cannot be confined behind bars, in spite of the best efforts of those who want to silence that message. The Easter proclamation cannot be imprisoned, just as the guards at the tomb of Easter could not prevent Jesus bursting forth into new life. The light that shone from the risen Lord and from the preaching of the Easter Gospel could not be extinguished by the powers of darkness. The gospel reading acknowledges that even though the light has come into the world, some have shown that they prefer darkness to the light. They hate and avoid the light because they feel threatened by it, as if it will expose what is wrong in them. Yet the light of Easter is not like the light of the interrogation room. It is not a light to be feared. It is the light of God, who so loved the world that he gave his only Son, in the language of the gospel reading. It is not a condemnatory light; God did not send his Son into the world to condemn the world but so that, through him, the world may have life and have it to the full. This is a light to be warmly welcomed, not to be extinguished or imprisoned. God has embraced the world through the death and resurrection of his Son. It falls to us now to embrace God's Son, the light of the world, who declared that whoever follows him will never walk in darkness but will have the light of life

15 April, Thursday, Second Week of Easter
John 3:31–36
The Acts of the Apostles suggests that as soon as the Gospel began to be preached after Pentecost efforts were made by people in authority to suppress it. The Gospel was not experienced as good news by some and they made every effort to silence those who were preaching it. However, today's first reading shows that the efforts of those in authority to silence the Gospel were not successful. Although Peter and the other apostles had been given a formal warning by the religious authorities not to preach the Gospel, they carried on regardless because they understood that this was their calling in life, the mission they had received from the risen Lord. As they say to the religious authorities in that first reading, 'Obedience to God comes before obedience to men'. It is a statement worth reflecting upon. It invites us to ask, 'Who shapes our lives? Is it the Lord or someone or something else?' Or, to put the question in another way, 'Who or what is Lord of our lives?' The apostles were clear that Jesus was Lord of their lives and not the religious authorities. It was to him that they must submit, not to them. The attitude of the apostles shows us what is at the heart of our own lives

as Christians. We are those who seek to take Jesus as the Lord of our lives. We recognise in the words of today's gospel reading that 'he is above all others', including all human authority, be it religious or political. We spend our lives trying to submit ourselves to the Lordship of Jesus. In submitting to his Lordship, we are assured that we will experience true freedom, what Saint Paul calls 'the glorious freedom of the children of God', the freedom to live in the fully human way that God desires for us.

16 April, Friday, Second Week of Easter
John 6:1–15
It is difficult to know exactly what happened that day in the wilderness when Jesus and his disciples found themselves before a large hungry crowd. However, the message that the evangelist seeks to communicate through his telling of that event is reasonably clear. Jesus is presented as working powerfully through very meagre resources. He feeds a multitude with five loaves and two fish. The Lord can work powerfully through our own rather limited resources, if we are generous with those resources and place them at the Lord's disposal. A little can go a long way when it is placed in the hands of the Lord. Saint Paul expresses that truth in these terms: 'God's power is made perfect in weakness'. The tendency of Philip and Andrew in the gospel story was to complain about the hopelessness of the situation, 'Two hundred denarii would not buy enough … What is that between so many?' We are all prone to throwing our hands up to the heavens in exasperation and even despair at the perceived extent of some problem. The gospel reading calls on us rather to have an expectant faith, a faith in the Lord's power to work wonders with even the little that we give him.

17 April, Saturday, Second Week of Easter

John 6:16–21

The first reading from the Acts of the Apostles shows some tension in the church of Jerusalem. Something of a storm was brewing in this young church, which became the mother church, because it was from the church in Jerusalem that the other churches were founded. The Hellenists, Greek-speaking believers, were complaining about the Hebrews, Aramaic-speaking believers, because the Hellenists felt that their widows were not being as well provided for as the widows of the Hebrews. The leaders of the Jerusalem church, the twelve, realised that this problem would not be resolved unless they drew other members of the church into this ministry of providing for all the widows and the other vulnerable people in the church. The twelve could not do everything; they had to prioritise. They declared to the other members of the church that as the leaders they should be devoting themselves to prayer and to the service of God's word. As a result, they invited the members of the church to choose people of wisdom and of the Spirit who could attend to this important work of providing for the most vulnerable. Seven suitable people were chosen, allowing the twelve to focus on what was important in their calling. Here, at the very early days of the Church we have a good example of how the Church must function in every age. No one group within the Church can do everything. There is a need for different groups of people to take responsibility for different ministries. This is how the Spirit continues to shape the life of the Church today. There will always be the kind of tensions or storms within the Church that we find in today's first reading. However, such stormy moments can be times of grace, opportunities for the Spirit in work in new ways in the Church. In today's gospel reading, the Lord came to his disciples as they were struggling with a strong wind and a rough sea and brought them to a safe haven. The Lord is always with his Church in the various storms that will assail it. His presence at the heart of the storm can help to ensure that moments of crisis in the Church can also be times of new life.

19 April, Monday, Third Week of Easter
John 6:22–29

At some level we are all seekers or searchers. We never stand still; we are always looking for more. At the heart of that search for more is a search for God, a search for the Lord who is Emmanuel, God-with-us. At the beginning of today's gospel reading we find the people of Galilee searching for Jesus. They get into boats by the shore of the Sea of Galilee after Jesus and his disciples and cross to Capernaum looking for him. When they find Jesus, he addresses them and declares that they are looking for him for the wrong reasons. They want more of the bread that he multiplied in the wilderness. Jesus challenges them to look for him not as the provider of food that cannot last but as the provider of food that endures to eternal life. We can all look for Jesus for the wrong reasons. What we want from him does not always correspond to what he wants for us. What we want from him can be far too limited. He wants to give us what endures and we look for what perishes. We struggle to bring our prayers of petition into line with what the Lord wants to give us. Saint Paul says in his letter to the Romans that we do not know how to pray as we ought. He immediately goes on to say, 'the Spirit helps us in our weakness'. This Easter season, we ask the Holy Spirit to shape our longing, our desires and our prayers so that they correspond more to the Lord's desire for us.

20 April, Tuesday, Third Week of Easter

John 6:30–35

Chapter six of John's Gospel, from which we are reading all this week, is very much a Eucharistic chapter. Unlike the other three gospels, John's Gospel has no account of the actual institution of the Eucharist, but it does have this wonderful chapter, which is unique to this gospel and which is full of Eucharistic themes. In today's gospel reading Jesus contrasts the bread with which the people of Israel were fed by Moses on their way through the wilderness en route to the promised land with the true bread, the bread of God, which is given not just to the people of Israel but to the world. What is this true bread, this bread of God? Jesus goes on to identify himself as this bread, 'I am the bread of life', he says. Jesus gives himself to us as the bread of life on our own journey towards the promised land of heaven. Jesus is our fundamental resource on our pilgrimage through life. He nourishes us spiritually in the Eucharist, but in other ways as well, such as in and through his word. His word is in its own way bread of life. He nourishes us with his Spirit, the Holy Spirit. Our calling is, in the words of the gospel reading, to come to him and to receive. He has much to give us.

21 April, Wednesday, Third Week of Easter

John 6:35–40

There is a striking statement in today's first reading, 'Saul then worked for the total destruction of the church'. In the immediate aftermath of the martyrdom of Stephen, Saul, the zealous Pharisee, set himself the task of destroying this heretical Jewish movement. It was this same Saul who went on to become the greatest missionary in the early Church, bringing the Gospel to major cities in modern-day Turkey and Greece. In the gospel reading, Jesus declares that he came to do his Father's will, which is that all who see the Son and believe in him shall have eternal life. Saul or Paul, while in the very act of persecuting the Church, came to see the Son and believe in him and received the gift of eternal life. Paul saw the Son because the risen Lord appeared to him just outside Damascus. We have not seen the Son in the way Paul did, yet we see him with the eyes of faith. We recognise him in the Eucharist as 'the bread of life', in the language of today's gospel reading. It is Paul who, in his letters, teaches us that through baptism we have become members of the Lord's body, temples of the Holy Spirit, sons and daughters of God, sharing in Jesus' own relationship with God. Although Paul had seen the risen Lord in a unique sense, he didn't consider the members of the Church to whom he wrote, including ourselves, to be any less privileged than himself. It is Paul, the former persecutor of the Church, who reminds us in his letters that the bread that we break and the cup that we bless in the Eucharist is a communion with the body and blood of Christ. Our union with Christ through baptism is thereby strengthened in the Eucharist. It is Paul who teaches us in his letters that this communion with the Lord that we enjoy in this life will not be broken by death, because our ultimate destiny is 'to be with the Lord for ever'. We can be grateful to this former persecutor of the Church for opening up for us the riches of our Christian identity and destiny.

22 April, Thursday, Third Week of Easter
John 6:44–51

In today's gospel reading Jesus declares that 'everybody who believes has eternal life' and 'anyone who eats this bread will live for ever'. It appears that eating Jesus, the bread of life, is an image for believing in Jesus. However, when Jesus goes on to say, 'the bread that I shall give is my flesh for the life of the world', the term 'bread' begins to acquire a Eucharistic meaning. Jesus will go on to speak about the need to eat his flesh and drink his blood, which has even clearer Eucharistic overtones. Yet eating the bread that is Jesus, in the sense of believing in Jesus, comes before eating his flesh, or his body, in the Eucharist. The Eucharist, like all the sacraments, presupposes faith. We first come to Jesus in faith before we come to him in the Eucharist. We find a similar pattern in the first reading. The faith of the Ethiopian is first nurtured by Philip through his proclamation of the word before the Ethiopian comes to celebrate the Sacrament of Baptism. The Sacrament of Baptism, like the Sacrament of the Eucharist, also presupposes faith. In the case of infants, it is the faith of the parents and family and the faith of the believing community that is presupposed. The first reading reminds us that an encounter with the Lord in his word is often prior to an encounter with him in the Sacraments. The word of the Lord nurtures our faith in preparation for our encounter with him in the Sacraments.

23 April, Friday, Third Week of Easter
John 6:52–59

Syria has been in the news in recent years because of the unrest there and Damascus, the capital, has been mentioned more than once. Today's first reading is set in Damascus and its vicinity. The story of Paul's conversion on the road to Damascus has captured the imagination of many people in the course of the centuries, including the imagination of many artists. As a result of his meeting with the risen Lord outside Damascus Saul, the violent persecutor of the Church, became the great apostle to the Gentiles. Yet according to Luke in the reading we have just heard, in the immediate aftermath of his meeting with the Lord, Paul was first struck blind and had to be led by the hand into the city of Damascus. The self-assured Pharisee suddenly found himself completely dependent on others. He was dependent on Ananias, a member of the church of Damascus, to receive back his sight, be baptised and received into the Church. Before he began his missionary career the Lord gave Paul this profound experience of his dependence on others and, ultimately, on the Lord. We can only work for the Lord and serve the Lord to the extent that we are aware of and acknowledge our total dependence on him. As Jesus says in John's Gospel, 'apart from me you can do nothing'.

24 April, Saturday, Third Week of Easter
John 6:60–69

There is a striking image of the churches in the land where Jesus lived and worked at the beginning of today's second reading. It is said that 'the churches throughout Judea, Galilee and Samaria were left in peace, building themselves up, living in the fear of the Lord, and filled with the consolation of the Holy Spirit'. The 'fear' referred to is a reverential awe at all the Lord was doing among them and through them. The members of the Church were building themselves up. The ministry of encouragement, of building up, seems to have been a very important one in the early Church. The earliest Christian document we possess is Paul's first letter to the Thessalonians, written about twenty years after the death and resurrection of Jesus. Towards the end of that letter, Paul calls on the members of the Church to 'encourage one another with these words', and then, again, to 'encourage one another and build up each other, as indeed you are doing'. This is a ministry we all share, because it is rooted in our baptism. Of course, we can sometimes be a source of discouragement to one another in regard to faith in the Lord. It was surely discouraging for Jesus and the other disciples when, in the words of today's gospel reading, 'many of his disciples left him, and stopped going with him'. Jesus risked being discouraged further by asking the twelve, 'what about you, do you want to go away too?' It must have been a source of great encouragement to Jesus and to the other eleven disciples when Peter, speaking on behalf of all, said, 'Lord, who shall we go to? You have the message of eternal life'. At a discouraging moment for the group of Jesus' disciples, Peter was an encouraging presence. The ministry of mutual encouragement is all the more important when there are grounds for discouragement, such as in these times. The Lord is always the great encourager, and he continues to empower us to encourage one another in faith, and to build up one another in the Lord.

26 April, Monday, Fourth Week of Easter
John 10:1–10

In today's gospel reading, Jesus says 'I am the gate'. We tend to think of gates as fixed in one place. They give access to something, whether it is a building or a field. The gate doesn't move, but people move through it. Jesus is not a gate in that fixed sense. Earlier in today's gospel reading, Jesus identifies himself not so much with the gate of the sheepfold but with the shepherd who enters the sheepfold through the gate and then leads the sheep out through the gate to pasture. He goes ahead of the flock and they follow him because they know his voice. Jesus is both the shepherd and the gate. As the shepherd he is always going ahead of us, calling us to follow him. As the gate, he invites us to keep entering through him. Because he is also a shepherd, entering through him as the gate will mean something different at different times in our lives. According to today's first reading, for the early Church, entering through Jesus, the risen Lord, meant breaking new ground, preaching the Gospel to pagans for the first time. For us too, as followers of Jesus today, entering through Jesus, the gate, will often mean taking a new direction on our faith journey, taking a new step we haven't taken before. There is nothing static about our relationship with the Lord. He is always leading us to new pastures, personally and as a community of faith. Like Peter in the first reading, we need to be attentive and sensitive to the Lord's leading, even when he seems to be leading us to places that some might be very wary of.

27 April, Tuesday, Fourth Week of Easter

John 10:22–30

Today's first reading makes reference to the persecution of the early church. After the execution of Stephen, the church in Jerusalem experienced a time of persecution. As a result, many of the Jewish Christians there had to flee from the city. Yet Luke, who wrote the Acts of the Apostles, highlights that this experience of persecution was actually a blessing for the Church. Some of those who fled Jerusalem brought the Gospel to places where it had not been preached, including the city of Antioch, where the gospel was preached for the first time to pagans. As a result of the success of this mission, Barnabas came from Jerusalem to Antioch to give encouragement to this new development and, in his wisdom, he went to Tarsus and brought Saul to Antioch, recognising that this was a church where someone like Saul or Paul could flourish. Barnabas was proved right. The church of Antioch became Paul's spiritual home and the base for his missionary journeys. So, according to Luke, great good came from the persecution of the church in Jerusalem. Difficult times for the Church can often be moments of renewal, times of new and unexpected growth. The Lord works in life-giving ways in what can seem to be desolate places. Resistance, even hostility, to the Church's message can allow the Lord to work in new ways. In the gospel reading, Jesus speaks out of an experience of resistance on the part of some to what he says and does. Yet, as Jesus declares there, 'the Father … is greater than anyone'. God's work will not ultimately be derailed. This realisation can keep us hopeful and energised in difficult times.

28 April, Wednesday, Fourth Week of Easter

John 12:44–50

The Acts of the Apostles tells the story of the spread of the Gospel from Jerusalem outwards into the Roman Empire. Today's first reading is the moment when the Gospel makes the first significant spread westwards from the land of Israel, to the island of Cyprus. It was the generosity of a church in Syria, to the north of Israel, that made this possible. The church of Antioch, in response to the promptings of the Holy Spirit, set aside two of their own leading members for this mission, Barnabas and Saul. They allowed themselves to become poorer so that others would be enriched. This was the pattern of Jesus' own life. In one of his subsequent letters Paul will say of Jesus that 'though he was rich, yet for your sakes he became poor, so that by his poverty you might become rich'. Jesus emptied himself, taking the form of a servant, so that we all might have life and have it to the full. This is to be the pattern of our own lives too. We all have some gift or grace that we can give away so that others might live more fully in some way. When we let go in this way, after the example of the church in Antioch, we not only make others more alive but we become more alive ourselves, the Spirit grows more fully within us. In the gospel reading, Jesus says that he came as light into the world so that others might not stay in the dark any more. Whenever the pattern of Jesus' life becomes the pattern of our lives, then his light continues to shine through us.

29 April, Thursday, Feast of Saint Catherine of Siena

Matthew 11:25–30

Catherine was one of the great mystics of the church. She was born in 1347, the daughter of a prosperous wool dyer, and died in 1380, at the age of thirty-three. At a young age, she decided to give herself to the Lord, and resisted the attempts of her family to find her a good husband. She insisted that she was betrothed to Christ. Eventually, her father relented. Rather than join a religious order, she became a Dominican tertiary. For a three-year period she devoted herself to prayer and seclusion. Early on in this period, she was tormented by doubt, but this gave way to mystical encounters with Christ. After three years, she began the second great phase of her career. She set about serving her neighbours, distributing alms to the poor, ministering to the sick and to prisoners. She began gathering about herself a group of followers, men and women, priests and religious. After a profoundly mystical experience she had a sense of Christ calling her to take a further step, to serve the wider world and universal Church. She commenced her role as a public figure, dictating hundreds of letters to popes, monarchs and other leaders of note. She also wrote her great work, the *Dialogues*, describing the contents of her mystical conversations with Christ. As she learned to write only towards the very end of her life, she dictated these writings. It is evident that Catherine's mysticism did not withdraw her from the world. She was deeply involved in what was happening in Europe and in the Church in her time. Because of the chaos and dangers of Rome, the popes had left Rome for Avignon. She worked to persuade Pope Gregory XI to return to Rome from Avignon. She insisted that the pope's place was beside the bones of the martyrs. Her mission in person to the pope was a surprising success. Shortly after his return, Pope Gregory died. He was succeeded by Pope Urban VI who turned out to be a disastrous pope. The cardinals regretted their decision and elected a second pope but could not persuade Pope Urban to retire. The Church now had two rival popes, one in Rome and one in Avignon, a situation that lasted for several decades. Catherine remained faithful to Pope Urban, in spite of his faults, because he had been duly elected. She was convinced that the wound in the body of Christ could be healed only by great sacrifice. She prayed that she might atone for the sins of the Church and, shortly afterwards, she collapsed and died. Catherine stood out as a beacon of light in a dark time in Europe and in the Church. She was such a light because of her deeply personal and mystical relationship with Jesus. The Lord's invitation, 'Come to me, all who labour and are overburdened', was one she responded to every day of her life. Her life shows us very clearly that the life of faith has both an inward and outward dimension. The Lord calls out to all of us to come to him, to know and love him as he knows and loves us. In calling us to himself he also sends us into the world afire with the flame of his love. Pope Paul VI declared Catherine a doctor of the Church in 1970. In doing so he was stating that her life and writings have something important to say to the Church of every generation.

30 April, Friday, Fourth Week of Easter
John 14:1–6
When someone you love deeply is seriously ill and is not going to get better, it is a real way of the cross. You feel helpless before the physical decline of the person who has meant so much to you for so long. You sense that all you can do is travel this difficult journey with your loved one, doing all you can to make that journey a little easier. At the Last Supper, the disciples were aware that Jesus who had come to mean so much to them was soon to die, and there was nothing they could do about it. That is the setting of today's gospel reading. In that highly charged moment, Jesus turns to his disciples and says, 'Do not let your hearts be troubled. Trust in God, and trust in me'. It is a word that Jesus speaks to all those who are being called to let go of those they love because of illness. It is not easy to trust in God at such times. When Jesus calls on his disciples to trust, he also gives them a reason to trust. He assures them that in dying he will be going to the many-roomed house of God his Father; he will

be returning home to God his Father. Jesus also assures them that where he is going is where he will bring all who trust in him when they come to the end of their earthly lives. 'I will return to take you with me', he says, 'so that where I am, you may be too'. Jesus has passed through death to a new and fuller life for all of us. Where he has gone, he wants us to follow. The decline associated with approaching death is the prelude to a great fullness of life in God our Father's heavenly home. These words of Jesus to his disciples on the night before his own death give hope and comfort to us all as we face into the death of our loved ones and our own death.

1 May, Saturday, Fourth Week of Easter
John 14:7–14

At the end of today's gospel reading, Jesus says something that can seem strange to our ears. He declares that whoever believes in him will do even greater works than he has done. It is tempting to ask, 'How could this be possible?' 'How could Jesus' disciples do greater works than Jesus himself?' Jesus often speaks in the gospels in ways that leave us perplexed and wondering what he means. Jesus was speaking to his disciples in the context of the Last Supper. He was assuring them that his leaving on the following afternoon, his 'going to the Father', his death, would not be the disaster it seemed to be. His 'going to the Father' entails not only his death but his resurrection, his glorification. It will result in the sending of the Paraclete, the Holy Spirit. The coming of the Holy Spirit to the disciples will enable the risen Lord to continue to do his work in and through them. As risen Lord, he will do even greater works through his disciples, in the power of the Spirit, than he could have done during his earthly life. His earthly ministry was confined to a particular place and time. His ministry as risen Lord will be in every generation and throughout the world. Yet he can only do his greater works through disciples who believe in him and who remain in his love. 'Whoever believes in me … will perform even greater works.' As believers, we can be tempted to discouragement in these times. Today's gospel reading assures us that the Lord's good work continues. The risen Lord is as active today, indeed, more active, than he was during his public ministry. We are all invited to be part of his great Spirit-empowered work, which no earthly power can halt.

3 May, Monday, Feast of Saints Philip and James
John 14:6–14

Today we celebrate the feast of two of the twelve apostles, Philip and James. According to the Fourth Gospel, Philip was from the same town as Andrew and Peter, Bethsaida on the north shore of the Sea of Galilee. James is identified as the brother or cousin of Jesus. After the death and resurrection of Jesus, he became the leading member of the church in Jerusalem. In today's first reading from the first letter to the Corinthians, Paul lists James as one of those to whom the risen Lord appeared. In today's gospel reading, Philip makes a request of Jesus, 'Lord, let us see the Father and then we shall be satisfied'. He recognises in that request that only God can satisfy the deepest longings of the human heart. We will never be fully satisfied until we see God. We look forward in hope to seeing God face to face beyond this earthly life. It is only then that the deepest hungers and thirsts of our hearts will be completely satisfied. Earlier in that first letter to the Corinthians, Paul had said, 'now we see in a mirror, dimly; but then we will see face to face'. For the moment, we have to make do with seeing in a mirror dimly, a poorer form of seeing compared to that which awaits us in eternity, the seeing face to face. Yet, even this seeing in a mirror dimly is potentially a very rich form of seeing. In the gospel reading, Jesus says to Philip, 'to have seen me, is to have seen the Father'. There is a very real sense in which we see Jesus, the risen Lord, in this earthly life, and through him see God. We see the Lord as he comes to us in his word and in the Eucharist, the breaking of bread. We see him in each other, in particular, the broken and vulnerable. We see him in creation. The poet James Mary Plunkett wrote, 'I see his blood upon the rose and in the stars the glory of his eyes; His body gleams amid eternal snows, His tears fall from the skies'. If our eyes were opened, we would see the Lord in his many guises and we would begin to experience in the here and now something of that rest and peace which is the fruit of seeing God face to face in eternity.

4 May, Tuesday, Fifth Week of Easter

John 14:27–31

I listened recently to an interview with the secretary of Goebbels, Hitler's Minister for Propaganda. She was 103 when the interview took place and could remember the outbreak of the First World War. She was reflecting aloud on her life, including her time as secretary to Goebbels, for which she spent fifteen years in a Russian prison. Towards the end of the interview she commented on all the evil in the world. She claims to have become aware of the evil of the Nazi regime only after the war. She then paused and hesitatingly said, 'I believe in the Devil, but I do not believe in God'. She had no doubt about the Devil's influence in the world, but could see no sign of God's influence. In today's gospel reading, Jesus speaks of the devil as 'the prince of this world'. On the night before his crucifixion, he says to his disciples, 'The prince of this world is on his way'. However, Jesus immediately goes on to say, 'He has no power over me'. Jesus was aware of the presence of the devil, but he knew that the devil was not the ultimate power. God was more powerful than the devil. If the devil was instrumental in Jesus' death, God overcame death and brought Jesus to a new life. Jesus continues to live with that new life, the life of heaven, which is the life of love. He releases that life of love into our hearts through the Holy Spirit. The power of the Spirit is greater than the power of evil, which is why Jesus teaches us to pray with confidence, 'Deliver us from evil'. God is always working to overcome evil and he empowers us to share in that work.

5 May, Wednesday, Fifth Week of Easter
John 15:1–8

Today's gospel reading is again taken from John's account of what Jesus said to his disciples on the night before he died. Jesus is taking his leave of his disciples but, before doing so, he wants to assure them that beyond his death and resurrection he will remain in communion with them. The image of the vine and the branches expresses the depth of his communion with his disciples, with all of us. The Lord wants to be in communion with all of us, but for that to happen we must seek to remain in communion with him by allowing his words to remain in us and to shape our lives. We can slip out of our communion with the Lord; we can cut ourselves off from him. However, his invitation is always there to return to him and to remain with him or in him. It is in returning to him, in remaining in him, in allowing his words to remain in us, that our lives bear rich fruit, what Paul calls the fruit of the Spirit. According to the last verse of our gospel reading, it is lives rich in the fruit of the Spirit that give glory to God. According to Saint Irenaeus, a second-century saint, it is the human person fully alive – alive with the fruit of the Spirit – that gives glory to God. Lives open to the Spirit are lives that are fully human, in the way God intended, because such lives are living images of his Son, the most fully alive human person ever to have lived.

6 May, Thursday, Fifth Week of Easter

John 15:9–11

It is inevitable that we make distinctions between people. We choose one person over another as a friend or a lifelong companion. We don't treat everyone equally, much as we might want to. In today's first reading, Peter declares to the leaders of the Church that 'God made no distinction between them [the pagans] and us'. There was no longer one chosen people. God had shown through the life, death and resurrection of Jesus that he was choosing everyone equally. God was giving the Holy Spirit, the Spirit of his love, to all equally, Jew and pagan. Peter was proclaiming a God who does not discriminate. This was in keeping with the teaching of Jesus. As Jesus says on one occasion, God 'makes his sun rise on the evil and the good'. What Jesus says to his disciples in today's gospel reading is said to all: 'As the Father has loved me, so I have loved you'. There is no discrimination on God's side. The discrimination is on our side. Not everyone responds to the gift of God's love in the same way. Not everyone remains in the Lord's love to the same degree and each one of us does not remain in his love to the same extent in the course of our lives. We remain in his love, Jesus says, by keeping his commandments, especially the great commandment to love one another as he has loved us. The capacity to receive the Lord's love and to reflect it in our dealings with each other is what distinguishes people, and what can distinguish different moments of our own lives. At the end of the gospel reading, Jesus assures us that in so far as we learn to receive his love and share it with others, we will come to experience something of his own joy.

7 May, Friday, Fifth Week of Easter

John 15:12–17

The ministry of encouragement is a very important one in the Church. It is one we are all called to engage in. We find that ministry at work in the early Church in today's first reading. The members of the church in Antioch were mostly of pagan background. They had been disturbed by other members of the church whose background was Jewish; they felt pressured to submit to certain aspects of the Jewish Law. As a result, the leaders of the church in Jerusalem wrote a letter to the members of the church of Antioch who were of pagan background. According to our reading, when the church in Antioch read this letter, they were delighted with the encouragement it gave them. They had been unnecessarily disturbed by some and now they were greatly encouraged by this letter from the leaders of the Jerusalem church. Encouraging one another on the journey of faith is one expression of the commandment of Jesus in the gospel reading to 'love one another, as I have loved you'. Jesus refers to this love as the love of friendship. Jesus has befriended us by laying down his life for us, by revealing God to us, and now he calls on his disciples, on us, to befriend one another as he has befriended us. We have an image here of the Church as a community of friends, a community of believers who love one another as the Lord loves us, who encourage one another as the Lord keeps encouraging us. There are many ways of thinking about the Church; there are many models or images of the church. However, I have always found the Fourth Gospel's image of church as a community of friends to be one of the most appealing of all.

8 May, Saturday, Fifth Week of Easter

John 15:18–21

In today's first reading, Luke, the author of the Acts of the Apostles, gives us a strong sense of the early Church being guided by the Holy Spirit. Paul and his companions travelled through the countryside of the Roman province of Galatia, having been told by the Holy Spirit not to preach the word in the Roman province of Asia, both provinces being in modern-day Turkey. The Spirit would not allow them to cross into the province of Bithynia either, so, instead, they came to the city of Troas, on the north-western coast of modern-day Turkey. There Paul experienced the prompting of the Spirit once more in the form of a vision in which a person from Macedonia in Northern Greece called on Paul and his companions to come over and help them. Luke was showing that the Holy Spirit was guiding the early Church, especially the missionary journeys of Paul. We can be confident that the Holy Spirit continues to guide the Church today. The Church is not just a human organisation, a kind of religious multinational corporation. Yes, it has elements that are typical of any worldwide organisation. It is a human institution. More fundamentally, however, the Church is a spiritual reality. The risen Lord, through the Spirit, is present in the Church, shaping it and guiding it. The Church cannot be shaped by opinion polls. It can only be shaped by the Lord and his Spirit. Sometimes, as Jesus says in the gospel reading today, this will put the church into conflict with the prevailing culture, 'if they persecuted me, they will persecute you too'. The Church is in the midst of the world, but it is not of the world. As Jesus declares in that gospel reading, 'you do not belong to the world'. The really important question for the Church is not, 'What do people think of us?', but 'What is the Lord saying to us?', or 'Where is the Spirit leading us?' Answering those questions requires prayerful discernment from us all.

10 May, Monday, Sixth Week of Easter

John 15:26–16:4

According to the Acts of the Apostles from which we are reading these weeks, there were a number of prominent women in the early Church. We find one such woman in today's first reading, Lydia, a devout woman who was a dealer in the purple-dye trade. In that culture, the colour purple was associated with honour and prestige, and purple cloth was the most expensive cloth of all. She must have been a woman of some means. When Paul preached the Gospel to her and some other women in Philippi, the reading says that 'the Lord opened her heart to accept what Paul was saying'. She and her household were then baptised. Having received this gift of the Gospel, this gift of faith, of belonging to the community of believers, she immediately gave generously from what she had received. She insisted that Paul and his companions would stay at her home as her guests. Freely she had received, and, now, she was freely giving. Having responded to Paul's witness of his faith, she now witnesses to her own faith by showing this hospitable spirit. In the gospel reading, Jesus promises to send the Advocate, the Spirit of truth, from the Father, to empower us to witness to our relationship with him. Lydia shows us that one aspect of witnessing to our faith in the Lord is giving to others out of what we have received from the Lord. This is our baptismal calling, and we are promised the gift of the Holy Spirit to help us to live out this calling.

11 May, Tuesday, Sixth Week of Easter

John 16:5–11

In the Acts of the Apostles, Paul preaches the Gospel in a whole variety of situations and places. In today's gospel reading, he preaches the Gospel in prison to his jailer and the jailer's family. We are being reminded that there is no place or situation in which the Gospel can't be preached. The jailer and his family responded to Paul's preaching of the Gospel and were baptised and received into the Church. Immediately, the jailer gave something back to Paul. Having received the wonderful gift of the Gospel and of faith, he washed Paul's wounds and then, with his family, he showed hospitality to Paul and his companions. Having freely received from the Lord through Paul, he freely gave to Paul. We have all been greatly graced by the Lord, and we are called to give generously from what we have received. This pattern of people receiving the Gospel and then giving from what they received is frequently found in the Acts of the Apostles. It is the pattern of the Christian life. In the gospel reading, Jesus speaks about the gift of the Holy Spirit he will give beyond his death and resurrection, a gift we are invited to receive. We have all received this gift of the Spirit and we are called to give from what we have received, to live in accordance with the Spirit we have received. The Lord's giving and our receiving from him, and our giving from what we have received is to be the shape of our lives.

12 May, Wednesday, Sixth Week of Easter

John 16:12–15

I was in Athens a couple of years ago with a group of priests and, at the spot where the Council of the Areopagus would have met, we read the passage from the Acts of the Apostles that was today's first reading. In that speech Paul begins by acknowledging the religious sensibilities of the Athenians. He goes on to announce that the God whom he proclaims, the God who raised Jesus from the dead, is the God for whom they are searching without realising it. Paul begins by recognising the Athenians' pursuit of truth and then offers them the gospel as the embodiment of that truth for which they long. In John's Gospel Jesus declares himself to be the truth, and in today's gospel reading from that gospel Jesus announces the coming of the Spirit of truth who will lead us to the complete truth. The Spirit will lead us to the complete truth by drawing us to Jesus, by leading us to a deeper grasp of all that Jesus said and did. The Spirit of truth, the Spirit of Jesus who is the truth, will satisfy our own longings for ultimate truth, for the truth that sets us free. That is why in the run up to the feast of Pentecost it is good to pray, 'Come Holy Spirit, enlighten the eyes of our minds and hearts'.

13 May, Thursday, Sixth Week of Easter

John 16:16–20

We have all experienced the sorrow associated with the loss of a loved one, the sorrow of bereavement. When we are in the throes of grief, it can be difficult to see any further than our grief. We find it hard to imagine any other condition. In today's gospel reading, Jesus is speaking to his disciples on the night before his death, in the setting of the Last Supper. He is aware that they are already troubled and distressed at what is unfolding and he tells them that very soon, in a short while, they will be 'weeping and wailing', they will be 'sorrowful'. His imminent death would bring them deep sorrow. Yet he goes on to say, 'Your sorrow will turn into joy'. In a further short while, they will see him again, when he rises from the dead, and they will rejoice. 'Your sorrow will turn into joy.' When we find ourselves engulfed by sorrow, we need to remind ourselves of those words of Jesus. Death and the sorrow associated with death will not have the last word. The resurrection of Jesus shows that life is stronger than death and that sorrow will eventually give way to joy. Because the risen Lord is with us at all times, life, his life, is always present in the midst of death, and a deeper joy is always possible for us even in times of sorrow. As Jesus says elsewhere in John's Gospel, those who follow him, the light of the world, will never walk in darkness, because the light of his presence, the light of life, is always shining even in our darkness.

14 May, Friday, Feast of Saint Matthias

John 15:9–17

The verb 'to choose' is common to both readings for this feast of Saint Matthias. After the death of Judas, the members of the early Church realised that they needed to choose someone to replace him. However, they were aware that the person they chose must also be someone whom the Lord was choosing. That is why, having gone through the human process of nominating two suitable candidates, they then presented the two candidates to the Lord and invited him to show them which of the two he had chosen. They were aware that they had a role to play in finding someone to replace Judas, but that the final choice was the Lord's. In the gospel reading, Jesus says to his disciples in the context of the Last Supper, 'You did not choose me, no, I chose you'. The Lord's choice of us is always prior to our choice of him. Our choice of him is a response to his prior loving choice of us. Earlier in that gospel reading, Jesus had said, 'As the Father has loved me, so I have loved you'. God's love for us through Jesus comes first. That constitutes the Gospel, good news. Having stated that fundamental truth of God's prior loving choice of us, Jesus then calls on his disciples and on us all to 'remain in my love', and he goes on to state that we remain in his love by keeping his commandment to love, by loving one another as he has loved us. The Lord's love for us is a given. We are invited to remain in his love by sharing it with each other. We have all been chosen in love; we respond to such a rich gift by living lives that bear fruit, in the words of the gospel reading, the fruit of the love that we have received.

15 May, Saturday, Sixth Week of Easter

John 16:23–28

In today's gospel reading, Jesus is very clear about his identity, where he has come from and where he is going. He declares, 'I came from the Father and have come into the world and now I leave the world to go to the Father'. There is a wonderful sweep in that statement. Jesus speaks of a great sweeping journey from God and back to God. There is a sense in which what Jesus says of himself can be said of every human person. We have all come from the Father and we are on a lifelong journey towards the Father. This is the essential truth about human life that Jesus has come to reveal to us. Jesus' journey to the Father helps us to travel our journey to the Father well. He shows us the way to the Father. Indeed, he says of himself, 'I am the way'. The way he travelled to the Father was the way of love. He gave himself in love to all, even to the point of giving his life for all. This is the way he sets before all of us: 'Love one another as I have loved you'. Jesus not only shows us the way to the Father, but he also empowers us to take that way. He has sent us the Paraclete, the Holy Spirit, to lead us to the complete truth, to lead us to God who is Truth. The Spirit leads us to God by empowering us to love one another as Jesus has loved us. We have an example of such love in action in the first reading, when a married couple, Priscilla and Aquila, gave further instruction about Jesus to a young convert, Apollo. They helped him to grow in his relationship with the Lord. Bringing each other closer to the Lord is one of the greatest loving services we can render each to each other. We do that by revealing the Lord's love to one another. Helping to bring each other to the Lord is a privileged expression of that way of love that leads us to the Father.

17 May, Monday, Seventh Week of Easter

John 16:29–33

The disciples speak with great confidence about Jesus at the beginning of today's gospel reading, 'Now we see that you know everything ... we believe that you came from God'. They speak almost as if they have finally reached their goal in their relationship with the Lord: 'We see ... we believe'. Jesus immediately punctures their self-confidence, declaring very bluntly that the time has arrived when they will abandon him, when they will be scattered, each going his own way, and leaving Jesus alone. This is what happened when Jesus entered into the journey of his passion and death. The gospel reading reminds us that we can never become too complacent about our relationship with the Lord. No matter how much progress we think we have made in the faith, there is always the possibility that we will go our own way rather than the Lord's way, and that we will be unfaithful to him in one way or another. When the disciples went their own way, it was not the end of the road for them. The risen Lord recommissioned them, breathing the Holy Spirit upon them, sending them out as he had been sent by his Father. When we go our own way, it is not the end of the road for us either. The same risen Lord stands ready to receive us when we turn back to him and will empower us afresh to be his followers through the gift of the Holy Spirit.

18 May, Tuesday, Seventh Week of Easter

John 17:1–11

Today we begin reading from the great prayer of Jesus in chapter 17 of John's Gospel. At the beginning of our reading we hear Jesus say, 'And eternal life is this: to know you, the only true God, and Jesus Christ whom you have sent'. The 'knowing' referred to there is not only a knowing with the mind but also that deeper knowing of the heart, the knowing that comes from love. We only really know those we love. Jesus declares that eternal life consists in a loving relationship with God and God's Son, Jesus, as a result of which we know God as God is, as Love. The first letter of John declares that in eternal life we will see God as God is, and, as a result, we shall be like God. It has been said that we become what we contemplate. In eternity we will contemplate God, we will see and know God, as Love, so we will become as loving as God is loving. We can anticipate that eternal destiny in the course of our earthly lives. Because, in the words of the gospel reading, Jesus has made known God's name, God's identity, to us, we can already know God with our mind and with our heart in this earthly life. We can contemplate the face of God in the person of Jesus, enter into a loving relationship with God, through Jesus, and, thereby, begin to become what we contemplate. Our heavenly destiny can begin in this earthly life. Through our loving relationship with God who is Love we can begin to become the loving person we will become fully in eternity.

19 May, Wednesday, Seventh Week of Easter
John 17:11–19

In today's gospel reading, Jesus continues his prayer for his disciples, the beginning of which we heard in yesterday's gospel reading. In the section of the prayer that we have just heard, Jesus prays that God would protect his disciples from the evil one. You may hear there an echo of one of the petitions of the Lord's Prayer, the prayer that Jesus taught to his disciples, 'Lead us not into temptation, but deliver us from evil'. Jesus, it seems, was very aware of the presence of evil, of the evil one, in the world. He also knew that such evil would always be a threat to the lives of his disciples. Jesus took evil seriously. He knew his disciples needed to be protected from the power of evil. Yet he was not overly preoccupied with evil, because he knew that the power of God was greater than the power of evil. He knew that, in the words of Paul, 'where sin abounds, grace abounds all the more'. Just before Jesus began his great prayer in John's Gospel, he said to his disciples, 'In the world you face persecution, but take courage, I have conquered the world'. We take evil seriously, yes, but we never allow its presence to make us despondent because we know that the light of the risen Lord's presence will never be overcome by the power of darkness and his light shining through our lives can face down the power of evil in our world.

20 May, Thursday, Seventh Week of Easter
John 17:20–26
Today's gospel reading is the conclusion of the great prayer of Jesus in chapter 17 of John's Gospel. In the course of this prayer, Jesus has been praying for his disciples, which is all of us. The disciples in John's Gospel represent all future disciples. Jesus' final prayer for his disciples, for us, is that 'the love with which you have loved me may be in them, and so that I may be in them'. It is a wonderful vision for the Christian life, according to which the love that God the Father has for Jesus would be in us, that we would love others in the same way that God loves Jesus and, in that way, that Jesus himself would live in us. There is a wonderful simplicity about that vision for our lives, even if it is supremely challenging. A few verses earlier, Jesus had given us his vision for our lives beyond this earthly life. He prays that we would be with him where he is, seeing his glory that God the Father gave him before the foundation of the world. Our ultimate destiny is to be with Jesus in God's presence. Our present destiny is to allow Jesus to be with us, to live in us, through his love, God's love, becoming incarnate in our

lives. What is common to both our present and eternal destiny is our communion with the Lord, his living in us in this life, and our living with him in the next life. It is clear from what Jesus says that our communion with him will always entail a communion with others. The Lord wants to live in us in this life so that he can continue to express his love for others through us, and he desires for all of us to be with him as a community of disciples in the next life. That is why Jesus' earlier prayer in our gospel reading is that we may be one, in the way he and the Father are one. This communion of love, flowing from our shared relationship with Jesus, is both our present and future destiny.

21 May, Friday, Seventh Week of Easter
John 21:15–19

We live in a somewhat unforgiving culture. If people in positions of leadership make a mistake, there is often a call for their immediate resignation. The possibility of someone learning from his or her mistake and becoming a better leader because of it never seems to be a consideration. Jesus did not work on that principle when it came to the leader of the twelve, Peter. He had failed in the most serious manner imaginable, denying publicly three times any association with Jesus, his Lord. Jesus did not transfer the leadership of the twelve to someone else, as a result. Rather, as today's gospel reading shows, the risen Lord gave Peter the opportunity to reverse his three–fold denial, asking Peter three times, 'Do you love me?' At the hour of Jesus' passion and death, Peter's love for Jesus, his loving fidelity to Jesus, had fallen away. Now Peter is being invited to renew his love for Jesus. Once Peter did so, Jesus re-instated him in his leadership role in the community, calling upon him to be the chief shepherd of Jesus' church, feeding his flock. The way Jesus related to Peter is how he relates to us all. When we fail him, he does not give up on us. When we don't live as his faithful disciples, he continues to love us, and he continues to call out to us to renew our love of him. His question to Peter, 'Do you love me?', is always being addressed to us, and we are always given the opportunity to answer his question as Peter did, 'Lord, you know I love you'. The Lord will then ask us, as he asked Peter, to express our love for him by being a good shepherd to others, revealing to others the Lord's faithful love for us.

22 May, Saturday, Seventh Week of Easter
John 21:20–25
It is extraordinary to think that of all the billions of people in the world no two people are exactly the same. We are each a unique image of God. The risen Lord can work through any one of us in a way that is distinctive to each of us. In the passage before today's gospel reading, Jesus had called Peter to be the chief shepherd of the Church: 'Feed my sheep'. He intimated that his shepherding of Jesus' flock would cost him not less than everything, as he would be taken 'where you do not wish to go'. He would be a shepherd in the mould of the Good Shepherd who laid down his life for his flock. There is another disciple present in today's gospel reading, alongside Peter, that nameless disciple who is always referred to in the Fourth Gospel as 'the disciple whom Jesus loved'. Having received his commission from the risen Lord, Peter seems curious about the role this disciple will have in the Church, 'Lord, what about him?' Jesus does not give a direct answer to Peter's question, but implies that the role of this disciple will be quite different from Peter's. Indeed, this is the disciple whose preaching and teaching stands behind the composition of the Fourth Gospel. If Peter witnessed to Jesus by laying down his life for the flock, the Fourth Gospel is this disciple's witness to Jesus. How we witness to Jesus is distinctive to each one

of us, reflecting our unique gifts, abilities and temperament. The Lord needs a rich diversity of disciples if he is to express himself fully in today's world. Paul, whose final preaching in Rome features in the first reading, tells us in his letters that the Church is the body of Christ, with a great diversity of members, every one of which is vital for the full functioning of the body.

24 May, Monday, Blessed Virgin Mary, Mother of the Church
John 19:25–34

Pope Francis recently introduced this new memorial of the Blessed Virgin Mary, Mother of the Church, to be celebrated on the Monday after the Feast of Pentecost. The second reading for this memorial comes just before the first reading for the feast of Pentecost from the Acts of the Apostles. Today's reading portrays the moment just before the coming of the Holy Spirit. The disciples, Mary, the mother of Jesus, some other women and Jesus' relatives are joined together in prayer, waiting for the coming of the Spirit. She is portrayed there as at the heart of the Church just before Pentecost. She remains at the heart of the Church today, and today's memorial reminds us that she is at the heart of the Church as mother. In today's gospel reading, Jesus says to the disciple he loved, the beloved disciple, 'This is your mother'. In John's Gospel, the beloved disciple represents all beloved disciples. What Jesus said at the Last Supper is said to all disciples of every generation, 'As the Father has loved me, so I have loved you; abide in my love'. The beloved disciple abided in Jesus' love even when the other disciples deserted Jesus. The same is true of the mother of Jesus who stood at the foot of the cross alongside the beloved disciple and some other women. The gospel writer is suggesting that the Church, the community of disciples, is already present at the foot of the cross, with the mother of Jesus as mother of this emerging church. Today's memorial celebrates the good news that the mother of Jesus is also our mother, which means Jesus is our brother. For most of us, our earthly mother remains a significant presence throughout our lives. Mary is a hugely significant presence in our faith life. She is one of Jesus' great gifts to us, to accompany us on our life journey as a helpful and supportive presence. She prays for us not just at the hour of our death but here and now, in the concrete circumstances of our daily lives. Today is a good day to remind ourselves that she is there as mother for us all throughout our lives, and that her primary role is to lead us to her Son, who is our way, our truth and our life.

25 May, Tuesday, Eighth Week in Ordinary Time
Mark 10:28–31

There is a lot of wisdom in the Jewish Scriptures. We are reading these days from the Book of Ecclesiasticus, which is one of the Wisdom books of the Bible. In today's first reading, the author calls on people to honour God not just by offering sacrifices in the Temple but by the way that they live: 'a virtuous person's offering graces the altar'. The author goes on to say that serving the Lord by both our worship and our way of life is to be done cheerfully: 'Add a smiling face to all your gifts, and be cheerful as you dedicate your tithes'. I am reminded of a verse from Paul's second letter to the Corinthians: 'Each of you must give as you have made up your mind, not reluctantly or under compulsion, for God loves a cheerful giver'. Sometimes our giving to the Lord and to others can be reluctant and a little begrudging, as if we were putting everyone under a complement to us. To give joyfully is a sign, a fruit, of the Spirit in our lives. Peter's question to Jesus in today's gospel reading, reveals something of that attitude of reluctant giving. 'What about us? We have left everything and followed you.' It is as if he were saying, 'We have given a lot. Now what's in it for us?'

Jesus takes his question seriously, however, and promises Peter that having given up everything to become a disciple, he will experience a rich reward in the form of a new family, a family of faith, brothers and sisters in the Lord, and Jesus adds, 'not without persecutions'. For all its blessings, the path of discipleship won't always be easy. Even when it is not easy, our following of the Lord is to be cheerful. It is always a joyful response to God's prior goodness to us.

26 May, Wednesday, Eighth Week in Ordinary Time
Mark 10:32–45

There are times in the gospels when Jesus seems aware that he is calling his disciples to a way of life that is out of sync with the culture around them. Today's gospel reading is a good example of this awareness of Jesus. He looks out at the pagan world of his day and he sees how the rulers and those in authority govern. He says that they lord it over their subjects and make their authority felt. He then very pointedly says to his disciples, 'This is not to happen among you'. He had noticed that his disciples were speaking and behaving in ways that reflected the world's understanding of authority as conferring status and power. James and John had just been looking for the places of honour in Jesus' kingdom. The other disciples became indignant with James and John, thinking perhaps that they had stolen a march on them. Jesus did not want his community of disciples to learn the ways of the world when it came to exercising authority. 'This is not to happen among you.' Unfortunately, this strong admonition has not always been heeded by the Church in the course of its history. Jesus understands authority purely in terms of service: 'Anyone who wants to become great among you must be your servant'. This was Jesus' teaching, but, even more so, this was Jesus' way of life, 'the Son of Man came not to be served but to serve, and to give his life'. Jesus embodied the authority of self-emptying service of others, especially of the most vulnerable. He declares in today's gospel reading that this is the only exercise of authority that is valid for his followers.

27 May, Thursday, Eighth Week in Ordinary Time
Mark 10:46–52

Bartimaeus, who features in today's gospel reading, always strikes me as someone with a great spirit, in spite of the very difficult circumstances of his life. He was clearly very determined to make contact with Jesus. He didn't speak politely to Jesus; he shouted at him, 'Son of David, Jesus, have pity on me'. When the crowds scolded him and told him to be quiet, he shouted all the louder. Here was someone who was totally focused on making contact with the Lord and he wasn't going to be put off by people who were trying to put him in his place. It was his desperate need that drove him to seek out the Lord with such single-minded determination. His determination brought results. Jesus paid attention and he asked the very people who were telling Bartimaeus to be quiet to call him over. We can allow that story to speak to us in a whole variety of ways, but the first part of the story encourages us to keep seeking the Lord, even in the face of those who would try to block us from relating to the Lord. In various ways, the culture in which we live can demand that we keep quiet in regard to our faith and our efforts to grow closer to the Lord. We need something of the spirit of Bartimaeus today. The gospel reading assures us that if we have that spirit, the Lord will not be found wanting. He will respond to us and empower us to follow him along the road, as Bartimaeus ended up doing.

28 May, Friday, Eighth Week in Ordinary Time
Mark 11:11–26

The evangelist Mark often links two stories together that he perceives to have something in common. In today's gospel reading he links the story of Jesus in the Temple with the story of Jesus and the fig tree. Jesus could not find any fruit on the fig tree, and he declared that the tree had no future. Mark is implying that when Jesus entered the Temple he found that it was not bearing the fruit it was meant to bear. Instead of being a house of prayer it had become a robber's den. Like the fig tree, it too had no future. At the end of the gospel reading, Jesus speaks again about prayer. The Temple is to be replaced by a new house of prayer, a new praying community, the community of those who do the will of God as Jesus has revealed it, the community of Jesus' brothers and sisters, what came to be called the Church. The Church is to be a prayerful community. It is also to be a community that is marked by forgiveness. When Jesus speaks about prayer at the end of the gospel reading, he links it to forgiveness. 'When you stand in prayer, forgive whatever you have against anybody, so that your Father in heaven may forgive your failings too'. The readiness to forgive as we have been forgiven is one of the primary fruits that God would expect to find among this new community of prayer.

29 May, Saturday, Eighth Week in Ordinary Time
Mark 11:27–33

The question of authority is always a lively one. Who has authority? How is it exercised? Where is it exercised? The gospels suggest that the issue of authority was a controversial one in relation to Jesus. On one occasion when Jesus declared to a paralysed man that his sins were forgiven, the religious leaders asked, 'Who can forgive sins but God alone?' Jesus went on to declare that the Son of Man had authority on earth to forgive sins, and to show this authority he healed the paralysed man. In today's gospel reading, the religious authorities ask Jesus, 'What authority have you for acting like this? Or who gave you authority to do these things?' Jesus had just caused mayhem in the Temple area, driving out those who were buying and selling and overturning the tables of the money changers and the seats of those who sold doves. The second question that Jesus was asked on this occasion is the crucial one: 'Who gave you authority to do these things?' We all know the answer to that question. God gave Jesus the authority to do what he did in the Temple, attacking the self-serving practices of the Temple authorities. Jesus is God's authoritative presence. A little before today's gospel reading in Mark, Jesus had defined authority in terms of service of others. 'Whoever wishes to become great among you must be your servant'. Jesus' authority was always in the service of others; he always used it to promote human well-being at every level. It is the authority of self-emptying love. This is the kind of authority that Jesus wishes to share with us all. He sends us out in the power of the Spirit to be his authoritative presence in the world, displaying the power of a love that promotes the well-being of all human life.

31 May, Monday, The Visitation of the Blessed Virgin Mary
Luke 1:39–56

In today's gospel reading, Mary is portrayed as a caring, considerate woman and as a prayerful woman. Many of us know or have known such women whose faith in the Lord found expression in faithful prayer and in loving consideration for others. Mary, who is pregnant with Jesus, is portrayed in that reading as going on a long journey from her home in Nazareth of Galilee to the hill country of Judah to be with her older cousin, Elizabeth, who was also expecting a child, who would become known as John the Baptist. Mary goes out of herself to be with her cousin whose need is greater than her own. In a very real, physical sense, Mary was bringing the Lord to Elizabeth, because she was carrying him in her womb. When Mary arrived at Elizabeth's house, Elizabeth exclaimed, 'Why should I be honoured with a visit from the mother of my Lord?' Mary's journey to Elizabeth expresses what is at the heart of our own baptismal calling. We are all called to bring the Lord to each other by our caring and considerate presence to them. Any time we set out on a journey towards someone whose need is greater than ours, as Mary did, we are bringing the Lord to them. Mary's movement in love towards others was matched by her movement in faith towards God in prayer. Her visit to Elizabeth and the way Elizabeth greeted her inspired Mary to pray that wonderful prayer which has come to be known as the Magnificat. Here again, Mary gives expression to what is at the heart of our baptismal calling. Our movement towards others in love is to be matched by our movement towards God in faith, expressed through prayer. Like Mary, we recognise the great things that God has done for us, and we respond by praising and thanking God. This feast of the Visitation of Mary is not just about Mary; it is also about us. It offers each of us a portrait of that way of life which flows from our baptismal identity and to which Mary gives expression so fully.

1 June, Tuesday, Ninth Week in Ordinary Time
Mark 12:13–17

Tobit was a very good and generous man who had a reputation for looking after those in need. He was suddenly struck blind, as we read in today's gospel reading. His wife asked a very understandable question, 'What about your own alms? What about your own good works? Everyone knows what return you have had for them'. She was saying, in other words, 'You have been doing all these good deeds and look at what has happened to you?' It is a question that people of faith continue to ask today. 'He was such a good person. What did this happen to him?' Yet, Tobit remained faithful to God, even after his personal tragedy. He didn't cease relating to God and living out of that relationship, in spite of his misfortune. In the gospel reading, Jesus gives a thought-provoking response to a trick question about paying taxes to Caesar that was intended to trap him: 'Give back to Caesar what belongs to Caesar, and give back to God what belongs to God'. The coin his questioners were carrying, with Caesar's head on it, belongs to Caesar and should be given back to him. What is it that belongs to God? For Jesus, everything belongs to God. All of our being belongs to God, our heart, soul, strength and mind. Even when life goes against us, we still belong to God. Tobit displays this giving of one's whole self to God, even in times of great personal distress. We don't relate to God for what God can give us, but because of who God is. He alone is worthy of all our reverence and devotion, regardless of the circumstances in which we find ourselves.

2 June, Wednesday, Ninth Week in Ordinary Time
Mark 12:18–27
In the time of Jesus there was more than one understanding of death within the Jewish tradition. One group, the Sadducees, did not believe in life after death in any real sense; they dismissed any notion of resurrection from the dead. In today's gospel reading they try to ridicule Jesus' belief in the resurrection of the dead. According to the Jewish Law, if the husband of a woman died, his brother should marry her to ensure the deceased brother lived on through his wife's children. The Sadducees put before Jesus the preposterous scenario of this situation repeating itself seven times, and they ask which of the seven brothers will the woman be wife to in the afterlife. In

his response to the Sadducees, Jesus declares that there is a radical difference between life in this world and life in what he calls 'the other world'. In this world we all die sooner or later. In the other world, Jesus says, people no longer die. Jesus does not spell out what life in this other world will look like. However, he does say that the children of the resurrection will be sons and daughters of God. In other words, our primary relationship will be with God rather than with each other. We will come to share in Jesus's own relationship with God as Son to a greater degree than is possible in this life. Jesus' answer does not mean that deep human relationships based on love will not endure. In growing closer to God we grow closer to each other. As we are drawn into Jesus' own relationship with God, we believe that our capacity to love is purified and perfected, and our loving relationships are brought to completion.

3 June, Thursday, Ninth Week in Ordinary Time
Mark 12:28–34

The first reading tells of the coming together in marriage of Tobias, Tobit's son, and Sarah, the daughter of Raguel. On their wedding night, they both prayed to God. The prayer first acknowledges God as worthy of blessing – 'Let the heavens bless you … ' – and only then moves to petition: 'Be kind enough to have pity on her and on me and bring us to old age together'. There is a similar pattern in the prayer that Jesus taught his disciples to pray. They are first to acknowledge God as worthy of blessing, 'hallowed by your name', and only then are they to petition God for their needs, 'give us this day our daily bread … '. The focus on God is prior to the focus on ourselves. There is a similar pattern in Jesus' reply to the question of the scribe in the gospel reading, 'Which is the first of all the commandments?' Jesus declares that the first commandment is fully focused on God. It is only God who is to be loved with all our heart, soul, mind and strength. Jesus immediately gives what he considers to be the second most important commandment, which has a focus on ourselves, 'you must love your neighbour as yourselves'. Jesus is saying that even in the midst of our most precious human relationships our primary focus is to be on God, because God alone is deserving of all our love. It is in loving God with all our being that our human loves, including the most intimate of human loves, can become complete.

4 June, Friday, Ninth Week in Ordinary Time

Mark 12:35–37

Today's gospel reading is short but it may sound a little confusing on first hearing. Many Jews expected the coming Messiah to be a son of David, a descendant of David. Jesus suggests that the title, 'Son of David', is not adequate for God's Messiah, for himself, Jesus. In the manner of a discussion among rabbis, Jesus argues his case on the basis of a verse of Scripture, a verse from the Psalms. It was generally understood in the time of Jesus that King David was the author of the Psalms. In one psalm, the person praying, understood to be David, refers to the coming anointed one, the coming Messiah, as 'my Lord'. Jesus argues that if David refers to the coming Messiah as 'my Lord', then the Messiah cannot simply be David's son. He is clearly David's Lord. Jesus is really saying that there is much more to him than people imagine. Yes, he is a son of David, a Jew from the line of David, yet his full identity is not exhausted by the title Son of David. We are being reminded that there is always more to Jesus than we imagine. Our ways of thinking and speaking about Jesus will always fall short of his full identity. He is always more mysterious, more wonderful, than we can possible conceive. Saint Paul speaks of 'the love of Christ that surpasses knowledge'. It is because Jesus is the love of God in human form that he is beyond any title we could give him. Our thoughts and words never do justice to him, and that is ultimately very consoling.

5 June, Saturday, Ninth Week in Ordinary Time
Mark 12:38–44

In today's first reading, the angel Raphael declares to Tobit and his son Tobias, 'better to practise almsgiving than to hoard up gold'. The gospel reading could be read as a commentary on that saying of Raphael. The scribes, regarded as experts in the Jewish Law, are identified by Jesus as 'men who swallow the property of widows, while making a show of lengthy prayers'. They have the visible trappings of piety while hoarding up gold in the form of stealing the property of the most vulnerable in society, widows. One of those widows reveals an extraordinary generosity of spirit in the presence of Jesus and his disciples. She gave alms to the Temple treasury, only two small copper coins, but it was all she had to live on. If generosity is measured not in terms of how much one gives but in terms of what one has left after one gives, then her generosity knew no bounds. She gave until she had nothing left to give. In a sense, she anticipates the giving of Jesus, who would give himself to others until there was nothing left to give; he gave his all on the cross. Perhaps this is why it was only Jesus who noticed her and then immediately called over his disciples so that they too would see this living parable of the kingdom of God. There are times in our lives when we seem to have little to give, little in the way of material resources, or, perhaps, little in the way of time or energy or imagination. Yet, the widow shows us that we can be just as generous, if not more so, at such times than when we seem to have a great deal more to give.

7 June, Monday, Tenth Week in Ordinary Time
Matthew 5:1–12

The Beatitudes are one of the best known texts in the gospels. Jesus declares 'blessed' or 'happy' those who live by a certain set of values that Jesus himself gives expression to in his own life. They are 'blessed' not so much because of their present situation but because of the ultimate future that these values open up for them in eternity. Jesus promises that for those who live by these values, 'theirs is the kingdom of heaven'. He outlines a set of attitudes and values that leads to life in God's kingdom. He is describing the way of life that God desires for us and which Jesus himself lived to the full. Jesus is giving us a portrait both of himself and of his disciples. Such people will be poor in spirit, acknowledging their poverty before God and their need of God. They will be gentle rather than arrogantly insisting on their own way. They will mourn because the world is out of sorts and not as God wants it. They will have a deep hunger and thirst for God's justice to come into our world. They will reveal God's merciful love to the broken and work for peace and reconciliation in the world. They will have that purity of intention which keeps putting what God desires first. They are ready to suffer for the sake of a right and just way of life for all. Jesus promises that if we travel this path as he did, then we will come to share in the fullness of God's blessing.

8 June, Tuesday, Tenth Week in Ordinary Time
Matthew 5:13–16

Today's gospel reading follows on immediately from the gospel of the Beatitudes. Jesus is declaring that it is those who live by the values proclaimed in the Beatitudes who are salt of the earth and light of the world. The horizon of both these images is very wide: 'earth' and 'world'. The way of life that Jesus describes in the Beatitudes, the way of life for his disciples, is with a view to the earth and the world. Jesus envisages that those who live by the values of the Beatitudes will have an impact for good far beyond their own circle. The images of salt and light capture something of this impact for good. Salt was a very important commodity in the world of Jesus. It was used to preserve food and to enhance its flavour. Jesus' disciples, by living the beatitudes, are called to preserve what is best in the world and to enhance the lives of others. In a culture without electricity, the flickering light of a lamp or torch was essential when darkness fell. It allowed people to find their way without damaging themselves or others. Jesus is declaring that when his followers live by the Beatitudes, their resultant good works are like a light in a dark world, showing people the way. This is not with a view to Jesus' followers drawing attention to themselves but so as to lead people to give glory and praise to God who has inspired such a way of life. The gospel reading reminds us that individually and as a community of faith we have been entrusted with a worldwide mission as disciples of the Lord.

9 June, Wednesday, Feast of Saint Columba
Matthew 8:18–27
Columba was born in Gartan, County Donegal in 521 and was of royal lineage. He founded monasteries in Derry, Durrow and, possibly, Kells. In 565 he left Ireland with twelve companions and founded a monastery on the island of Iona off south-western Scotland, which was given to him by the ruler of the Irish Dal Riada. Columba remained in Scotland, mainly Iona, for the rest of his life, returning to Ireland only for occasional visits. He died on 9 June 597. Columba and his companions preached the Gospel in the western part of Scotland. In the words of the first reading from the letter to the Colossians, he made the word of God fully known

wherever he went. That reading describes God's word as the mystery hidden throughout the ages but now revealed. The content of this mystery, according to that reading, is 'Christ among you, the hope of glory'. This is the heart of the good news. Christ is among us and his presence among us gives us hope, hope of sharing in the glory that he now enjoys. As we journey towards that glory, our calling in this life is, in the words of that same reading, to become 'mature in Christ'. We are to grow up into Christ who lives among us, and to the extent we do that we will become fully mature human beings, as Columba was. Our becoming mature in Christ, our growing up into Christ, is a lifetime's work, and this work is not just our work; more fundamentally it is the work of the Holy Spirit within us. Today we ask the Spirit to conform us more and more to the image of Christ.

10 June, Thursday, Tenth Week in Ordinary Time
Matthew 5:20–26

Saint Paul makes a striking statement in today's first reading: 'This Lord is the Spirit, and where the Spirit of the Lord is, there is freedom'. 'Freedom' is one of the great values of our age. There is an emphasis on people's freedom to choose. Paul had a very particular understanding of freedom, 'where the Spirit is, there is freedom'. For him, the truly free person is the person whose life is shaped by the Spirit, who is led by Spirit, in whose life is to be found the fruit of the Spirit. The primary fruit of the Spirit for Paul is love, love as it was revealed in the life of Christ, self-emptying love in the service of others. For Paul the truly free person is the person who is free to love in the way Jesus loved, to whom such a way of love comes easily and naturally. For Paul, the more we grow up into the loving person that Jesus was, the freer we are. The more we live out of that deeper virtue that Jesus speaks about in the gospel reading the more we display what Paul calls in his letter to the Romans 'the glorious freedom of the children of God'. Paul would say that we will only have that glorious freedom to the full when all is made new, beyond this earthly life. Yet he would also say that here and now we can begin to taste that glorious freedom of God's children in so far as we live our lives under the influence of the Lord's Spirit, the Holy Spirit.

11 June, Friday, The Most Sacred Heart of Jesus
John 19:31–37
The traditional image of the Sacred Heart of Jesus shows Jesus with a pierced heart. Such an image is influenced by today's gospel reading, although the reference there is to the piercing of Jesus' side rather than his heart. It is only in the Gospel of John that we find this detail of a Roman soldier piercing the side of Jesus with a lance, resulting in a flow of blood and water. This scene is an echo of an earlier passage in John's Gospel. There, on the last day of the feast of Tabernacles in Jerusalem, Jesus cries out, 'Let anyone who is thirsty come to me, and let the one who believes in me drink. As the scripture has said, "Out of his heart shall flow rivers of living water".' The fourth evangelist then comments on this saying of Jesus: 'Now he said this about the Spirit, which believers in him were to receive'. It is very likely that the fourth evangelist understood the flow of blood and water from the side of Jesus as a symbol of the life-giving Spirit, the Holy Spirit, the Spirit of God's love. When Jesus was lifted up on the cross, he poured out this Spirit of God's love on all humanity, and those who look up at the crucified Jesus with the eyes of faith receive this gift of God's love into their lives. The death of Jesus reveals the love of the good shepherd for his own and also the love of God for all humanity. Jesus' death not only reveals God's love for the world but makes that love tangible and personal for each one through the outpouring of the Holy Spirit into our hearts.

Saint Paul in his letter to the Romans expresses this wonderful truth of Jesus' death very succinctly. He declares that 'God proves his love for us in that while we were still sinners Christ died for us', and also states, 'God's love has been poured into our hearts through the Holy Spirit that has been given to us'. Today's feast is a feast of love. It is the feast of God's love, revealed in Christ, especially in his death, and given personally to each one of us through the Holy Spirit. This love is a given; it is ours to receive. In the second reading today, Paul calls on us to be planted in this love, and to allow ourselves to be built on this love, a love which, as he says in that reading, is 'beyond all knowledge'.

12 June, Saturday, Tenth Week in Ordinary Time

Matthew 5:33–37

I have often been struck by the last sentence in today's first reading from Paul's second letter to the Corinthians: 'For our sake God made the sinless one into sin, so that in him we might become the goodness of God.' According to Paul, God sent his Son into the sinfulness of the human condition, with all its tragic consequences for Jesus, so that we might come to share in Jesus' goodness, the goodness of God. God needed to get as close as possible to us through the sending of his Son, so that we could get as close as possible to God. Jesus revealed the goodness of God by his life, death and resurrection, and, as risen Lord, he poured the Spirit of this goodness, the Holy Spirit, into our hearts so that we might grow into his own goodness. There is a wonderful vision here of the goal of the Christian life, growing into the goodness of God. This is a journey that will never be complete in this life. It is only in eternity that we shall become like God, filled with the goodness of God, when we see God as God is. Yet, each day, with the help of the Holy Spirit, we can grow towards that goodness of God which is our ultimate destiny. In the gospel reading, Jesus highlights one manifestation of God's goodness in our lives. Our word is to be so reliable that we do not need to take an oath. The taking of an oath to guarantee the truthfulness of what we say becomes redundant. What we say reflects God's truth, which is one dimension of God's goodness. Only Jesus could say, 'I am the truth', because he was the fullest reflection of the truth of God's goodness. Each day, with the help of the Spirit, we seek to become more and more conformed to the image of God's Son.

14 June, Monday, Eleventh Week in Ordinary Time
Matthew 5:38–42
The principle of an eye for an eye and a tooth for a tooth, which Jesus quotes from the Jewish Scriptures, was meant at the time to put a restraint on the desire for revenge. There was only to be one eye for one eye, not a hundred eyes for one eye. In relatively recent times, some warring nations adopted the principle of taking ten or more times the number of lives for lives that were taken. It has always been a tendency of people to behave in this way in wartime. In that context, an eye for an eye could be understood as an enlightened policy. Revenge was to be proportionate. However, as in so much else in the Jewish Scriptures, Jesus goes beyond even this relatively enlightened principle. There is to be no place for revenge or retaliation within the community of his followers. 'Offer the wicked man no resistance.' In other words, evil is not to be met with evil, not even with proportionate evil. Rather, evil is to be met with goodness and generosity. Saint Paul in his letter to the Romans expressed this teaching of Jesus very succinctly: 'Do not be overcome by evil, but overcome evil with good. It is a hugely challenging teaching. Our human instinct is often to fight fire with fire, wrong with wrong, violence with violence, rejection with

rejection, insult with insult. It is the human instinct but it is clearly not the divine instinct. We can only operate out of the divine instinct of overcoming evil with good, with divine help, with the help of the Holy Spirit. We do occasionally witness within human relations evil being overcome by good. When that happens, we can be certain that there the Holy Spirit is at work.

15 June, Tuesday, Eleventh Week in Ordinary Time
Matthew 5:43–48
The word hate when applied to people always has a troublesome connotation. When someone says that they hate someone, it leaves us somewhat disturbed. The natural objects of our hate are those whom we perceive in some way or other to be our enemy. Perhaps they stand for everything we are opposed to, or perhaps they are responsible for some harm that has been done to us. In the gospel reading today Jesus declares that there is no room for hatred among his disciples, not even hatred of enemies. In fact, Jesus makes the extraordinary demand of his disciples to love their enemies. The love that the Jewish Law called on people to extend to their neighbour is now to be extended much, much further, to embracing the enemy. The kind of love that Jesus speaks about here is a divine love, a love that does not know how to discriminate in any way, a love that embraces the enemy as much as the friend. This is what the gospel reading refers to as perfection. 'Be perfect as your heavenly Father is perfect.' Perfection consists in loving as God loves. We can do that only with the help of the Spirit that God gives.

16 June, Wednesday, Eleventh Week in Ordinary Time
Matthew 6:1–6, 16–18
I have always been struck by that statement of Paul in today's first reading, 'God loves a cheerful giver'. He contrasts giving cheerfully

with giving grudgingly or under a sense of compulsion. What is it that makes our giving cheerful rather than grudging and resentful? I think it is ultimately a sense of gratitude. We give cheerfully to those whose presence we have experienced as a grace and a blessing, whose love has touched our lives deeply. As we grow in our appreciation of the ways God has blessed and graced us, as we come to know the depth of his love for us, our giving to God will be a cheerful giving, and that giving to God will express itself in a giving to all those whom God loves. Paul was a cheerful giver. Even as he wrote his letter to the Philippians while in prison, with a death sentence hanging over him, he was giving cheerfully to that church. The highest concentration of the noun 'joy' and the verb 'to rejoice' is to be found in that letter. His cheerful giving at that time was rooted in his profound sense of the many blessings and graces he was receiving from the Lord. 'I can do all things through him who strengthens me,' he wrote. Even if our situation leaves a lot to be desired, we can still give cheerfully, if we allow ourselves to appreciate just how much the Lord has blessed and graced us through his life, death and resurrection. In the gospel reading, Jesus warns against a giving that is calculating and self-serving, namely, giving alms, praying, fasting to attract the notice of others. Such giving is at the opposite end of the spectrum to the cheerful giving Paul speaks about and embodies in his own life. Paul assures us in that first reading that our cheerful giving will bring down upon us God's blessings and graces even more abundantly.

17 June, Thursday, Eleventh Week in Ordinary Time
Matthew 6:7–15

In today's gospel reading, Jesus teaches his disciples how to pray what has become known as 'the Lord's Prayer'. Pope Francis has approved a change to the wording of the Lord's Prayer after what was described as a 'flawed translation' from the original Greek wording. It comes two years after the pope expressed his dislike of the phrase 'Lead us not into temptation'. He said that this version implies that God, not Satan, leads people into temptation. Pope Francis has now approved a change from, 'lead us not into temptation', to 'do not let us fall into temptation'. Approval has been granted for the Italian version of the prayer to be updated but it's not known when the English version will be changed. It would seem there are no implications for the Irish translation of the Lord's Prayer. The relevant petition 'agus ná lig sinn i gcathú' translates roughly into English as 'and let us not succumb to temptation', which corresponds to the pope's favored phraseology, 'do not let us fall into temptation'. God does not lead us into temptation; God does not tempt us. Indeed, the letter of James in the New Testament says explicitly, 'No one, when tempted, should say, "I am being tempted by God"; for God cannot be tempted by evil and he himself tempts no one.' What God can do and wants to do is to strengthen us when we are tempted by evil. This understanding of God finds expression in Jesus' prayer to God on behalf of his disciples, as found in John's Gospel: 'I ask you to protect them from the evil one'. We desperately need the Lord to protect us from the evil one, to strengthen us when our faithfulness to his way is put to the test.

18 June, Friday, Eleventh Week in Ordinary Time
Matthew 6:19–23

I have often been struck by that saying of Paul that comes towards the conclusion of today's first reading. He speaks of his daily preoccupation, which he identifies as 'my anxiety for all the churches'. He had a daily concern for the members of the various churches he had founded. He goes so far as to say, 'when any person is made to fall, I am tortured'. He had a great concern for the community of faith, the life of the Church. In the gospel reading Jesus says, 'where your treasure is, there will your heart be also'. The members of the Church were Paul's treasure and, so, that is where his heart was. An even more fundamental treasure for Paul was the Lord himself, the Lord's Gospel, which he felt impelled to preach. His heart was above all with the Lord and his Gospel. When people responded to his preaching of the Lord, when they believed in the Gospel, they became his treasure, because they became the Lord's body on earth. Today's readings invite us to ask, 'Where is my treasure? Where is my heart?' Paul encourages us to take the Lord and his Gospel as our primary treasure, our pearl of great price. If the Lord and his Gospel becomes our treasure, we too, like Paul, will feel a great concern for the life of the Church. We will rejoice to see the Church alive in the Lord and be distressed to see the Church decline and weaken. Earlier in this same letter to the Corinthians Paul had said that we have this treasure, the treasure of the Lord and his Gospel, in earthen vessels. As members of the Church, the Lord's body, we can be frail and vulnerable, prone to brokenness, like clay jars. Yet the treasure of the Lord and his Gospel remains and our frailties and weaknesses do not make it any less of a treasure.

19 June, Saturday, Eleventh Week in Ordinary Time
Matthew 6:24–34
The Jesus who calls on us in today's gospel reading not to be overly anxious about food or clothing is the same Jesus who, towards the end of this gospel of Matthew, calls on us to clothe the naked and to feed the hungry and who declares that whatever we do or fail to do for the naked and hungry we do or fail to do for him. Jesus was very aware that we all have a responsibility to ensure that everyone can enjoy the basic necessities of life, yet he was also aware that we

can be overly anxious about food and clothing in our own regard. He is inviting us in that gospel reading to reflect on what it is we set our hearts on. What drives us? Is it the desire for more food or clothing or money than we need? At the end of the gospel reading, Jesus identifies what it is we are to set our hearts on, 'Set your hearts on the kingdom first, and on his [God's] righteousness', God's righteousness being God's will for our lives. This corresponds to the opening petitions of the Lord's Prayer: 'Your kingdom come, your will be done on earth as it is in heaven'. It is further into that prayer that we pray, 'Give us this day our daily bread'. The fundamental question that Jesus wants us to ask ourselves is, 'What is God's will for my life, for the life of the Church, for our world? How can I, how can we, live in such a way that the kingdom of God, the reign of God, becomes more of a concrete reality in our world?' This is to be our primary desire, which is to shape all the other desires of our lives. This is to be our basic prayer which informs all our other prayers.

21 June, Monday, Twelfth Week in Ordinary Time
Matthew 7:1–5
We don't often think of Jesus as having a sense of humour. However, something of his sense of humour comes across in today's gospel reading. He paints an amusing picture – amusing because it is ridiculous and incongruous – of someone with a plank in his or her eye struggling to take a splinter out of someone else's eye. Yet behind the humour there is a serious point. Jesus is alerting us to the human tendency to be very aware of the failings of others while at the same time being blind to our own failings. In a sense, wagging the finger at the perceived failings of others is always a strong temptation for all of us. I was struck some time ago by an exchange on television between an Irish bishop and a certain well-

known newspaper correspondent. What remained with me after the exchange was not anything either of them said but the sight of the correspondent continually wagging his finger at the bishop in the course of the exchange. Bishops, of course, have done their own share of finger wagging in the past, as, indeed, we all have. In today's gospel reading, Jesus encourages us to be constantly looking at ourselves when we come to turn the spotlight on others. We need to be in touch with our own humanity before we can comment on the humanity of others, and, it is probably true to say that the more we know ourselves the less inclined we will be to judge or accuse others.

22 June, Tuesday, Twelfth Week in Ordinary Time
Matthew 7:6, 12–14

There have been many disputes about land in human history. Land can be a highly contentious matter in our own culture. We are familiar with John B. Keane's play, *The Field*. In today's first reading, we are told that the land that Abraham and Lot came to was 'not sufficient to accommodate them both'. A dispute broke out between the herdsmen of Abraham and the herdsmen of Lot. There wasn't enough room in this land for the livestock of both. The potential for serious conflict was very real. However, Abraham's magnanimous attitude nipped the dispute in the bud. He said to Lot, 'Let there be no dispute between me and you, nor between my herdsmen and yours, for we are brothers ... Part company with me: if you take the left, I will go right; if you take the right, I will go left'. Abraham's conciliatory attitude served God's purpose for his people and through them for all humanity. In a way, Abraham's attitude anticipated the call of Jesus in the gospel reading, 'So always treat others as you would like them to treat you'. If everyone were to live by that principle, it would be a very different world. There would certainly be much less conflict. Jesus goes on to acknowledge that embracing such an attitude involves going through the narrow gate and taking the hard road. Yet, according to Jesus, it is the road that leads to life, life for ourselves and for others. It is a road we can take with the Lord's help, in the power of his Spirit of life.

23 June, Wednesday, Twelfth Week in Ordinary Time
Matthew 7:15–20

We are familiar with the proverbs, 'you cannot judge a book by its cover' and 'all that glitters is not gold'. Like all proverbs, they express a truth about human reality that has been gleaned from people's experience over a long period of time. People have learned, sometimes from all-too-bitter experience, that what you see is not always what you get when it comes to other people. Jesus makes the same observation in today's gospel reading when he speaks of those who 'come to you disguised as sheep but underneath are ravenous wolves'. There is a sharp contrast between a sheep and a wolf, the latter being a dangerous enemy of the former. In John's Gospel, Jesus makes reference to the hired hand, as distinct from the shepherd, who 'sees the wolf coming and leaves the sheep and runs away'. Jesus declares in today's gospel reading that we judge a person's character not by how they appear to us but by what he calls 'their fruits'. This gospel reading is part of the conclusion of the Sermon on the Mount. By 'fruits' Jesus means the fundamental attitudes and values, along with the actions or 'good works' that flow from them, which he has been portraying throughout the Sermon, beginning with the Beatitudes. This is not far removed from what Paul, in his letter to the Galatians, calls the fruit of the Spirit: 'love, joy, peace, patience, kindness, generosity, faithfulness, gentleness and self-control'. It is Paul who reminds us that if Jesus' gospel message is to bear the appropriate fruit in our lives, we will need to open our lives to the Holy Spirit who, as Paul declares in his letter to the Romans, 'helps us in our weakness'.

24 June, Thursday, Feast of the Birth of John the Baptist
Luke 1:57–66, 80

Many of the questions that people ask in the gospels are worth pondering. In today's gospel reading, we find one such question: 'What will this child turn out to be?' The question was people's response to the unusual circumstances surrounding the birth of John the Baptist. His father, Zechariah, had insisted that his newborn child was to be called 'John', even though no one in the family ever had the name 'John'. However, this was the name the angel Gabriel had given to the child who was to be born of Zechariah and Elizabeth when Gabriel appeared to Zechariah. Zechariah, who had lost his power of speech when he doubted the word of Gabriel, now received it back when he named his newborn son 'John'. The circumstances of John the Baptist's birth were unusual indeed. No wonder those present asked, 'What will this child turn out to be?' It is a question that could be asked of any newborn child. Indeed, it is a question that could be asked of any one of us, at any stage of our lives. We are always a work in progress, all of us. None of us are the finished product, regardless of our age or stage in life. We can all ask ourselves, 'What will I turn out to be – today, tomorrow, next week, next month, next year?' Shortly after the crowd asked that question in relation to the newborn child of Zechariah and Elizabeth, the evangelist said that 'the child grew up and his spirit matured'. John's human spirit matured because he was open to God's Spirit. This is how the Lord would want us all to turn out. He calls us every day to keep maturing in spirit, by opening ourselves more fully to the presence of the Holy Spirit in our lives. In today's responsorial psalm, the psalmist turns to God and says, 'I thank you for the wonder of my being'. The Lord calls us to allow the wonder of our being to flourish by surrendering ourselves to the movement of the Holy Spirit within us, after the example of John the Baptist who lived the wonder of his being to the full.

25 June, Friday, Twelfth Week in Ordinary Time
Matthew 8:1–4

Today's gospel presents us with that very striking meeting between Jesus and the leper. The term 'leprosy' was used to describe a variety of contagious skin diseases. Those who suffered from this disease were not only physically afflicted. They were also religiously afflicted, many believing that their disease was a punishment for sin. They were socially afflicted, in that they lived alone with only other lepers for company. The leper in the gospel reading shows great courage in breaking through all these barriers and approaching Jesus directly. He shows his faith in Jesus by saying, 'if you choose, you can make me clean'. In response, Jesus also breaks through the barriers that separated this man from himself, from God and from the community, and touches him, and in touching him, heals him. Both Jesus and the leper have something to teach us. The leper teaches us never to be afraid to reach out to the Lord in our need, no matter how separated from him we may feel. Jesus shows us that there is no condition in our lives, in our world, that he cannot touch with his loving presence. There is no situation, no matter how awful and desperate, that he cannot enter into and transform.

26 June, Saturday, Twelfth Week in Ordinary Time
Matthew 8:5–17

The gospels often make reference to people being astonished at Jesus, either at what he says or what he does. In today's gospel reading, however, it is Jesus who is described as being astonished at someone. He is astonished at the quality of faith in him shown by a Roman centurion, a pagan, a member of the occupying power. Jesus sees this centurion as an example of the many from east and west who will take their place with the Jewish patriarchs at the feast in the kingdom of heaven. There are elements of the centurion's faith that are instructive for us today. He showed great humility in recognising his unworthiness to have Jesus come to his home. As a Roman centurion, he was a person of some status and influence, yet he recognised that Jesus was his superior. We all need to come before the Lord in that same spirit of humility, recognising our unworthiness before him. We always come before the Lord as sinners, before one who is all good and all loving. Yet this recognition of our unworthiness to be in the Lord's presence does not make us fearful. This brings us to the second element of the centurion's faith, his profound trust in the healing and life-giving power of the Lord's word, 'just give the word ... '. In coming before the Lord in our unworthiness, we too, at the same time, recognise his healing and life-giving word. In coming before the Lord in our weakness, he gives us his strength; in coming before him in our sinfulness, he gives us his mercy; in coming before him in our brokenness, he brings us healing.

28 June, Monday, Thirteenth Week in Ordinary Time
Matthew 8:18–22

It can often happen that people take on some task or commit to some cause or set out on some journey without fully appreciating all that is involved. When it turns out to be a lot more difficult than they anticipated, they quickly fall away. A desire to do somewhat worthwhile is a wonderful quality but our desire also needs to be grounded in the reality of what will be asked of us. Jesus welcomed the desire of people to follow him along his way, but he also wanted to be sure that they knew what lay ahead. In today's gospel reading, when a Jewish scribe comes up to Jesus and says, 'I will follow you wherever you go', Jesus was no doubt very pleased with this man's enthusiastic desire to become his follower, but he also reminded him of the harsh reality of what was involved in following him,: 'The Son of Man has nowhere to lay his head'. In other words, you will be following someone who doesn't have a stable home, but will be constantly on the move. We know from the gospels that it was only when Jesus got to Jerusalem for the last time that he was finally forced to stop his travels, and that was because he was nailed to a cross. How does this encounter between Jesus and the scribe speak to us today? The Lord continues to call us to follow him, not in the sense of physically going where he goes, but in the sense of walking in his way, living in the same generous, loving, way as he did. If we are to respond to the Lord's call today, we need a strong desire to be his follower. We need something of the desire of the scribe in the gospel reading. We also need a realistic recognition that following the Lord today won't always be easy. In many ways, being the Lord's disciple today is as countercultural as it was in the time of Jesus. To decide to become the Lord's disciple is a big step and won't always be easy, yet it is always a step we take with the Lord at our side. He takes that step with us, and will help us every step of the way to remain his faithful disciple to the end.

29 June, Tuesday, Feast of Saints Peter and Paul

Matthew 16:13–19

Peter, the leader of the twelve, and Paul, the great apostle to the Gentiles, have been remembered together on this date since ancient times. According to very ancient tradition, both were put to death for their faith in Jesus during the persecution of the church in Rome by the Emperor Nero in AD 64. Successive generations of

Christians remembered where the two leaders of the early Church were buried and, when Christianity became legal under the Emperor Constantine, a basilica was built over the tomb of each of them, the Basilica of Saint Peter on the Vatican Hill and the Basilica of Saint Paul outside the Walls. Both basilicas remain places of pilgrimage to this day. Peter and Paul had very different backgrounds. Peter was a fisherman by the Sea of Galilee in modern-day Israel. Paul was a learned Pharisee from the university city of Tarsus in modern-day Turkey. Peter journeyed with Jesus from the beginning of Jesus' public ministry until the time of his passion and death; the risen Lord appeared to Peter. Paul had never met Jesus until the risen Lord appeared to him on the road to Damascus in modern-day Syria. According to Paul's letter to the Galatians the two of them met in the city of Jerusalem probably less than twenty years after the death and resurrection of Jesus and they went on to have a major disagreement in the church of Antioch about the terms on which pagans should be admitted to the Church. Even great apostles and saints can disagree over matters of fundamental importance. However, what united them, their faith in and love for the Lord, was far more significant than what divided them. They were very different people and they didn't always see eye to eye, but the Lord needed both of them. He had a very different but equally vital role for each of them to play in spreading the Gospel. Today's feast reminds us that the Lord has a role for each of us to play in his work today. Our very different backgrounds, and even our disagreements over Church-related matters, are not an issue for the Lord. Rather, it is our very diversity which allows the Lord to work through us in a whole variety of ways. The Church is never uniform, but the Lord asks to be united in our faith in and love for the Lord, as Peter and Paul were.

30 June, Wednesday, Thirteenth Week in Ordinary Time
Matthew 8:28–34

In the gospel reading Jesus is met by two very disturbed people. They were so disturbed that they lived among the tombs and no one would pass that way for fear of them. Jesus, however, was not afraid of them, even though they initially addressed him in a very aggressive way. Undisturbed by their aggression, Jesus went on to heal them and to restore them to themselves and to the community. Jesus' power to give life was stronger than the power to damage, destroy and disturb which he confronted. That remains true today. The risen Lord's life-giving power at work in our lives is stronger than the forces in our world that dehumanise and damage. That is why we need always to be people of hope. The Lord at work among us and through us can do immeasurably more than all we ask or imagine, in the words of Saint Paul. We need to open ourselves to the Lord's presence so that he can work through us. In contrast to the townspeople in the gospel reading who asked Jesus to leave the neighbourhood, we invite the risen Lord to use us as his instruments in his healing and life-giving work.

1 July, Thursday, Thirteenth Week in Ordinary Time
Matthew 9:1–8

People who have lost bodily powers that we can so easily take for granted depend on others to do things for them that they cannot do for themselves. We often associate such a level of dependency with advanced years, yet people can become dependent on others at a much earlier stage in life. We are not told the age of the paralytic in today's gospel reading, but he was likely a relatively young man by today's standards. He was completely dependent on others to bring him where he wanted to go. When it was heard that Jesus had arrived in the town, he must have expressed some desire to be brought to Jesus. Clearly this man was not alone in his paralysis because people quickly gathered around him to carry him to Jesus. There is a striking image here of who we are all called to be as church. In various ways we are to bring each other to the Lord. We never make our way to the Lord on our own. The journey to the Lord is always a shared journey. We need other people of faith around us, if not physically, then spiritually. When the paralytic reached Jesus, the gospel reading says that Jesus saw 'their faith', not just the faith of the paralytic but the faith of those who carried him. We have much to receive from other believers on this journey, as well as much to give. Today's gospel reading invites us to give thanks to God for all those who have brought us to the Lord in some way, perhaps teachers, priests, religious sisters or brothers, friends and, for most of us, parents, who were the first to bring us to the Lord when presenting us for baptism.

2 July, Friday, Thirteenth Week in Ordinary Time
Matthew 9:9–13

One of my favourite paintings is *The Calling of Matthew* by Caravaggio. The artist depicts Jesus to the right of the painting pointing towards Matthew. It is the moment of Jesus' call to Matthew to be his disciple. Matthew is seated with others; he has one hand on the money he is counting and with his right hand he points to himself, his hand almost in line with the pointing hand of Jesus. It is as if Matthew is saying, 'Who? Me?' Matthew's world of commerce was very different from the world of Jesus, even though they both inhabited much the same space. Yet Jesus was capable of breaking into Matthew's world and calling him to a very different way of life from the one he had known. Matthew went on to become a significant member of the group of twelve that Jesus gathered around him; he was the inspiration behind the gospel we know as the Gospel according to Matthew. We are being reminded that one of the foundational pillars of the Church included someone who, by reason of his profession, was considered a sinner at the time. In the person of Jesus, Matthew experienced both God's forgiveness and God's call to a new way of life. Jesus reveals God to be someone who desires more that mercy be shown than that sacrifices be offered, and who seeks out sinners more than the virtuous. The call of Matthew reminds us that the Lord is always seeking to break into our world, whatever state our personal world is in. The Lord breaks in there to communicate his boundless mercy towards us, so that we can share more fully in the Lord's work in the world. Every day, we can ask ourselves the question, 'Who? Me?' to which the Lord will always answer, 'Yes, you'.

3 July, Saturday, Saint Thomas, apostle
John 20:24–29

Perhaps, we will find it easy to identify with Thomas in today's gospel reading. When the other disciples approached him with the good news of Easter – 'We have seen the Lord' – their message did not resonate with him in any way. The darkness of Good Friday was still too real for him and prevented him from being moved by their Easter proclamation. His own reasoning did not allow him to believe that life had triumphed over death, that the crucified Jesus was now the risen Lord. Thomas stood in the light of Easter, yet that light did not dispel his darkness. If his fellow disciples were full of Easter faith, he was full of doubt. They claimed to have seen the risen Lord; Thomas declared that he would not believe until he not only saw the Lord but touched his wounds. In his doubting, Thomas may be like many other disciples today. Many believers can be troubled by their sense that the light of Easter does not seem to have penetrated their lives sufficiently. We can be distressed at the degree of doubt that we experience within ourselves, troubled that such doubts may even become more pronounced as we get older. Like Thomas, we can struggle to identify fully with those whose faith seems so much more assured than ours. The prayer of one of the more minor Gospel characters, 'Lord, I believe, help my unbelief', may find a ready place in our heart. Today's gospel reading assures us that the Lord understands a doubting, questioning faith. When the Lord appeared to Thomas, he did not rebuke him. His first words to him were, 'Peace be with you'. He invited Thomas to touch his wounds as he had requested. The gospel reading does not state that Thomas actually touched the wounds of Jesus. Seeing the risen Lord was enough to dispel his doubt. Then, out of the mouth of the great sceptic came one of the most complete professions of faith in Jesus to be found in all the gospels, 'My Lord and my God'. We are being reminded that serious doubt and great faith can reside in one and the same person. The Lord considers anyone who is a seeker and who wishes to believe as a believer already. If we remain true to our spiritual search, even as we struggle with doubt, the Lord will keep drawing near to us, inviting us, as he invited Thomas, 'Doubt no longer but believe'.

5 July, Monday, Fourteenth Week in Ordinary Time
Matthew 9:18–26

I am always struck by the contrast in the way that the two people approach Jesus in today's gospel reading. The synagogue leader approached Jesus in a very public way on behalf of his daughter's healing, bowing low before Jesus in the presence of others. The woman approached Jesus in a very private way, coming up behind him to touch the fringe of his cloak for her own healing. She would have been quite happy not to be noticed by anyone. We each approach the Lord differently because we are all different and the circumstances of our lives are different. Our relationship with the Lord is a deeply personal one. As we relate to each other out of our uniqueness, so too we relate to the Lord out of our unique personality and history. Even when we are praying together, as we do at Mass, reciting the same prayers together, we do so in a way that is personal to each one of us. The Lord respected the very different way that the two people approached him and responded to each of them equally. The Lord respects us in our uniqueness. He recognises and rejoices in the personal nature of our faith. He calls us by name, respecting our individuality. The Christian faith is a communal faith; we journey together to the Lord who is always at work to form a community of believers. Yet, that communal nature of our faith never eradicates what is unique to each of us. As Paul recognised very clearly, the Church is a unity in diversity, like a human body.

6 July, Tuesday, Fourteenth Week in Ordinary Time
Matthew 9:32–38
The sense that Matthew gives us in today's gospel reading is of a Jesus who is constantly on the go. He heals a man who cannot speak; he goes through the towns and villages of Galilee, teaching in the synagogues, proclaiming the presence of God's kingdom and curing the sick. He begins to minister to a crowd whom he recognises to be harassed and dejected, like sheep without a shepherd. Is it any wonder that Jesus then goes on to ask his disciples to pray to God, the Lord of this rich harvest, to send more labourers into the harvest. Not even Jesus could meet the needs of people on his own; he needed helpers. It is probably always the case in every age of the Church that the harvest is rich and the labourers are few. There was a time when we understood that call of Jesus to pray for more labourers as a call to pray for vocations to the priesthood and religious life. However, the decline in vocations to the priesthood and religious

life has sharpened our awareness that the labourers the Lord needs are to be found among all the baptised. The Lord needs all kinds of labourers, with a whole variety of gifts and temperaments. We can look around our parishes and give thanks for the many labourers that are already serving the parish community in some way. We need to pray for more such labourers. Even a small service can bear rich fruit for the life of a parish, like the mustard seed that became a large shrub. The widow's gift of two small coins to the Temple treasury shows that great generosity can be manifest in small ways.

7 July, Wednesday, Fourteenth Week in Ordinary Time
Matthew 10:1–7

The person of Joseph in today's first reading illustrates the truth of the line from one of the Psalms, 'the stone which the builders rejected has become the cornerstone'. Joseph had been rejected by his brothers, thrown into a pit and left for dead. However, he was eventually rescued by travellers and brought to Egypt. There his natural gifts ensured that he rose up in the Egyptian civil service. Eventually, he had the responsibility for distributing food to the hungry in time of famine. Egypt's reserves of food meant that it remained a source of food for other peoples who were beset by famine. When Jacob's brothers came from the land of Israel to look for food, it was Joseph who had the power and the ability to meet their need. The rejected stone had become the keystone. What we reject can sometimes turn out to be of crucial importance for us. Our initial inclination to say 'no' to something or someone is not always the best response. Yet our saying 'no' can itself serves God's purpose, just as the brothers' rejection of Joseph ended up serving God's purpose for his people. Jesus is the supreme example of the rejected stone becoming the cornerstone. The rejection of God's Son went on to serve God's purpose for humanity. Among those who rejected Jesus was one of the twelve he chose in today's gospel reading. Yet even Judas's betrayal of Jesus came to serve God's greater purpose of revealing God's unconditional love for all humankind. The story of Joseph and Jesus reminds us that, in the words of Paul's letter to the Romans, 'all things work together for good for those who love God'.

8 July, Thursday, Fourteenth Week in Ordinary Time
Matthew 10:7–15

When Jesus sends out the twelve to share in his mission in today's gospel reading, it seems as if he is sending them out in a general state of unpreparedness. The usual resources that people would take with them for a long and demanding journey are being denied to them. From a human point of view, Jesus sending out his disciples almost devoid of the usual resources seems foolhardy. Jesus had a habit of speaking or behaving in an exaggerated way to make his point strongly. In sending out his disciples in such a vulnerable state, Jesus was teaching them not to be over-reliant on their own human resources, but to rely on the Lord to provide for them. The value of self-reliance is an even stronger one today than it would have been in the much more communal culture of Jesus. We have been taught to leave nothing to chance. We must plan for every eventuality. Yet, when it comes to the work of the Lord in our time, we need to have a light hold on all possible resources and to allow room for the Lord himself to work. We can be so absorbed in the work of the Lord that we can sideline the Lord of the work. If we provide excessively for ourselves, including our work in the Lord's service, we can forget that the Lord is the ultimate provider. Poverty of resources can sometimes allow the Lord to work more powerfully than he could if we had every eventuality covered in advance. The Lord is always inviting us to step out of the boat, trusting that he will not let us sink.

9 July, Friday, Fourteenth Week in Ordinary Time
Matthew 10:16–23

There is a very moving scene at the end of today's first reading as Jacob (Israel) meets with his long-lost son, Joseph, whom he had presumed to have been killed. Joseph embraced his father and wept on his shoulder, and Jacob declared, 'Now I can die, now that I have seen you again, and seen you still alive'. We are reminded of the prayer of Simeon at the beginning of Luke's Gospel after he had set eyes on the child Jesus, the 'salvation' he had been waiting for, 'Now, Master, you can let your servant go in peace'. Jacob could have said of Joseph what the father said of his son in one of the parables in Luke's Gospel, 'this son of mine was dead and is alive again; he was lost and is found!' The son in that parable had chosen to leave his father, whereas Joseph had been forcibly removed from his father by his brothers, who had sold him into slavery. Joseph's situation is more akin to the situation that Jesus envisages in the gospel reading, 'brother will betray brother to death'. Conflict in families is as old as the story of Cain and Abel, where again a brother betrays a brother to death. It was jealousy that prompted Joseph's brothers to sell him into slavery. Jesus envisages a situation where he himself will be the cause of brother betraying brother to death. Those who believe in Jesus and bear witness to him will be hated even by members of their own family. Our attempts to be faithful to the Lord's way can continue to cause family tensions today. In such moments, Jesus assures us that we will not be left to our own resources. The Holy Spirit, the Spirit of Jesus and of God the Father, will be given to us as strength in our weakness, just as God promised Jacob in the first reading, 'I myself will go down to Egypt with you'.

11 July, Saturday, Fourteenth Week in Ordinary Time
Matthew 10:24–38

Twice in the course of today's gospel reading Jesus says to his disciples, 'Do not be afraid'. He was sending them out on mission. He had just been very honest with them about the hostility they were likely to encounter. As Jesus says in the gospel reading, if they have called the master of the household, Jesus, Beelzebul, accusing him of being in league with Satan, what will they not say of the members of his household, Jesus' followers? When it comes to witnessing publicly to our faith in the Lord, we can all be held back by fear. Yet it is striking how many times in the gospels Jesus calls on his disciples not to be afraid. On one occasion, he said to his disciples in the boat in the midst of a storm on the Sea of Galilee, 'Why are you afraid, you of little faith?' Jesus identifies fear as a sign of little faith. So often in the gospels the opposite of faith is not doubt but fear. Genuine faith is always a courageous faith. In the gospel reading today, Jesus gives us a reason why we can be courageous in witnessing to our faith in him. God who cares for the humble sparrow cares for us even more, who are worth 'more than hundreds of sparrows'. God holds us in the palm of his hand, especially when we witness publicly to our faith in his Son, when, in the words of Jesus at the end of the gospel reading, we declare ourselves publicly for him before others. It is above all at such times that God is our refuge and our strength, in the language of one of the Psalms.

12 July, Monday, Fifteenth Week in Ordinary Time
Matthew 10:34–11:1

The cruel treatment of the Hebrew people in Egypt, as told to us in today's first reading, is an all too familiar one. Ethnic or religious groups in a country can be seen as a threat because they embody a different set of values from the dominant culture. They can become a scapegoat for the ills of the nation. People suspect them of cooperating with the nation's enemies, 'if war should break out, they might add to the number of our enemies'. Minority groups in a society can suddenly find themselves very vulnerable. Jesus was aware that his followers would be a minority group within the larger society and, therefore, would be very vulnerable. Even within their own families, his disciples would be vulnerable to the attacks of parents, siblings, sons or daughters: 'A person's enemies will be those of his own household'. When Jesus says that he came to bring not peace to the earth but a sword, he was looking ahead to the consequences of his coming, rather than expressing his intention for his mission. The Lord's disciples can continue to feel vulnerable today, especially in certain parts of the world. The vulnerable status of believers can help to make the Church more attentive to the presence of the vulnerable in our world. In the gospel reading, Jesus highlights the value of showing even the smallest act of kindness towards the vulnerable, such as a cup of cold water to the 'little ones', those who have no power or influence in the world. Jesus also identifies with his own vulnerable disciples, 'whoever welcomes you welcomes me'. Elsewhere he identifies with other categories of vulnerable people, such as the children, the sick, the imprisoned, the hungry, the thirsty, the stranger. He assures us that in serving them, we are serving him.

13 July, Tuesday, Fifteenth Week in Ordinary Time
Matthew 11:20–24

We can get very discouraged when we encounter a poor response to our efforts to offer something we consider worthwhile. Those of us who work in parishes may get a speaker who has something valuable to say about the life of faith and only a handful turn up, in spite of our best efforts to promote it. Within a family, parents give exemplary witness to their faith in the Lord, and their children do not come to share their faith. In the gospel reading, Jesus shows his discouragement, indeed, his exasperation, at the indifferent response of the towns of Chorazin, Bethsaida and Capernaum to his healing and life-giving ministry. On another occasion he wept over the city of Jerusalem, because in spite of his best efforts to gather them to himself as a hen gathers her brood, they were unwilling. Jesus bemoaned his deep disappointment in all these cases. However, when Moses saw an Egyptian strike a Hebrew his reaction went beyond bemoaning to violent behaviour that resulted in the death of the Egyptian. How do we respond to situations we find deeply disappointing and upsetting? Jesus has something to teach us in this regard as in all others. In Luke's Gospel a Samaritan town rejected Jesus' offer of the Gospel. His disciples wanted the townspeople struck dead from heaven, which was akin to Moses' reaction. Jesus simply went on his way to the next town. As risen Lord he reached out to the Samaritan towns with the Gospel through the ministry of Philip, and on this occasion the Samaritans responded with joy. We sometimes need that kind of patience. Yes, we can bemoan people's lack of response to our offer of the gospel message, but we do not allow such experiences to embitter us. We keep offering, trusting that the Lord will bring some good out of our persistence.

14 July, Wednesday, Fifteenth Week in Ordinary Time
Matthew 11:25–27

The account of Moses' call by God in the first reading is one of the key texts in the Jewish Scriptures. Moses' encounter with God at the burning bush would transform him from a humble shepherd to the great liberator of the people of Israel from the slavery of Egypt. This profound spiritual experience was as significant for Moses as Paul's encounter with the risen Lord on the road to Damascus was significant for him. In that highly charged moment, according to our first reading, Moses heard God call on him to take off his shoes, 'for the place on which you stand is holy ground'. Every prayerful encounter between ourselves and the Lord generates holy ground. In the gospel reading we are given an insight into a moment of Jesus' prayerful encounter with God. He thanks God that it is 'mere children' who are receiving his revelation of God the Father. It is not the 'learned and the clever', the experts in the Jewish Law, who are receiving this revelation, but those considered to be uneducated in the ways of God, such as sinners, tax collectors, people from all walks of life who do not keep the details of the Jewish Law. Jesus says that we need to 'become like children' if we are to enter the kingdom of God. We need a humble openness to God's presence, such as Moses showed while shepherding his sheep. Prayer is a moment when we come before the Lord in our poverty, conscious that we have nothing to offer that God needs but that we need everything that God has to offer. When in prayer we come before the Lord in such poverty of spirit, we are truly on holy ground.

15 July, Thursday, Fifteenth Week in Ordinary Time
Matthew 11:28–30

In today's first reading, Moses asks God for his name. It is a bold request. In the biblical tradition, someone's name reveals their core identity. In his reply to Moses' request, God reveals his name to be 'I am' – 'This is what you must say to the sons of Israel: "I am" has sent me to you'. The name 'I am' suggests God's presence to his people, and the larger context of the passage indicates that it is God's saving and liberating presence that is to the fore, 'I have resolved to bring you out of Egypt'. Jesus is the fullest revelation of God in human form and in John's Gospel, in particular, he often speaks of himself as 'I am', as in 'before Abraham was, I am'. In today's gospel reading, Jesus speaks as one who has a uniquely intimate relationship with God: 'No one knows the Son except the Father, just as no one knows the Father except the Son'. Yet his closeness to God is matched by his closeness to men and women, especially to those who labour and are overburdened because of an oppressive interpretation of the Jewish Law by those considered 'learned' and 'clever'. Jesus issues a very personal invitation to the burdened: 'Come to me ... learn from me'. Jesus does not invite people to a new code but to an intimate relationship with himself, comparable to his intimate relationship with God. It is in allowing Jesus to draw us to himself that we will come to share in his 'rest'. 'Rest' here is not the absence of activity. It suggests the 'restful waters' of Psalm 23, to which the Lord leads us to revive our drooping spirits. As we draw close to the Lord, our spirits are revived and we are empowered to live by his teaching, which, while demanding, will be experienced as 'light'.

16 July, Friday, Fifteenth Week in Ordinary Time
Matthew 12:1–8

In today's gospel reading, the Pharisees criticise Jesus' disciples for satisfying their hunger in a way they considered inappropriate on the sabbath, by eating some of the grain as they walk through a cornfield. However, Jesus defends what his disciples are doing. He gives priority to human need over a strict interpretation of a religious law, even a law as important as the sabbath law. This exchange between Jesus and the Pharisees shows us something of Jesus' priorities. He was concerned for human well-being. He wanted the hungry to be fed, the thirsty to have clean water, the homeless to be housed, the sick to be cared for, the rejected to be welcomed. These were the values that he lived by and religious law was at the service of those values. Jesus lived by these values because he knew that they were God's values. This is why he goes on to quote from the prophet Hosea, 'What I want is mercy, not sacrifice'. God gives greater priority to people showing mercy to others than to people offering him sacrifice in the Temple. Showing mercy to others entails providing for people's basic needs, such as ensuring that the hungry are fed. Jesus could speak as God's representative. As he says in the gospel reading, 'Here, I tell you, is something greater than the Temple'. The Temple was traditionally understood to be the privileged place of God's presence in the world. Jesus, however, is now that privileged place of God's presence. He speaks and acts as God would speak and act. Jesus shows that God's highest value is mercy, the loving care of others in their need. Jesus wants us, his followers, to make God's highest value our own in the way we relate to others.

17 July, Saturday, Fifteenth Week in Ordinary Time
Matthew 12:14–21

Just as according to the first reading the people of Israel leave Egypt because of the deadly hostility of the Egyptians towards them, so, according to the gospel reading, Jesus withdraws from the district where he had been because of the deadly hostility of the Pharisees towards him. Matthew goes on to interpret Jesus' healing ministry in the light of one of the 'Servant Songs' to be found in the prophet Isaiah. Jesus had spoken about himself as 'gentle and humble in heart' (11:29). Such a figure does not 'brawl or shout' in the language of the quotation. The primary focus of his mission was the afflicted crowds, the 'crushed reeds' and 'smouldering wicks'. Pope Francis often speaks about the need for tenderness in our relationship with others. The quotation from Isaiah evokes Jesus' tender love towards others. Jesus could be angry when anger was called for, towards his opponents and even towards his own disciples. Towards the most vulnerable, however, he showed tender loving care. Rather than breaking the crushed reed, he helped to mend it. Rather than putting out the smouldering wick, he fanned it into a living flame. Such tender love was the visible expression of the Spirit in his life. In the words of the quotation from Isaiah, Jesus is the servant whom God has endowed with his Spirit. The risen Lord has poured that same Spirit into all our hearts so that we can become servants in the mould of Jesus, giving expression to his tender love for the weak and vulnerable among us.

19 July, Monday, Sixteenth Week in Ordinary Time
Matthew 12:38–42
In the gospel reading Jesus makes reference to the prophet Jonah and to King Solomon. He highlights different elements of the story of both of these figures from the Jewish Scriptures. It was clear that for Jesus the story of Jonah and the story of Solomon spoke to the present. The religious leaders who look to Jesus to give them a sign need to listen to the stories of their Scriptures carefully and learn from them. For Jesus all of the Scriptures were ultimately about the here and now. They did not just belong to the past. God continued to speak through his past word to the present. Jesus seems to have read the Jewish Scriptures as a word about himself and about how people were relating to him and to God and how they were being called to relate to him and to God. If the pagan people of Nineveh responded to the preaching of the Jewish prophet Jonah, if a pagan queen travelled to see the Jewish king Solomon, surely Jesus' own contemporaries could respond positively to his mission because he was so much greater than all the prophets and kings of Israel. We too can read the Scriptures, both the Jewish Scriptures and the Christian Scriptures, the Old and the New Testament, as a word from God to us today. In some sense, all of the Scriptures speak to us about Jesus

and about our relationship with him and his relationship with us. Whenever we open any part of the Scriptures Jesus is saying to us, 'there is something greater than Jonah here ... there is something greater than Solomon here'. It is Jesus, God-with-us, who is present in all of God's word to us.

20 July, Tuesday, Sixteenth week in Ordinary Time
Matthew 12:46–50

Jesus' response to his mother and brothers in today's gospel reading seems a little uncaring. They were anxious to see him, presumably out of concern for his well-being. However, when this message was passed through to Jesus, his focus was not on his blood family but on the disciples around him whom he immediately identified as his new family, mother, brothers and sisters. This gospel reading gives us a little insight into the struggle of Jesus' family, and of Jesus' mother in particular, to let him go to a much larger family, a family not defined by blood but by a willingness to follow in the way of Jesus. Luke's Gospel suggests that this struggle to let Jesus go was experienced by Mary (and Joseph) when Jesus was only twelve years of age. On that occasion, Jesus identified his Father as God rather than Joseph and declared to his anxious and perplexed parents that his primary concern was God his Father's business rather than his parents' business. Jesus had to move on from his blood family to do the work God sent him to do, which involved the forming of a new family of disciples who would become known as the Church, a family of which we are all members in virtue of our baptism. In this family we can look to Jesus as a brother, to God as our Father, and to Mary as a mother. It is often the way that we too have to move on from something or someone very significant for us so as to do the work God is asking us to do. Such moving on will often be painful both for ourselves and for the people from whom we are moving on. However, if we can make this move, this exodus, in the imagery of the first reading, it will often be the necessary step to some important work that the Lord wants to do through us.

21 July, Wednesday, Sixteenth Week in Ordinary Time
Matthew 13:1–9

Jesus noticed that the farmer scattered the seed with abandon, almost recklessly, not knowing what kind of soil it would fall on. Inevitably, a great deal of the seed that was scattered was lost; it never germinated, yet some of the seed fell on good soil and produced an extraordinary harvest. God was scattering the seed of his life-giving word through Jesus' ministry. God's favour was being scattered abroad in an almost reckless manner. Through Jesus, God wanted to touch the lives of everyone, regardless of how they were perceived by others or by themselves. God gave the most unlikely places the opportunity of receiving the life-giving seed of his word. There was nothing selective about Jesus' ministry. As with the farmer in the parable, much of what Jesus scattered was lost. Yet Jesus knew that some people were receiving his word, and that would be enough to bring about the harvest of God's kingdom. In speaking this parable, Jesus may have been encouraging his disciples, saying to them, 'Despite all the setbacks, God is working to bring about something wonderful'. We are as much in need of Jesus' encouraging word today as the disciples were. We can be very aware of the obstacles to the growth of the Gospel in our world, in our Church, and, in our own lives. Yet, the parable assures us that these obstacles will not ultimately deter God's desire to fill our lives and our world with his bountiful presence. God is willing to be reckless and wasteful in our regard with his gracious favour because he knows that there is good soil there somewhere.

22 July, Thursday, Feast of Saint Mary Magdalene
John 20:1–2, 11–18

According to John's Gospel, the new tomb in which Joseph of Arimathea and Nicodemus buried Jesus was located in a garden, close to the place where Jesus was crucified. In today's gospel reading, Mary Magdalene comes to the tomb in the garden. When the risen Lord appeared to her and spoke to her, she presumed that the person before her was the gardener. The risen Lord was living with a very different kind of life from the life he had before he was crucified, yet he seemed to Mary Magdalene to be the gardener. It is interesting to think of the risen Lord as a gardener. A gardener works to nurture the life of nature; gardeners make God's good creation bloom and blossom. The risen Lord also works to nurture life; he came that we may have life and have it to the full. Fullness of life is a sharing in the Lord's own risen life. Whenever we nurture life, in whatever form, be it human life or the life of our created world, the risen Lord is working through us. It was only when the risen Lord addressed Mary by name that she realised that the person before her was Jesus whom she had been following and who had been crucified. The Lord calls each of us by name, but we don't always allow ourselves to hear him speak our name. If we seek after the Lord, in the way Mary Magdalene is portrayed as doing in the gospel reading, we will hear the Lord speak our name in love. After the risen Lord spoke Mary's name, he sends her out as his messenger to the other disciples. She becomes the apostle to the disciples. The Lord who calls us by name sends us out in the same way. The Living One who calls us by name sends us out into the world as life givers, to protect, sustain and nurture life in all its forms.

23 July, Friday, Feast of Saint Bridget of Sweden
John 15:1–8

Bridget was born in the year 1303. She was the daughter of a wealthy governor in Sweden. She married a well-to-do man and they had eight children. She went on to serve as the principal lady-in-waiting to the queen of Sweden. She had a reputation as a woman of great prayer. After her husband died she founded a monastery for sixty nuns and twenty-five monks who lived in separate enclosures but shared the same church. She journeyed to Rome in 1349 to obtain papal approval for the order, known as the Bridgettines. She never returned to Sweden from Rome. She spent the rest of her life in Italy or on various pilgrimages. She impressed with her simplicity of life and her devotion to pilgrims, to the poor and the sick. She died in Rome in 1373. Brigid had a deep prayer life which overflowed in a life of extraordinary service of others. The gospel reading of the vine and the branches is very appropriate for her feast day. Jesus' image of the vine is an image of the intimate relationship between himself and his disciples. He has created this intimate relationship through his life, death, resurrection and sending of the Holy Spirit. Jesus is the entire vine, root, stem and branches and his disciples are the branches. It is difficult to say where the vine ends and the branches begin, because the branches are part of the vine. Saint Paul expresses this profound relationship between the Lord and the baptised in different language, declaring that we are members of his body, that he is in us and we are in him. The fundamental call of Jesus in the gospel reading is 'Make your home in me', or 'Remain in me'. Jesus has united us to himself in the most wonderful way, and now we have to preserve that unity, that deep relationship with him. Saint Brigid shows us that one of the ways we cultivate the relationship Jesus has formed with us is through prayer. Such remaining in the Lord 'will bear fruit in plenty', what Saint Paul calls the fruit of the

Spirit, which is the fruit of love. Brigid shows us one shape of such a loving life. If we nurture our relationship with the Lord, our lives will bear that same rich fruit of love, whereas, in contrast, as Jesus says in the gospel reading, 'cut off from me you can do nothing'.

24 July, Saturday, Sixteenth Week in Ordinary Time
Matthew 13:24–30

We are all familiar with weeds in our gardens. We have a tendency to root them out immediately. However, sometimes the weeds are so close to the shrub or flower that to take out the weed risks disturbing the plant. We sometimes have to let the weeds be for the sake of the shrub or flower. We are also aware in recent times that the blossoms that weeds generate can be great pollinators for our bees. We are now being told not to be rooting out our dandelions so quickly and ruthlessly. Weeds are making a comeback! In the parable Jesus speaks in today's gospel reading, the servants of the landowner wanted to pull up the weeds that had appeared among the wheat. However, the landowner himself was a more patient man. He was aware that pulling up the weeds could pull up some wheat as well and he advised letting both weed and wheat grow until harvest time, and then they could be separated. There is always a deeper meaning to Jesus' parables. He wasn't primarily talking about gardens or fields of wheat. After all, he began the parable with the words, 'The kingdom of God may be compared to … '. Jesus was really talking about God and how God relates to us. He is suggesting that God can be patient with our weaknesses because God recognises that they are often closely aligned with our strengths. An angry person may have a passion for justice; a lazy person may be a great listener; an overly anxious person may be very dutiful and conscientious. God recognises that we are all a mixture of wheat and weed, of good and evil, of strength and weakness, and he is patient with our mixture. We, too, need to be patient, with ourselves and with others. In striving after a perfect garden, a gardener risks doing harm as well as good. In striving too hard to make ourselves perfect or, more worryingly still, to make others perfect, we risk doing as much harm as good. We need to learn to live with the mixture we and others are, while celebrating and working to enhance all that is good there.

26 July, Monday, Seventeenth Week in Ordinary Time
Matthew 13:31–35

It is likely that Jesus spoke the two parables we have just heard as a word of encouragement to his disciples. God's kingdom was not coming through the ministry of Jesus as quickly and as powerfully as many of Jesus' followers might have expected. Indeed, the longer Jesus' ministry went on, the more opposition and hostility he encountered, especially from those in powerful positions. In this setting of growing hostility, Jesus reassures his disciples that, in spite of the small and insignificant progress being made, God's good work would come to pass, and God's kingdom would come in all its fullness. The seed, small as it was, had been sown, and its growth is assured. Similarly, just as a small amount of yeast has a significant impact on a large amount of flour, Jesus' ministry will eventually have an enormous impact for good. Jesus' words of encouragement are as necessary for disciples and the Church today, for our own lives and for the world, as they were for the Lord's disciples. Today's gospel reading assures us that a seed has been sown by the Lord and its growth is assured, a power for good has been released, the power of the Spirit, and its impact for good is not in doubt. There is no room for complacency, but there is also no room for despondency. As Saint Paul reminds us in his letter to the Ephesians, God's 'power at work within us is able to accomplish abundantly far more than all we can ask or imagine'.

27 July, Tuesday, Seventeenth Week in Ordinary Time

Matthew 13:36–43

The question 'Who is God?' has intrigued curious people down through the centuries. Many different answers have been given to that question. Perhaps one of the most attractive answers from the Jewish Scriptures is to be found in today's first reading. It declares God to be a 'God of tenderness and compassion, slow to anger, rich in kindness and faithfulness'. This is the God revealed by Jesus in his teaching, his whole way of life, his death and his resurrection. The words used to speak of God there are thought-provoking and reassuring, 'tenderness, compassion, kindness, faithfulness'. When we encounter these qualities in someone we meet, we consider ourselves blessed to be in their company. These are the people who are spoken of in the gospel reading as 'the subjects of the kingdom'. They bring something of the kingdom of God to earth. The gospel reading realistically identifies a different kind of presence in our world, namely, 'the subjects of the evil one'. We are only too well aware of the evil that is being constantly perpetuated by some people, and the painful consequences of such evil for others. We recognise clearly that the kingdom of God has not yet fully come into our world. Indeed, we know that it has not yet fully come into our own lives either. We often fall short of revealing in our lives those divine qualities of tenderness, compassion, kindness and faithfulness. Yet, because these are the qualities of the Lord and he has poured his Spirit into our hearts, we can confidently reach towards these wonderful life-giving qualities, knowing that they are attainable because of the help the Lord gives us.

28 July, Wednesday, Seventeenth Week in Ordinary Time

Matthew 13:44–46

We sometimes use the word 'radiant' with reference to people. We might refer to a bride on her wedding day as 'radiant'. It is a word that suggests some kind of glow, not primarily in a physical sense but in a deeper sense. It is said of Moses in today's first reading that after he came down the mountain, having communed with God, 'the skin of his face was radiant'. Indeed, the reading says that his skin 'shone so much' that the people of Israel 'would not venture near him'. We are put in mind of that moment, which we refer to as the transfiguration, when Jesus' face 'shone like the sun', having gone up the mountain to be in communion with God. When we open ourselves to God's presence in life and in prayer, we too can become radiant in a similar way. Our inner spirit comes more alive and the light of God's presence shines through us more clearly. Moses and Jesus sought after God on the mountain of prayer. We too need to be seekers in that sense. We seek the Lord whose face, according to Saint Paul, reflects fully the light of the glory of God. The parables that Jesus speaks in our gospel reading portray that seeking spirit. The day labourer seeks the treasure he unexpectedly found buried in a field and joyfully sells all he owns to buy it. The merchant had long been seeking the pearl of great value that he came upon and he gladly sells everything he owns to buy it. The Lord who spoke those parables is, himself, the treasure hidden in the field, the pearl of great price. He is worth seeking with all our heart, soul and mind. We seek him in our day-to-day lives, and, in a more focused way, we seek him in prayer. When we seek him in prayer, we open ourselves to the radiant light of his presence, and he empowers us to reflect to others something of his radiance, as Moses does in our first reading.

29 July, Thursday, Feast of Saint Martha

John 11:19–27

One of the most profound statements ever made about God is present in today's first reading, from the first letter of Saint John: 'God is love'. Those three words express the fullest possible insight into God. At this point in his letter, the author wants to stress not what he calls 'our love for God', but, as he says, 'God's love for us'. He also states that God revealed his identity as 'Love', his love for us, by sending his Son into the world so that we could have life through him. All authentic love, all self-giving love, is always life-giving for others. This is supremely true of God's love for us. It is a love that is life-giving in the sense that it brings us into a sharing in God's own life, what we call eternal life. This is the promise that Jesus makes to Martha in today's gospel reading, in the wake of the death of her brother Lazarus. It is a promise that has given hope to believers ever since in the face of death: 'I am the resurrection and the life. If anyone believes in me, even though they die they will live, and whoever lives and believes in me will never die.' Jesus acknowledges there the reality of physical death for those who believe in him, 'even though they die'. Yet, he affirms that our life-giving communion with him which our faith creates will not be broken by death. Rather, our communion with the Lord will be deepened beyond the moment of physical death and we will come to share more fully in his risen life. Martha, the woman of faith, whose feast we celebrate today, was the recipient of that great promise of Jesus on behalf of us all. In speaking to her, the Lord was speaking to each of us. Her question to her is addressed to each one of us: 'Do you believe this?' Today's feast of Saint Martha is an appropriate moment to make our own her response to Jesus' question: 'Yes, Lord, I believe that you are the Christ, the Son of God, the one who has come into this world'. To

Martha's answer we can add, 'Yes, Lord, I believe that you are the resurrection and the life'.

30 July, Friday, Seventeenth Week in Ordinary Time
Matthew 13:54–58

A lot had happened between the time Jesus left Nazareth to travel south to be baptised by John the Baptist in the River Jordan and the day when he returned to Nazareth some time into his public ministry. In that intervening time his ministry of word and deed had been amazing people throughout Galilee, as well as gaining Jesus many enemies. When he returned to his home town of Nazareth for the first time since his ministry began, today's gospel reading suggests that some people felt he was getting too big for his boots and wanted to take him down a peg or two. The questions they asked – 'Where did this man get this wisdom and these miraculous powers? This is the carpenter's son, surely?' – amount to asking, 'Who does this local man, whose family we all know, think he is?' Many people seemed to think that God could not have been working so powerfully through someone so ordinary, so like themselves in so many ways. The very ordinariness of Jesus prevented some people from recognising that God was indeed working powerfully in and through him. The kingdom of God was at hand in one like themselves, like us in all things but sin, as the letter to the Hebrews says. Just as God was at work in the humanity of Jesus, the risen Lord is at work in the humanity of us all today. The Lord is powerfully at work in and through the ordinary acts of loving kindness and goodness that we see all around us today. It is the evil in the world that tends to make the headlines, but we, as followers of a living, risen Lord, need to be alert to the signs of his loving presence in our world and to rejoice in them. The power of the Spirit that the risen Lord released into the world is stronger than the evil forces that are there.

31 July, Saturday, Seventeenth Week in Ordinary Time
Matthew 14:1–12

Today's gospel reading is one of the more violent stories in the Gospels. An innocent and good man, John the Baptist, is unjustly executed by a ruler who had wanted to kill John but had refrained from doing so because of John's reputation among the people. However, he eventually ordered John's execution to uphold his honour, having sworn on oath to give his stepdaughter anything she wanted. John's only crime in the eyes of Herod and his wife was to proclaim God's word as revealed in the Jewish Law. What happens to John foreshadows what would happen to Jesus. As John was executed by Herod under pressure from his wife, Jesus was executed by Pilate under pressure from the religious leaders. Jesus' only crime was to proclaim God's word, the coming of God's kingdom, to announce that God's hospitable love was embracing all of humanity, and not just a chosen few. John and Jesus were innocent victims of self-serving power. There have been many such innocent victims throughout history. At some moments of our lives, we may have been one of those innocent victims of the self-serving actions of others and, if we are completely honest, at times our own less than worthy motives may have helped to create innocent victims. Of the two great prophets, John and Jesus, it is above all Jesus who shows us that the suffering we endure at the hands of others can be redeemed by love and forgiveness. As he suffered on the cross, his love for humanity was at its most selfless and life-giving, and his capacity to forgive, to share God's forgiveness, was at its most powerful. His Spirit at work in our lives can empower us to be as loving and forgiving as he was, when we find ourselves on the cross because of the attitudes and actions of others. When that happens, the mystery of the cross, the mystery of God's love which embraces all, becomes tangibly present in our own time and place through us.

2 August, Monday, Eighteenth Week in Ordinary Time

Matthew 14:13–21

We know from our own experience that different people can react to the same situation in different ways. In today's gospel reading, Jesus and his disciples reacted very differently to the challenge of a large hungry crowd in a deserted place late in the day. The disciples wanted Jesus to send the crowd away so that they could buy some food for themselves somewhere in the vicinity. Jesus seems to have reacted to the word 'buy'. 'There is no need for them to go', he says. Rather than sending them away to buy food, Jesus was going to feed the crowd freely, without charge, thereby revealing God's generosity. Jesus would need the disciples to help him to feed the crowd, getting the disciples to bring to him whatever little food was out there among the crowd. However, he fed them abundantly out of his own generous love. They say 'there is no such thing as a free dinner'. Well, that calculating mind-set does not apply to Jesus. He fed the crowd freely and abundantly without asking or looking for payment. There is an image here of how the Lord relates to us all. He pours his love into our lives freely and generously, without asking us to do anything to earn or deserve it. As John's Gospel puts it, 'from his fullness we have all received'. What Jesus did on this occasion anticipated what he would do at the Last Supper, taking, blessing, breaking and giving bread. At the Last Supper Jesus freely and generously gave of his love to his disciples, and he does the same at every Eucharist. Every Mass is pure gift. It is the sacrament of the Lord's freely given love poured out abundantly into our lives. All that is asked of us is that we receive what the Lord generously gives us and then live out of that abundance in our dealings with each other.

3 August, Tuesday, Eighteenth Week in Ordinary Time
Matthew 14:22–36

There was a conviction in the Jewish Scriptures that a person cannot see God and live. For someone to see God, to come close to God, was such an overpowering experience that death would ensue. It was not considered safe to come too close to God. The New Testament has a slightly different perspective. In Matthew's Gospel, one of the names the evangelist gives to Jesus is Emmanuel, which is Hebrew for 'God is with us'. God was drawing close to us in Jesus. We find that reflected in today's gospel reading. While the disciples were out in a boat on the Sea of Galilee battling with a strong headwind and a heavy sea, Jesus went towards them, walking on the sea. In the Jewish Scriptures, it was God who trod the waves, who walked on the sea. When Jesus reached the boat, he said to his frightened disciples, 'Courage! It is I! Do not be afraid'. The literal version of 'It is I' would be 'I am', which is an echo of that scene by the burning bush in the Book of Exodus where God gives his name to Moses as 'I am'. It is God who is coming to the frightened disciples through the person of Jesus. At the heart of our faith is the conviction that God has come close to us through Jesus and continues to come close to us today through the risen Jesus. God comes close to us especially when we find ourselves, like the disciples, battling with the storms of life, or, like Peter, sensing that we are sinking down into the waters of chaos. At such moments, the Lord is there with his reassuring word, 'Courage! It is I!', and with his strong hand to hold us and bring us to a place of calm, a sharing in his own calm and peace.

4 August, Wednesday, Eighteenth Week in Ordinary Time
Matthew 15:21–28

Sometimes in the story of the gospels, it is not the disciples chosen by the Lord who display great faith but the minor characters, those who appear once in the Gospel story and then are never heard of again. It is these minor characters, rather than the leading ones, who are often the most attractive and inspiring. We have an example of one such minor gospel character in today's gospel reading. We never hear of this pagan woman again, outside of this story, yet she displays a depth and strength of faith in Jesus, persuading him to do something he was initially very reluctant to do. At this point in his ministry, Jesus' focus was the people of Israel. He wanted to proclaim the Gospel in word and deed to his own people first, so that a renewed Israel could then bring the Gospel to the pagans. This is what Jesus means by his very short parable that seems harsh to our ears: 'It is not fair to take the children's food and throw it to the house-dogs'. The children, the people of Israel, have to be fed first. However, this persistent woman was not prepared to go along with Jesus' timetable. Her daughter was desperately ill, and she couldn't wait. Jesus came to recognise that her need was more important than his timetable: 'Woman, you have great faith. Let your wise be granted'. This woman displayed a determined, passionate, unflinching faith in the Lord's healing power, even in the face of his initial refusal to respond to her. We need something of her faith today. We need a quality of faith that keeps us engaged with the Lord, even when the Lord seems unresponsive. In reality, the Lord always responds to us when we engage with him, even if it is in ways we don't fully understand at the time.

5 August, Thursday, Eighteenth Week in Ordinary Time
Matthew 16:13–23

In today's gospel reading, Simon Peter shows great insight into Jesus, when he confesses him to be the Christ, the Son of the living God. This is the insight of faith. Jesus tells Peter that his insight is a graced insight. It is given to him by God. Faith, and the insight it gives rise to, is not just a human quality. It is a gift from God. It is because of Peter's faith that Jesus declares him to be the rock on which he will build his Church. Peter will have a foundational role in Jesus' Church. Jesus gives him a special authority, symbolised by the keys, and then identifies this authority as a teaching authority. The task of binding and loosing refers to Peter's authoritative role in interpreting the teaching of Jesus for the community of believers. We have here a very exalted portrait of Peter as a man of deep faith, a faith that equips him for a teaching role in the Church. Yet this teacher immediately shows himself to be a slow learner. Jesus began to teach his disciples about the need for him to go to Jerusalem where he would suffer and die. Peter would have none of this talk; he rebuked Jesus for it. Peter's faith in Jesus did not embrace the cross. The Son of the living God could not suffer and be crucified. Because of Peter's resistance to this vulnerable dimension of Jesus' identity, Jesus now addresses him as an obstacle, a stumbling stone, an agent of Satan. The rock becomes a stumbling stone to trip Jesus up. Within one short reading, we see the best of Peter and the worst of Peter. He clearly had a lot of growing in faith to do. We are all people of faith here at this Mass. Yet we all need to grow in faith as well. We can never become complacent about our faith; we are always on a journey. God may have begun a good work in us, but he has yet to bring it to completion. Like Peter we can all have our bad moments when it comes to our relationship with Jesus and the living out of that relationship. Yet the Lord continues to invest in us, as he continued to invest in Peter. We are not defined by our failures. They do not block the Lord from continuing his good work of bringing us to an ever deeper relationship with himself.

6 August, Friday, The Transfiguration of the Lord

Mark 9:2–10

Today's second reading contains a lovely image. It speaks of a 'lamp for lighting a way through the dark until the dawn comes'. The author understood the lamp as the words of the prophets, the word of the Lord. We all need a lamp or light to shine through the dark until the dawn comes. We are familiar with the prayer of the recently canonised John Henry Newman which has been put to music, 'Lead, kindly light, amid the encircling gloom, thou me on. The night is dark and I am far from home, lead thou me on'. He was addressing the Lord as his kindly light amid the gloom that seemed to encircle him at that time. The Lord is our kindly light too. He lights our way through the dark until the dawn comes. In today's gospel reading, Peter, James and John had a wonderful experience of Jesus as a kindly light in the darkness. Jesus had just been speaking to them for the first time about the darkness that lay ahead, the great suffering he would soon undergo, how he would be rejected by the religious leaders and put to death by Rome, and how they too would have to take up the cross as his followers. As Jesus and his disciples were about to set out on the journey to Jerusalem, the city that kills the prophets, there was this moment of glorious light on the mountain for Jesus and his disciples. A light was shining in the darkness and would continue to shine there. Peter's response to this experience of God's heavenly light shining through Jesus was one of wonder and gratitude: 'Master, it is wonderful for us to be here'. The transfigured, risen Lord continues to journey with us today. The light of God's life-giving love continues to shine through Jesus on all of us, regardless of where we are on our life journey, and no matter how great the darkness that seems to envelop us. That heavenly light continues to shine upon us every moment of every day until the dawn of the eternal day comes and eternal light shines upon us.

7 August, Saturday, Eighteenth Week in Ordinary Time
Matthew 17:14–20

One of the questions that people often ask of God in the Psalms, especially the psalms of lament, is, 'How much longer?' People who find themselves in dire straits turn to God and ask how much longer this situation is going to last, how much longer before God takes action to deliver the person praying. In today's gospel reading, this very question is to be found on the lips of Jesus: 'How much longer must I be with you? How much longer must I put up with you?' Even Jesus had his limits. What gave rise to Jesus' frustrated question was the comment by the father of the sick boy that Jesus' disciples had been unable to cure his son. Yet Jesus had empowered his disciples for precisely this kind of healing work. Perhaps we have all had a similar experience to that of Jesus. We give someone the wherewithal to do a task on our behalf and they don't do it; in frustration we ask, 'How much longer must I put up with you?' When the disciples subsequently asked Jesus why they couldn't heal the boy, Jesus answered, 'Because you have little faith'. Jesus did not say they had no faith, but that they had little faith. Little faith is a faith that is lacking in trust. They did not trust sufficiently that the Lord could work through them on this occasion. We can all be people of little faith. The Lord wants to work through each of us in a life-giving way, but our little faith, our failure to trust the Lord sufficiently, can inhibit him from working through us. The Lord needs a trusting faith if his presence and power is to become effective in the world.

9 August, Monday, Saint Teresa Benedicta of the Cross
Matthew 25:1–13

Saint Teresa Benedict of the Cross, also known as Edith Stein, was born a Jew in 1891 in Poland. She had abandoned her Jewish faith by the time that she was thirteen and declared herself an atheist. A brilliant student, she gained her doctorate in philosophy at the age of twenty-three, in 1914. In the wake of the awful slaughter of World War 1 Edith began to feel a growing interest in religion. In 1921 she happened upon the autobiography of Saint Teresa of Avila, the sixteenth-century Carmelite nun. With fascination, she read through the night and by morning concluded, 'This is the truth'. She was baptised a Catholic the following New Year's Day in 1922. Edith felt that by accepting Christ she had been reunited with her Jewish roots. She went on to obtain an academic post in the University of Munster in Germany in 1932. However, with the rise of Nazism she was dismissed from her post because she was considered a Jew by the Nazis. The loss of her job enabled her to pursue her growing attraction to the religious life. She applied to enter the Carmelite convent in Cologne and was formally clothed with the Carmelite habit on 15 April 1934. She took as her religious name, Sister Teresa Benedicta of the Cross. Believing that her presence in the convent endangered the sisters, she allowed herself to be smuggled out of Germany to a Carmelite convent in Holland. In 1940 the Nazis occupied Holland. She was captured and sent to Auschwitz where she died in the gas chamber on 9 August 1942. In 1998 she was canonised by Pope John Paul II as a confessor and martyr of the Church. Edith Stein responded to the Lord's call. In the end it brought her into a wilderness, the awful wilderness of Auschwitz. When Jesus responded to the call of God the Father, it led him to the wilderness of Calvary. We can all find ourselves in something of a wilderness because of our commitment to the Lord and his way. Yet, in today's first reading, God promises his people that he will speak to their heart in the wilderness. The Lord does not abandon us in our wilderness; he speaks to our heart when we are at our most vulnerable. God spoke a word of love to Jesus on the cross which brought him through death into risen life and he did the same for Edith Stein in her wilderness. The Lord will speak a word of love to our heart in our own wilderness moments. The Lord remains faithful to us, especially when we walk through fire. The life and death of Edith Stein encourages us to remain faithful to the Lord in bad times as well as good. In the language of the parable in today's gospel reading, she inspires us to keep the lamp of our faith burning brightly when all seems dark.

10 August, Tuesday, Saint Lawrence, deacon and martyr
John 12:24–26

Jesus often used the image of the sowing of seed to speak about God's relationship with us and our relationship with God. Several parables come to mind in that regard, such as the parable of the sower going out to sow, the parable of the mustard seed, the parable of the seed growing secretly, the parable of the wheat and the weeds. In today's gospel reading, Jesus again speaks of the sowing of seed, declaring that 'unless a wheat grain falls to the ground and dies, it remains only a single grain; but if it dies, it yields a rich harvest'. The seed that is sown has to die to being a seed if it is to grow to its potential as a wheat stalk that can be used for the making of bread to feed the hungry. It is often the way with life generally that something has to die for something new to emerge. In the gospel reading, Jesus is addressing us as his potential followers and servants, and he is declaring that we need to die to ourselves if we are to become fully alive with the life of God. We have to die to ourselves in the sense of dying to our self-centred selves, that tendency in us to live for ourselves alone. If we live our life in that self-centred, self-regarding, way, Jesus says that we will lose our life; we won't be alive with the life of the Spirit. In the first reading, Paul echoes what Jesus says, declaring that if we give generously and cheerfully, if we reach beyond ourselves, then we will open ourselves up to God's blessing: 'there is no limit to the blessings God can send you'. The deacon, Lawrence, whose feast we celebrate today, exemplifies that truth in a striking way. He gave his life generously for the Lord and, in doing so, yielded a rich harvest, not just for himself but for the whole Church. In less dramatic ways, we are all called to die to ourselves so as to live for God and for others. In doing so, we not only find life for ourselves but we also bring life to others.

11 August, Wednesday, Nineteenth Week in Ordinary Time
Matthew 18:15–20
In the time of Jesus, various Jewish rabbis claimed that when two pious Jews sat together to discuss the words of the Jewish Law, the divine presence was with them. In today's gospel reading, Jesus is presented as making a related but different claim. He declares that where two or three are gathered in his name, he himself is there in their midst. Jesus, in Matthew's Gospel, is Emmanuel, God-with-us. He himself is the divine presence among us. When his followers gather in his name, on account of him, he is with them as Emmanuel, God-with-us. Only two followers are necessary to ensure the presence of Emmanuel. When we gather in the Lord's name to pray, whether it is the prayer of the Eucharist or some other form of prayer, the Lord is there. We don't have to enter into the Lord's presence on such occasions, we are already in it. We only have to become aware of the one who is present among us. That is why attentiveness, awareness, is always at the heart of prayer, especially communal prayer. In prayer we allow ourselves to be present to the one who is present to us.

12 August, Thursday, Nineteenth Week in Ordinary Time
Matthew 18:21–19:1

Learning to forgive those who have hurt us is probably one of the greatest challenges in life. Peter's question to Jesus at the beginning of the gospel reading comes of out that sense of how difficult it is to forgive someone. 'How often must I forgive my brother?' The implication of his question is that there has to be a limit to forgiveness. Peter decides to err on the generous side, suggesting that seven times would be often enough. In the biblical culture of the time, seven was considered to be the complete number. To forgive seven times is complete forgiveness; surely, no more could be asked of someone. Yet Jesus does ask more, not seven times, but seventy-seven times. There is to be no limit to our willingness to forgive. Jesus underpins this very challenging call with the parable that he tells. In that parable the servant owes his master ten thousand talents. This was a massive sum of money, equivalent to billions of euro today. It simply could never be paid back. In the parable the master felt so sorry for his servant that he simply cancelled the debt completely. Here we have the triumph of grace over justice. There is an image here of the gracious and generous way that God deals with us. Jesus reveals a God whose mercy triumphs over justice. The most memorable image of such a God is the father in the story of the prodigal son. The remainder of the parable in today's gospel reading tells us that we must allow the mercy that God freely pours into our lives to flow through us to touch others. This is what the servant who was forgiven failed to do. One of the sayings of Jesus expresses the message of today's parable very succinctly: 'Be merciful as your Father is merciful'.

13 August, Friday, Nineteenth Week in Ordinary Time
Matthew 19:3–12

In today's first reading, Joshua reminds the people of Israel of the many ways they have been blessed and graced since God first called Abraham. The land they had recently entered with its towns, vineyards and olive groves was not the result of their own efforts but was much more by way of a gift from God. We all need to be reminded of how much we have received, the extent to which we have been graced by God. The more aware we are of the giftedness of life, the more thankful we will be. Saint Paul often called upon the first Christians to be thankful. In his first letter to the Thessalonians, which is the earliest Christian document that has come to us, he says, 'give thanks in all circumstances'. We are to live out of a sense of gratitude to God for what we have received from God. We express our gratitude to God in prayer but also in life, by our willingness to give to others out of what we have received from God, by seeking to love others in the way we have been loved by God. In the gospel reading, this is the kind of love Jesus calls for within marriage. For a couple to give to each other as they have received, to love one another as they have been loved by God, is to be faithful to each other for life, as God is faithful to us throughout our lives. Married love has the potential to be the greatest living sign of God's faithful love. Not everyone marries, of course, as Jesus recognises at the end of the gospel reading. Those who are not married can equally reflect the faithful nature of God's love in the way they live, through the love of friendship that they extend to others, and through their loving service of the community. Regardless of our state in life, we are all called to acknowledge how much we have received from God, and to give from what we have received.

14 August, Saturday, Nineteenth Week in Ordinary Time

Matthew 19:13–15

We often ask people to pray for us and people ask us to pray for them. In today's gospel reading, parents bring children to Jesus so that he may lay his hands on them and pray for them. Parents always want what is best for their children and, recognising Jesus as a man of God, they wanted to open their children up to God who was at work through Jesus. It is strange that Jesus' disciples would try to prevent this from happening, turning the children away. In the time of Jesus, children were way down the pecking order; they were without rights or status. Perhaps the disciples thought that these children were not 'worthy' of Jesus' attention. If so, they had a great deal to learn about the values of the kingdom of God that Jesus came to proclaim. Jesus insisted on allowing the children to come to him. He identifies them as those to whom the kingdom of God belongs in a special way. In the upside-down world of God's kingdom present in Jesus, those who have little or no status or importance in this world have a special place in the kingdom of God. St Paul was true to the teaching and actions of Jesus when he stated in his first letter to the Corinthians, 'God chose what is foolish in the world to shame the wise; God chose what is weak in the world to shame the strong'. In the previous chapter of Matthew's Gospel to today's reading, Jesus had told his disciples that they would not enter the kingdom of God unless they become like little children. Jesus seems to be saying that when it comes to our relationship with God, those who appear to have least of what the world considers important can have most to teach us.

16 August, Monday, Twentieth Week in Ordinary Time
Matthew 19:16–22

The young man in today's gospel reading clearly had a very good heart. There is something very appealing about him. He had very good values and had a clear goal in life. He wanted to live in such a way that he would inherit eternal life, life in God's presence. He kept the commandments God gave to Moses, including the great commandment to love one's neighbour as oneself. Yet, he wasn't satisfied. 'What more do I need to do?', he asked Jesus. There is such a thing as a holy restlessness. We are conscious of a 'more' we haven't yet attained. We sense the Lord calling us beyond where we are, even though where we are is good. We can point to good things we are doing, yet there are moments when we wonder if we are answering the Lord's call as fully as we might. A questioning restlessness creeps into our overall feeling of satisfaction with ourselves, with our relationship with God and others. Like the young man, we are drawn by a sense that there is 'more'. Jesus took the man's searching question seriously and called him to follow him in a very radical way, which entailed giving away all his great wealth. He was too attached to his wealth; he couldn't respond to Jesus' call, and a sadness came over him when he realised he couldn't reach towards the 'more' that he so desired. We are all held back in different ways from responding to the Lord's call to follow him more fully, to become even more authentic disciples than we are. The young man's struggle is the struggle of us all. At the very least, we need to remain alert to that deep desire within us for the 'more', even though we may struggle to follow through on it.

17 August, Tuesday, Twentieth Week in Ordinary Time
Matthew 19:23–30

Jesus uses many memorable images in the gospels and one is to be found in today's gospel reading, that of a camel passing through the eye of a needle. Needles in the time of Jesus, as today, had a tiny opening and camels were very large animals. To say that it is easier for a camel to pass through the eye of a needle than for a rich man to enter the kingdom of heaven is to say that the latter, a rich man entering the kingdom of heaven, is impossible. The kind of rich man Jesus has in mind is one who is possessed by his possessions. There is a striking portrayal of such a person in one of the parables of Luke's Gospel, the parable of the rich fool as it is often called. When riches become people's god, they cease to be aware of the true God, the God whom Jesus proclaimed. Feeling satisfied with their material possessions, they fail to appreciate their need of God and are unresponsive to the gift of the kingdom that God is offering. We can only receive God's gift of life in its fullness if we are aware of our need of that gift. If we don't experience thirst, we will never drink. Elsewhere, Jesus speaks of the poor in spirit and declares that the kingdom of heaven belongs to such people. This is the attitude of coming before God in our need, in recognition of our dependence upon God. Jesus declares in the gospel reading that the Lord can create this necessary attitude even in those to whom it seems foreign and impossible. When Peter asks, 'Who can be saved, then?' Jesus replies, 'for men, this is impossible; for God everything is possible'. There are no hopeless cases from God's perspective; God is always at work to bring about in us that poverty of spirit which creates the necessary opening for God to give us the riches of the gospel.

18 August, Wednesday, Twentieth Week in Ordinary Time
Matthew 20:1–16

Sometimes in the parables that Jesus speaks people behave in ways that others would find surprising or even foolish. The behaviour of the father in the parable of the prodigal son comes to mind. He gave an extraordinary welcome to a son who had done nothing to deserve it. The reaction of his older brother in the story is in keeping with how many people would have reacted if that had happened in real life. Today's parable of the workers in the vineyard is a little bit like that parable. The behaviour of the owner of the vineyard would have been considered very strange and even foolish in Jesus' time; he gave a day's wages to workers who worked only one hour. Many people tend to react to the parable somewhat negatively even today. Just as we often feel sorry for the elder son in the parable of the prodigal son, we tend to feel sorry for the workers who worked all day and yet got the same as those who worked for an hour. Yet the workers who worked all day got a day's wages for their work, which is what the vineyard owner promised them. What is strange and unsettling is that those who worked for only an hour also got a day's wages. Jesus began this parable with the words, 'the kingdom of heaven is like … '. The parable is saying something about how God relates to us. Jesus is saying that God is extraordinarily generous. There is nothing calculating about how God relates to us. God's giving is not dependent on our doing. There can come a time in our lives when, for one reason or another, we can't do a great deal. Jesus seems to be saying that this has no impact on how God relates to us. God does not ask us to be deserving but to be receptive, and then to share what we receive from him with each other.

19 August, Thursday, Twentieth Week in Ordinary Time
Matthew 22:1–14

An invitation is not a command. We receive many invitations in life, either verbally or in writing and we probably ignore or decline a good number of them. We are free to accept an invitation or not. God's way of relating to us is shaped more by invitation than by command. The parable Jesus speaks in the gospel reading is about God's invitation to all of us to the banquet of life. In the story, the king who invites chosen guests to his son's wedding banquet does not cancel the meal when those who were invited all refuse; instead he invites a whole new group. That aspect of the story speaks to us of God's persistence. When the human response to God's invitation is not forthcoming, God does not cancel anything; he simply intensifies his invitation. God continues to work to ensure that as many as possible approach the banquet of life. This banquet is in a sense embodied in the person of Christ who is the bread of life. The second part of the parable reminds us that saying 'yes' to God's invitation is not something we do once and then forget about. We have to say 'yes' to God's invitation every day of our lives. In the language of the parable, we are to keep putting on the wedding garment. Having been clothed with Christ at baptism, we need to keep clothing ourselves with Christ and all he stands for, day by day.

20 August, Friday, Twentieth Week in Ordinary Time
Matthew 22:34–40

People can ask questions for different reasons. In today's gospel reading we are told that the Pharisees ask Jesus a question to disconcert him. In other words, their question was not really a genuine question; it was a kind of a trick question intended to put Jesus on the spot. Yet Jesus appears to have treated the question, 'Which is the greatest commandment of the Law?', as a serious question because he gave it a very considered reply. He didn't exactly answer the question he was asked. He was asked for the greatest commandment of the Law, but he gave the greatest and the second greatest commandment of the Law, implying that both were inseparable. The commandment to love God with all one's heart, soul and mind and the commandment to love the neighbour as oneself belong together in the mind of Jesus. They belong together but they are not on the same level. One is more important that the other, one is first and the other is second. The love of God with all our being is prior to and somehow undergirds our love of neighbour. Jesus seems to be saying that we cannot really love our neighbour fully unless we give first place to God in our lives. Yet our failure to love our neighbour is a sign that God is not our first and most complete love. If we love God with all our being, we will be caught up into God's love of all humanity.

21 August, Saturday, Twentieth Week in Ordinary Time
Matthew 23:1–12

Today's gospel reading is one example of how the Church hasn't always taken everything Jesus says literally. Jesus declares, 'You must call no one on earth your father, since you have only one Father'. Clearly, we all have biological fathers whom we call 'father'. We even have a 'Father's Day'. Then Jesus goes on, 'nor must you allow yourselves to be called teachers, for you have only one Teacher, the Christ'. Again, there have always been teachers within the Church and outside of the Church, since the time of Jesus, and we have no difficulty in calling them teachers. Jesus didn't always intend himself to be taken literally. That is not to say that even on those occasions when he is not to be taken literally he doesn't have something very significant to say. We have only one Father, one heavenly Father. We would never dream of addressing the Lord's

Prayer, the Our Father, to any earthly father. Jesus called God 'Abba', Father, and he invites his followers to do the same. Through baptism we come to share in Jesus' own relationship with God. As Paul declares, God has poured the Spirit into our hearts, crying, 'Abba, Father'. We are privileged to be given the same intimate relationship with God that Jesus enjoys. Again, it is true to say that we have only one Teacher, the Christ. Jesus is unique among teachers because he alone is capable of teaching us fully about God. As John declares in the first chapter of his gospel, it is Jesus, 'the only Son, who is close to the Father's heart, who has made him known'. Because Jesus is one with God to a degree that is not true of any other human being, he is uniquely placed to make God known, to reveal God to us. Just as we are sons and daughters of the one Father, we are pupils of the one Teacher. From our baptism, we are called to allow Jesus to help us to know God more fully, not just with our minds but with our hearts. Jesus' knowledge of God was born out of love and that is the kind of knowledge of God that Jesus desires us all to have.

23 August, Monday, Twenty-First Week in Ordinary Time
Matthew 23:13–22

At the beginning of today's gospel reading, Jesus is very critical of those who shut up the kingdom of God in people's faces, refusing to go in themselves and preventing others from doing so. Jesus came to proclaim the presence of the kingdom of God and to invite people to savour the goodness of God's kingdom, the loving power of God's presence, here in this present life and, to a fuller extent, in eternity. Yet some of Jesus' contemporaries, the experts in the Jewish Law, were trying to close off this wonderful gift to others, as well as to themselves. John the Baptist had done the opposite. He had worked to open up people to the presence of God's kingdom in the person of Jesus. There will always be those who try to block others from coming to know the Lord and all that he offers and, thankfully, there will always be others who do the opposite, who try to open up others to faith in the Lord and all that flows from it. Because there will always be those who shut up the kingdom of God in people's faces, the Lord needs us to keep doing the opposite. He calls us to be John the Baptists in our day, to live in ways that open people up to the presence of the Lord and the fullness of life that he brings. It is a task that the Lord needs each of us to be engaged in, and there is no more important task in life.

24 August, Tuesday, Feast of Saint Bartholomew

John 1:45–51

The reason we read this gospel reading featuring Nathanael on the feast of Saint Bartholomew is because they have been traditionally regarded as the same person. There is something quite attractive about the portrayal of Nathanael in that gospel reading. His initial response to Philip's breathless witness to Jesus seems very gruff and dismissive: 'Can anything good come from Nazareth?' We are all familiar with the tendency to dismiss someone on the grounds of where they come from or who their parents are. Prejudice is always with us and can even lurk in our own hearts. Yet Nathanael didn't allow himself to get stuck in his prejudice. He went on to respond to Philip's gentle invitation to come and see Jesus. We are being reminded that it is not where we start that matters but where we end up. We are all capable of having a change of mind and heart for the better. This is a quality that Jesus clearly appreciates. When he sees Nathanael coming, he pays him a wonderful compliment, identifying him as a man 'incapable of deceit'. Where we are now is more important to the Lord than where we have been. Once Jesus engaged him in conversation, Nathanael made further progress, publicly declaring Jesus to be 'the Son of God' and 'the King of Israel'. He has come a long way from where he started; from dismissing Jesus, he now confesses him. The Lord invites us to keep travelling that same journey of deepening our relationship with him. Wherever we are on that journey, he will say to us what he went on to say to Nathanael, 'You will see great things'. Nathanael still had a long way to go on his journey towards Jesus and that is true of us all. The journey of coming to Jesus, seeing him with our heart and mind, staying with him and witnessing to him is a lifelong journey. It is one of the great journeys of life and the Lord travels it with us, constantly calling us to come and see.

25 August, Wednesday, Twenty-First Week in Ordinary Time
Matthew 23:27–32

Image and appearance are important values in our culture at the moment. There is an emphasis on looking well, and people can go to great lengths to look well. In the gospel reading, Jesus highlights the importance of what is within rather than what is without. How people are within themselves rather than how they appear to others is what matters. Jesus himself appeared at his most unattractive as he hung dying from the cross, yet that was the moment when the love that was within him was at its most intense. The poor widow who put two copper coins into the Temple treasury looked an insignificant figure contributing an insignificant amount of money. Yet Jesus saw through the unexceptional appearance of this woman to the generous heart within, a heart like his own, and he called over his disciples so that they could learn from her. Appearances can be deceptive. In the case of the scribes and Pharisees in today's gospel reading there was less there than met the eye. In the case of the widow and Christ crucified there was more than met the eye. The gospel reading encourages us not to work so much on our appearances as on what is within, the quality of the love in our heart.

26 August, Thursday, Twenty-First Week in Ordinary Time
Matthew 24:42–51

We continue to read today from Paul's first letter to the Thessalonians, the earliest Christian document we possess. At the beginning of that reading, Paul says to the church in Thessalonica, 'Your faith has been a great comfort to us'. He had founded the church in Thessalonica but he had to leave them much sooner than he would have wanted to, because there was so much hostility to him from various groupings in society. He was desperate to find out how his fledgling community of believers were doing, so he sent his trusted co-worker Timothy to visit the church and report back to him. Timothy returned with good news; this young church was standing in the faith. That is why Paul says in the reading today, 'Your faith has been a great comfort to us'. Paul was a man of great faith but he needed the faith of others to give life to his faith, to encourage him. We all need each other's faith if our own personal faith is to be strengthened. We can never walk the journey of faith alone. The Lord comes to us through the faith of others. When Jesus says at the beginning of today's gospel reading, 'Stay awake', one way of hearing that call is to stay awake to the various ways that the Lord comes to us each day of our lives. He will certainly come to us in and through the faith and love of other members of the believing community, the Church. Paul goes on to say to the church in Thessalonica in that reading, 'How can we thank God enough for you?' Because the Lord comes to us through each other's faith, we too can say to each other, 'How can we thank God enough for you?'

27 August, Friday, Twenty-First Week in Ordinary Time
Matthew 25:1–13

In today's first reading, Paul says, 'What God wants is for you all to be holy'. How did Paul understand 'holiness'? The end of that reading gives us a clue. Having declared, 'We have been called by God to be holy', he immediately goes on to speak of God 'who gives you his Holy Spirit'. In other words, 'holiness' for Paul is a life that is shaped by the Holy Spirit, a life that is rich in what he calls in his letter to the Galatians 'the fruit of the Spirit'. You are probably familiar with Paul's portrayal of the fruit of the Spirit, 'love, joy, peace, patience, kindness, gentleness and self-control'. This is Paul's depiction of a holy life, a life lived according to the Holy Spirit. This is our baptismal calling, which flows from our baptismal identity, our Spirit-shaped identity. The parable that Jesus spoke in today's gospel reading contrasts those bridesmaids who were ready to welcome the bridegroom with their lamps burning and those who were not. To the extent that we allow the Spirit to shape our lives, to bear fruit in our lives, we will be standing reading with lamps burning to welcome the Lord, the bridegroom, whenever he comes. He comes at the end of our lives but also in the course of our daily lives. In all the ways he comes to us, he will be hoping to find that our lives are burning brightly with the flame of the Spirit.

28 August, Saturday, Twenty-First Week in Ordinary Time
Matthew 25:14–30

When Jesus speaks a parable involving three characters, very often the emphasis falls on the third character. We can think of the parable of the Good Samaritan; it is the Samaritan, after the priest and Levite, who is the focus of the parable's attention. In the parable we have just heard the third servant had a very negative view of his master; he saw him as a hard man, reaping where he had not sown. Because this servant was so afraid of his master, he did nothing with what he had been given. The other two servants, in contrast, had a much more generous view of their master. As a result, they had the freedom to take initiatives and even to take risks with what they had been given. Jesus has revealed a very generous God to us; he has shown God to be someone whose generosity leaves us astonished, who remains faithful even when we are not faithful. Jesus does not reveal a God who is just waiting for us to fail, which is how the third servant saw his master. Rather, Jesus shows us a God who wants us to launch out into the deep and who continues to befriend us whether or not we catch anything. God does not ask us to be successful but to be courageous and faithful. God's loving fidelity should give us the courage to take risks with what God has given us. Perfect love drives out fear, according to the first letter of John. The assurance of God's perfect love should drive out the kind of fear that left the third servant in the parable crippled. God who has been generous with us asks us to be generous with what we have received, and then to leave the rest to God.

30 August, Monday, Twenty-Second Week in Ordinary Time
Luke 4:16–30

When Saint Paul speaks about eternal life in the first reading, he does so in very simple but very profound terms. He says, 'We will stay with the Lord for ever'. He is talking about a being with the Lord, a communion with the Lord. It is a communion with the Lord which is shared with others, 'We will stay…together'. Our being with the Lord fore ver can be anticipated in this earthly life, because the risen Lord promised us that he would be with us until the end of time. We can already enjoy something of that shared communion with the Lord in this earthly life, especially in and through the Church, the community of believers. In today's gospel reading, as Jesus announces the programme of his ministry in the synagogue of Nazareth, he promises to be in loving communion especially with the most vulnerable, the poor, the captive, the blind and the downtrodden. He promises to be with the most vulnerable regardless of their racial origin, just as Elijah was in loving communion with a widow from Sidon and Elisha with a Syrian who had leprosy. Jesus is with us all until the end of time, and he is with us in a special way when we are in greatest need. There are times in our lives when we feel poor, captive and downtrodden in some way. It is then that he is especially close to us. One of the psalms from the Jewish Scriptures puts it well: 'The Lord is near to the broken-hearted, and saves the crushed in spirit'. We can turn to the Lord in our weakness and experience his strength. The mission that the Lord announces for himself in Nazareth is one he calls us all to share in. The Lord seeks to be in communion with the most vulnerable in and through each one of us. In this season of creation, we are being reminded that our very planet is more vulnerable than ever and the Lord is urgently asking us to take much greater care of it.

31 August, Tuesday, Twenty-Second Week in Ordinary Time
Luke 4:31–37

At the end of today's first reading, Paul calls on the members of the Church in the city of Thessalonica to 'give encouragement to each other, and keep strengthening one another, as you do already'. This is the earliest Christian document we possess and, there, Paul is drawing attention to a very important ministry that everyone in the Church has been called to engage in since the Church's earliest days, the ministry of mutual encouragement. When Paul wrote, the Church consisted of a number of very small communities scattered throughout the Roman Empire, living in an environment that was hostile to them. They would not receive much encouragement from the society in which they lived, so they needed to encourage one another and to build up one another in the Lord. Today, two thousand years later, that ministry of encouragement in the Church is just as necessary as it ever was, especially in these times which can be so discouraging for people of faith. Our willingness to come together for worship as we are now doing is itself a source of encouragement for all present. In the gospel reading, Jesus engages in this ministry of encouragement and strengthening in the synagogue of Capernaum. He strengthens and builds up a disturbed person who had addressed him in a most aggressive way: 'What do you want with us, Jesus of Nazareth?' As a result of Jesus' ministry to this disturbed person, the gospel reading says that 'astonishment seized' all who witnessed it. Everyone who saw what happened was strengthened and encouraged. Whenever we do anything to encourage and strengthen one another in faith, we are doing the Lord's work in our own time.

1 September, Wednesday, Twenty-Second Week in Ordinary Time
Luke 4:38–44
The gospel reading suggests that there was a very definite rhythm to the life of Jesus, the rhythm of work and prayer. At sunset, according to the reading, Jesus is still working as people bring their sick friends to Simon Peter's house in Capernaum, where Jesus is based. At daybreak he left Simon's house and went to a lonely place to pray. The gospel reading suggests that whereas the crowds were delighted with Jesus as a healer of the sick, they were less impressed with him as a person of prayer. When he went off to pray, they went off looking for him, with a view to bringing him back to Capernaum where he could continue his healing work. Unlike the people of Capernaum Jesus placed as much value on prayer as on work. Perhaps our own age is not all that different. Prayer is not always seen as a good use of time, especially when there is so much work to be done. Yet, prayer helped Jesus to keep his focus on God and on what God wanted. The people of Capernaum wanted Jesus to stay with them. His prayer helped him to discern that staying put

was not what God wanted of him; he seems to have emerged from his prayer very clear that he must move on to preach the Gospel of God in other towns. Our own focus on the Lord in prayer can help us, too, to discern the Lord's will for our lives. Our prayer also gives us the strength to take the path the Lord wills us to take, even though it may not always be what others want from us.

2 September, Thursday, Twenty-Second Week in Ordinary Time
Luke 5:1–11

I remember that when I was a child, my father hired a rowing boat in Bray, County Wicklow, and took myself and my brothers out from the shore in it. It was one of the many activities that Bray offered at the time. After some time rowing, I can recall that my father struggled to turn the boat around to head back towards the shore because there was a very strong outgoing tide. None of us were great swimmers, and there was a moment of anxiety at the thought that the sea was getting deeper beneath the boat. Eventually he managed to turn around and get us to the shore. People not used to the sea are often nervous of deep water. When Jesus called on Peter and his companions to put out into deep water in today's gospel reading, they did so without anxiety because the sea was their livelihood. Having fished unsuccessfully all night, they now caught a huge number of fish, against all their expectations. The Lord is always asking us, as a church, as individual believers, to 'put out into the deep', to take new and even risky initiatives to promote his Gospel in today's world. We have a treasure, a pearl of great price, to share. At the end of today's first reading, Paul expresses what God has done for us, declaring that 'he has taken us out the power of darkness and created a place for us in the kingdom of the Son that he loves'. That is a good news story. The Lord calls on us to keep looking for new ways to tells it, to keep putting out into the deep, trusting that, just as in the gospel reading, the Lord will work powerfully through us, sometimes against all expectations.

3 September, Friday, Twenty-Second Week in Ordinary Time
Luke 5:33–39

I am sure every seamstress would agree with the statement of Jesus in today's gospel reading that 'no one tears a piece from a new cloak to put it on an old cloak'. It would make no sense. As Jesus says, the new cloak will have been damaged and the old cloak won't look well with a patch that doesn't match the rest of it. Jesus often uses images drawn from the daily lives of people to say something important about his relationship with us, and ours with him. Jesus was responding to the criticism of the Pharisees that he and his disciples were not fasting and praying in the traditional way, the way of the Pharisees. Jesus is suggesting, by means of the image of the new and old cloak, that he is doing something fundamentally new. God is working in a new way in and through his ministry. The old way of doing things, even the old way of fasting and praying, can no longer express God's new way of working through Jesus. Jesus also speaks in the gospel reading of new wine. Just as the new cloak cannot be used to patch up the old cloak, the new wine cannot be contained by the old wineskins. The risen Lord continues to work in a variety of new ways among us today. We have to keep renewing our old cloaks and old wineskins if the newness of the Spirit is to find full expression in our lives and in the life of the Church today. Saint Augustine addressed God as 'ever ancient and ever new'. There is something both ever ancient and ever new about the Lord and his work among us today. While being rooted in the ancient tradition, we need to keep opening ourselves to the new deed that the Lord is always seeking to do within us and among us.

4 September, Saturday, Twenty-Second Week in Ordinary Time
Luke 6:1–5

In today's first reading Paul calls upon the church in Colossae not to let themselves 'drift away from the hope promised by the Good News, which you have heard'. There is a lot of hopelessness in today's culture. Many people struggle with a sense of despondency. Paul is reminding us that the Gospel the Lord proclaimed gives us hope. Jesus has shown us by his life, death and resurrection that God is with us and for us. He has assured us that nothing need come between us and God's love for us. He has demonstrated that God's love is life-giving both in this earthly life and beyond it. God through Jesus wants to enter into a deeply personal relationship with us, a relationship that will endure beyond death. This good news gives us hope, even in our darkest moments. Our faith is always a hope-filled faith. As Paul says elsewhere in his letter, 'Hope does not disappoint us because God's love has been poured into our hearts through the Holy Spirit that has been given to us'. The Holy Spirit is the Paraclete, our Advocate, the one who stands alongside us to defend us. The Lord stands alongside us to defend us, to strengthen us, in and through the Spirit. This is what we find Jesus doing in the gospel reading. He stands alongside and defends his disciples against the unfair criticism of the Pharisees: 'Why are you doing something that is forbidden on the Sabbath day?' The answer Jesus gave to them was, 'The Son of Man is Lord of the Sabbath'. He is Lord of our lives, too, and his lordship is one of a life-giving love. Therein lies our hope.

6 September, Monday, Twenty-Third Week in Ordinary Time
Luke 6:6–11

In today's first reading, Paul speaks about the Gospel as a mystery that has now been revealed and he identifies this mystery as 'Christ among you, your hope of glory'. I often think that this phrase is a striking expression of the core of the Gospel. Christ, the risen Lord, is among us. He is among us above all in the community of believers, in the word of God, in the sacraments, in all who suffer. He is among us as our hope of glory. His presence among us is a foretaste of our ultimate and glorious destiny. Just as the risen Lord is present among us now, so he will be present among us in eternity. He is with us now, and we are destined to be with him in eternity. Just as we will be fully alive in his presence in eternity, so his presence among us now is life-giving for us. In the gospel reading, Jesus' presence in the synagogue was life-giving for the man with the withered hand. Yet, to others, Jesus' presence in the synagogue was threatening and his actions of healing the man made them furious. They rejected his life-giving presence among them. Our calling is to open our lives to Christ among us, our hope of eternal glory, so that we experience his life-giving presence in the here and now, as well as in eternity.

7 September, Tuesday, Twenty-Third Week in Ordinary Time
Luke 6:12–19
In today's first reading, Paul calls on us to be 'rooted in' Christ and to be 'built on him'. He uses two images, one which is more rural, 'rooted in', and the other more urban, 'built on'. Both images express equally the centrality and intimacy of our relationship with Christ. He is the soil in which we are rooted; he is the foundation on which we build our lives. He is to be the centre of our lives. Paul also declares in that reading why Christ is worthy to be the centre of our lives. It is because in him alone lives the fullness of divinity and in him we find our own fulfilment or fullness. He reveals God fully to us and, therefore, he can satisfy and fulfil the deepest longings of our heart. If Jesus, God incarnate, is to be the centre of our lives,

God the Father was the centre of his life. His relationship with God was the primary relationship of his life, the root and foundation of all he said and did. In the gospel reading, Jesus spent the whole night in prayer to God. His relationship with God was so central to his life that he wanted and needed to spend that amount of time in prayerful communion with God. That prayerful communion with God inspired both his choice of the twelve disciples and his teaching and healing the crowds that we hear about in the gospel reading. Because our relationship with Jesus is the central relationship in our lives, we will want and need to spend time with him in prayer. From that prayerful communion will flow our way of being in the world, our way of relating to others, especially those in greatest need.

8 September, Wednesday, The Nativity of the Blessed Virgin Mary
Matthew 1:1–16, 18–23

The Church has chosen this date, 8 September, to celebrate the day of Mary's birth. We celebrate the birth of Mary because in the words of today's gospel reading, she gave birth to a son who was named Jesus and who is Emmanuel, God-with-us. The name 'Jesus' is very akin to the name 'Joshua'. In the Hebrew language names often have a special meaning. Thus, the name 'John' means 'the Lord is gracious'. The name 'Jesus' means 'the Lord saves'. The gospel reading specifies that Mary's son was the one who would save God's people, Israel, and all of humanity, from their sins. At the Last Supper the adult Jesus, on the night before he died, would take a cup of wine, give it to his disciples to drink, while saying, 'This is my blood of the covenant, which is poured out for many for the forgiveness of sins'. Jesus was being true to his name at the Last Supper and, above all, on the cross, which the Last Supper anticipated in a symbolic way. We repeat those words of Jesus at every Eucharist, at the consecration of the Mass. Saint Paul says in his first letter to the Corinthians that 'every time we eat this bread and drink this cup, we proclaim the Lord's death, until he comes'. At every Eucharist, just as at the Last Supper, the Lord's total gift of himself for our sins is powerfully present. The Lord's death was the demonstration of God's love for us, a love that called out to all humanity, 'Be reconciled to God'. Jesus revealed by his life, and especially by his death, God's searching love for sinners. Mary's birth looks ahead to the birth of her son, Jesus, who revealed God's love to be stronger than human sin, if only we open ourselves to that love in our poverty. That is why we celebrate Mary's birth as a birth of great significance, not just for her own parents and family, but for all humanity.

9 September, Thursday, Twenty-Third Week in Ordinary Time
Luke 6:27–38
It is rare that the first reading and the gospel reading mirror each other as they do today. The call of Paul to be clothed in love, compassion, kindness, humility, gentleness, patience and forgiveness echoes the call of Jesus in the gospel reading to love even our enemies, to be compassionate, not to judge, to forgive and to give generously. We have two very powerful statements of the Christian way of life. There is a vision here for how we are to relate to each other as human beings, which, if lived to the full, would certainly lead to a greater flourishing of human life on earth. Yet it is clear from these two readings that prior to this vision of how we are to relate to others is the vision of how God relates to us. At the very beginning of that first reading, Paul says, 'You are God's chosen race, his saints; he loves you'. God's love for us is primary. The way of life Paul describes is a grateful response to God's loving choice of us. Similarly, in the gospel reading, the way of life Jesus portrays is

rooted in the way God has related and continues to relate to us. Jesus speaks of God who is kind to the ungrateful and the wicked. He calls on us to be compassionate as 'your Father is compassionate'. God's compassionate and unconditional love for us is the inspiration for the generous and loving way of life that Jesus portrays. The actual Gospel of God's love for us comes before the call of the Gospel to love one another as God has loved us. Learning to receive and experience God's personal love for each of us will inspire us to live in the way Paul and Jesus put before us in today's readings.

10 September, Friday, Twenty-Third Week in Ordinary Time
Luke 6:39–42

In the first reading, Paul reflects on his life before his meeting with the risen Lord near to Damascus. He is very honest about his past: 'I used to be a blasphemer and did all I could to injure and discredit the faith'. Yet he acknowledges that God was merciful to him: 'Mercy was shown me.' He also displays mercy towards himself. Looking back on that past, he says, 'Until I became a believer I had been acting in ignorance'. He tried to discredit the faith, out of ignorance. While acknowledging the gravity of what he did, he doesn't pass judgement on himself. We need to be able to forgive ourselves, as Paul was, to suspend judgement on past behaviour that we now recognise to be less than ideal. In the gospel reading, Jesus also calls upon us to be slow to pass judgement on others. We can be preoccupied with the splinter in someone's eye, while being oblivious to the plank in our own. Jesus is suggesting that it is very difficult for us to have the understanding of others that allows us to judge them fairly. We struggle to know what is really going on inside another person, and that limited perspective should make us slow to judge. We look at appearances, whereas only God sees the heart. It is because God sees the heart that he acts towards us with such generosity, understanding and compassion. We can all say with Paul in the first reading, 'Mercy was shown me'. Our calling is to be merciful to others as God has been merciful to us.

11 September, Saturday, Twenty-Third Week in Ordinary Time

Luke 6:43–49

We are always trying to find something or someone that we can rely on. We live in a world of much change but we all need to find reliability somewhere. We need some fixed points amid all the comings and goings of life. In the gospel reading, Jesus offers himself to us as the reliable foundation, the rock, on which we can build our lives. All that he asks of us for this to happen is that we listen to his words and try to live by them every day of our lives. Listening isn't sufficient, Jesus claims. We need to allow his words to shape how we live, every day of our lives. The Lord promises that if we try to be faithful to this calling, then we will discover that our lives have a stability because they are built on rock, the reliable rock that is Jesus. Paul was once a persecutor of the Church, but he went on to listen to the Lord's word and to live by that word. As a result, he came to discover that his life was founded on a reliable foundation, the Lord himself. In today's first reading, he highlights one dimension of the Lord's reliability. 'Here is a saying you can rely on,' Paul declares, 'Christ Jesus came into the world to save sinners'. Paul discovered above all the reliability of the Lord's mercy. As a persecutor of the church, he thinks of himself, in hindsight, as the greatest sinner. Yet, he went on to discover for himself the reliability of the Lord's mercy. If, in response to the Lord's calling, we seek to listen to the Lord's word and to live by it, we will discover the reliability of the Lord's mercy for ourselves, whenever we fail to answer that calling. Paul's experience of what the calls the Lord's inexhaustible patience is open to us all.

13 September, Monday, Twenty Fourth Week in Ordinary Time

Luke 7:1–10

Generally, the Jews saw the Romans as the enemy, as members of the occupying power. However, the relationship between the Jews and the Roman centurion in today's gospel reading is very different. There was a clearly warm and friendly relationship between the local Jewish community and this particular Roman centurion. He entrusted the Jewish elders with a special request, asking them to ask Jesus to heal his servant. They in turn spoke highly of him to Jesus, declaring that he deserved to have his request answered, remarking to Jesus on how friendly he was towards the Jewish people and how he had paid for the building of their synagogue. Jesus went on to discover for himself that there was something special about this Roman. He insisted that Jesus, a Jew, would not come to his pagan house to heal his servant. Instead he acknowledged that Jesus could heal his servant by speaking a word from a distance. Jesus could only respond, 'I tell you, not even in Israel have I found faith like this'. The Jewish community and Jesus discovered that goodness, generosity and faith can be found in unexpected people, in those who would normally have been written off as the disbelieving enemy. The gospel reading invites us to be open to the ways that God can be present in the lives of those whom we might be tempted to write off or dismiss. As the Gospel of John expresses it, 'the Spirit blows where it wills'.

14 September, Tuesday, The Exaltation of the Holy Cross

John 3:13–17

The words 'triumph' and 'cross' don't normally belong together. 'Triumph' suggests celebration, achievement, recognition. 'Cross' indicates suffering, humiliation, defeat. How could anyone who ended up crucified ever be said to have triumphed? It is hard to think of a greater paradox than the phrase 'the triumph of the cross'. Yet, as Christians, we don't find that phrase in any way strange. When we look on the cross with the eyes of faith, we don't simply see the tragic ending of a good man's life. We behold what Paul called the power and the wisdom of God. What is this power that shows itself in such degrading weakness? It is, of course, the power of love, the power of a love that is greater than any human love, the love spoken about in today's gospel reading. 'God so loved the world that he gave his only Son'. Here was a divine love that became a human love in the life and death of Jesus, a love so powerful that it was in no way diminished by the experience of rejection, hatred and all that was most sinister and corrupt in the human spirit. The triumph of the cross is the triumph of love over hatred, of life over death. The triumph of that Good Friday is a triumph in which we all continue to share. The light that shone in that awful darkness continues to shine on all of us. The love that burst forth from the hill of Golgotha two thousand years ago continues to flow into all our lives through the Holy Spirit.

15 September, Wednesday, Our Lady of Sorrows
Luke 2:33–35
I have a crucifix in my room that I like. It is a small replica of a crucifix in Assisi, the one before which Saint Francis was praying when he heard the Lord call on him to rebuild his Church. Initially, Francis understood that call in a very physical, practical way, and he started helping to repair the local churches. He came to see that the Lord was calling him to rebuild his Church in a much deeper sense. The Church was in need of reform and Francis was to be one of the Lord's instruments in that reform. Beneath the outstretched arms of Jesus are five figures, on one side is a man and a woman, Mary the mother of Jesus and the beloved disciple, traditionally understood

as John. This is the same scene that is depicted in words in today's gospel reading. Today's feast reminds us that Mary, more than any other human being, shared in the Lord's passion and death. When a young man dies, no one suffers more than his parents. Yet the cross of Jesus can never be separated from his resurrection. The same Mary who stood at the foot of the cross in deep sorrow and anguish was also present at Pentecost when the Holy Spirit came down upon her and the other disciples. Her sorrow, like that of the other disciples, turned to joy. It is striking that in the crucifix from Assisi, the crucified Jesus is depicted as calm and serene, almost glorious, and Mary and John and the other figures beneath the arms of Jesus appear to be smiling. It is a crucifix that is shot through with the light and joy of Easter. Even this feast of Our Lady of Sorrows is bathed in Easter light. All our sorrows are bathed in Easter light, because the risen Lord is our light in every darkness and our strength in every weakness.

16 September, Thursday, Twenty-Fourth Week in Ordinary Time
Luke 7:36–50

At the end of today's gospel reading, Jesus says that it is the one who is forgiven little who shows little love. The woman who had broken into the meal at which Jesus was a guest had been forgiven much. She had earlier experienced God's forgiving and unconditional love towards her through the person of Jesus. Having been forgiven much, she loved much. Her outpouring of loving gratitude to Jesus was lavish in the extreme. In contrast, Jesus' host, a Pharisee, had been forgiven little, in the sense that he had no awareness of his need for the forgiveness of God that Jesus had come to offer. Having been forgiven little, he loved little, denying Jesus even the ordinary rituals of hospitality, no basin of water for Jesus to wash his feet, no kiss of greeting, no anointing of his head with oil. The woman's loving gestures more than compensated for the Pharisee's lack of love. The story reminds us that receiving comes before giving. The woman recognised that she had received much from God through Jesus and, so, she gave much to Jesus in return. The Pharisee had received nothing from God through Jesus, he gave nothing to Jesus in return. We always come before the Lord as beggars, open to receive all those graces that only he can give, including the grace of God's forgiveness for our sins and failings. It is in learning to receive from the Lord in our poverty, like the woman, that we are empowered to give generously in gratitude for what we have been given.

17 September, Friday, Twenty-Fourth Week in Ordinary Time
Luke 8:1–3
There is a lot of human wisdom in today's first reading, from the first letter of Saint Paul to Timothy. He quotes an obvious truth: 'We brought nothing into the world, and we can take nothing out of it'. On that basis, he warns Timothy and his community against longing to be rich. Paul recognises that the excessive love of money can be the root of a lot of evils and declares, in particular, that those who set their hearts on wealth tend to wander away from the faith. It is a message that is very much in keeping with Pope Francis's call on us to live simply. In the gospel reading, we hear of a group of women who had not set their hearts on their wealth. These women weren't poor; they had material resources. One of them was the wife of the chief steward of Herod, the tetrarch of Galilee. Even though they seem to have been better off than many of their contemporaries, they were not attached to their resources, their wealth. The gospel reading says that they provided for Jesus and his disciples out of their resources. Jesus and his disciples were poor and they depended on the generosity of people like these women to continue with

their work. All of these woman had experienced the healing power of Jesus in their lives, and this was their way of expressing their gratitude to him. Today's readings remind us that it is not what we possess that matters so much, but what we do with what we possess. Like the women, we have all been blessed and graced by the Lord in various ways. Like them, we are called to use our resources, including our material resources, in grateful service of the Lord and his people.

18 September, Saturday, Twenty-Fourth Week in Ordinary Time
Luke 8:4–15

The parable of the sower is to be found in the three Synoptic Gospels, Matthew, Mark and Luke. In today's gospel reading we have Luke's version of this parable and its interpretation. His way of expressing the interpretation of the seed that fell on good soil is distinctive: 'This is the people with a noble and generous heart who have heard the word and take it to themselves and yield a harvest through their perseverance.' We are invited to hear God's word with a noble and generous heart. There is a great generosity about God's word because it expresses the generous heart of God. Jesus, God's Word made flesh, is the fullest expression of God's generous heart, but every word of God captures some dimension of the generous love of God. The generosity of God's word is to be responded to with a generous heart on our part. We give ourselves wholeheartedly to God's word, taking all of it to ourselves. We come before the Lord's word with an open and generous heart, ready to receive that word on the word's own terms. In the language of Saint Paul, we endeavour to allow the word of the Lord to find a home within us. We open wide the door of our lives to the Lord's word, displaying a generous hospitality to it. Having shown a generous hospitality to the Lord's word, we display the quality of 'perseverance'. We keep returning to this word of life, continuing to draw life from it, even in those times when we might be tempted to do otherwise. The gospel reading assures us that these qualities of generosity and perseverance towards the Lord's word will bear a rich harvest, not only in our own lives but in the lives of others.

20 September, Monday, Twenty-Fifth Week in Ordinary Time
Luke 8:16–18

Jesus often uses images from daily life to express some aspect of our relationship with God. He observes that when people light an oil lamp, they put it in a place where the light from the lamp can help people to navigate what would otherwise be a dark space. There would be no point in lighting such a lamp and then hiding it away and depriving others of its light. Jesus is suggesting that when the light of faith is lit in our lives, it is not meant to be covered or hidden. We need to allow the light of our faith to shine clearly and publicly so that it sheds light wherever we find ourselves, on all those whom we encounter. There can be pressure on people of faith today to hide their faith; in the imagery of today's gospel reading, to place the lighted lamp under a bed. Yet it is pressure we need to resist. If any one of us allows the light of our faith to shine publicly, it supports the rest of us in doing the same. Jesus goes on to say in the gospel reading, 'Take care how you hear, for anyone who has will be given more'. Attentive listening to the Lord's word keeps the light of our faith burning brightly and empowers us to allow that light to shine before all. When we listen and respond to the Lord's word, 'we will be given more', God's grace will invade our lives ever more abundantly and our faith, our relationship with the Lord, will shine ever more brightly.

21 September, Tuesday, Saint Matthew, apostle and evangelist
Matthew 9:9–13

Matthew was an unlikely candidate to be a member of Jesus' inner circle, the twelve apostles. He was very much an outsider among the Jewish community. He collected taxes for the Romans, the occupying power, and it was presumed that such people collected more money than was required, so as to enrich themselves. He would have been regarded as a sinner by those who thought of themselves as religious. It would have been tempting for many to ask, 'Can anything good come out of someone like Matthew?' Yet, not only did Jesus call him to become his disciple, one of the twelve, but Matthew went on to give his name to one of the four gospels. Matthew may not have personally written the gospel that has his name, but he was in some way influential in the writing of that gospel. The call of Matthew reminds us that the Lord relates to us as we are, not as we imagine that we should be or as other people think we should be. The Lord calls us to be his disciples, to share in his mission, even if there are all sorts of boxes we don't seem to tick. He does not wait for us to have it all together before calling us. As he says in the gospel reading, 'I did not come to call the virtuous, but sinners'. The Lord looks generously on each one of us; he has a purpose for our lives that is very ambitious. Paul describes that purpose in the first reading as becoming 'fully mature with the fullness of Christ himself'. It is an exciting call. All the Lord asks is that we respond generously to his call, as Matthew did. In responding to the Lord's call, we can rely on him to help us live out that call. As Paul says in that first reading, 'each one of us has been given their own share of grace, given as Christ allotted it'.

22 September, Wednesday, Twenty-Fifth Week in Ordinary Time
Luke 9:1–6

In today's gospel reading Jesus sends out the twelve whom he had earlier chosen to share in his mission. In the very next chapter of his gospel Luke reports that Jesus called and sent out a further seventy-two to share in his mission, and in that context Jesus says to the seventy-two, 'the harvest is plentiful, but the labourers are few; therefore, ask the Lord of the harvest to send out labourers into his harvest'. It seems that not only are twelve not enough, but seventy-two are not enough either. Prayers have to be made imploring God to keep sending labourers into the harvest. More than any other evangelist, Luke emphasises that sharing in the Lord's work, continuing the Lord's mission, is not the preserve of a select few. All of us are called to do the Lord's work, to do some labouring in the Lord's plentiful harvest. What that might mean for any one of us is something we have to try and discern with the Lord's help. In today's gospel reading, Jesus not only sent out the twelve, he also gave them power. In sending them, he empowered them. If we respond to the Lord's call to work in his harvest, we can be assured that the Lord will also empower us for the work he is calling us to do.

23 September, Thursday, Twenty-Fifth Week in Ordinary Time
Luke 9:7–9

Today's short gospel reading shows that Herod was puzzled by the reports he was hearing about Jesus. Other people were puzzled too, wondering if Jesus might be John the Baptist back from the dead, or if was Elijah or one of the ancient prophets come back to life. Herod's puzzlement about Jesus finds expression in his question, 'Who is this I hear such reports about?' His puzzlement made him anxious to see Jesus, so that his curiosity might be satisfied. Jesus was puzzling to many of his contemporaries. There was something strikingly different about his presence and his ministry. There is a sense in which Jesus remains something of a puzzle today. Herod's question, 'Who is this?', is a question that we can all ask. Because Jesus was the revelation of God in human form, and God is ultimately mysterious, Jesus will always remain something of a mystery to us. We can never fully answer the question, 'Who is this?, in this earthly life. We are always on a journey when it comes to Jesus. He knows us, as a shepherd knows his flock; he knows each of us by name. However, we do not know him as he knows us. Our sense of puzzlement about Jesus can be the driving force of the exciting journeying of coming to know him more fully, so as to follow him more closely and love him more dearly. As Saint Paul says, it is only beyond this earthly life that we will know the Lord fully, as we have been fully known by him. In the meantime, the Lord is always calling us to keep setting out on the journey of coming to know him more and more, not just with our mind but with our heart.

24 September, Friday, Twenty-Fifth Week in Ordinary Time
Luke 9:18–22

The first temple in Jerusalem was built by King Solomon. This temple was destroyed by the Babylonians at the beginning of what came to be called the Babylonian exile. When the people of Israel returned from exile they began to build a new temple, a second temple. According to today's first reading from the prophet Haggai, 'the new glory of this Temple is going to surpass the old'. This new second temple would be filled with the glorious presence of God in an even more wonderful way. In the course of his public ministry, Jesus said, 'Something greater than the Temple is here'. He was filled with the glorious presence of God in a way that was not true even of the Temple in Jerusalem which, in Jesus' time, was considered one of the Seven Wonders of the World. When Jesus asks his disciples in today's gospel reading, 'Who do the crowds say I am?' and Jesus learns that the crowd consider him to be John the Baptist back from the dead, or Elijah or one of the ancient prophets come back to life, it is clear that Jesus considers these answers inadequate. God is powerfully and gloriously present in Jesus in a way that wasn't true of John the Baptist or any of the prophets. When Jesus asks his disciples the question, 'Who do you say I am?', Peter's answer, 'the Christ of God', is much closer to the truth. Jesus' question to his disciples is addressed to us all. We are all invited to give our own answer to that question. Whatever answer we give, it needs to recognise that Jesus is filled with the glorious presence of God in a way that is unique among all that God has created. We are blessed because Jesus allows us to see the face of God, and he shows us that God's face is the face of love and mercy.

25 September, Saturday, Twenty-Fifth Week in Ordinary Time
Luke 9:43–45

In the first couple of hundred years of the Roman Empire, the city of Rome had no walls because they were not needed. Rome's enemies were a very long way away and were being kept at bay. It was only at the end of the third century AD that Rome's security became sufficiently precarious for the emperor of the time, Aurelius, to think it necessary to build gigantic walls, some of which still stand today. In today's first reading, the prophet Zechariah has a vision of a future Jerusalem without walls. Such walls would be a hindrance, given the envisioned growth of the city's population, and also, more fundamentally, because the Lord himself will be a wall of fire all around the city. The Lord will dwell in the midst of the city and he will be the city's protection. The building of walls is a sign of insecurity. The first reading suggests that the Lord himself will be people's ultimate security. In the gospel reading, Jesus' announcement of his forthcoming passion and death left his disciples feeling very insecure. They did not understand the meaning of what he said and were afraid to ask him for an explanation. Jesus could face into what lay ahead because his security lay in God his heavenly Father. At the moment of his death, in Luke's Gospel, he entrusts himself to his Father. When Jesus was arrested, according to Luke, some of his disciples struck out with the sword, suggesting that their security lay in force of arms rather than in God. The readings invite us to entrust our lives to the Lord, especially in times of trial, and to allow him to be the wall around us.

27 September, Monday, Twenty-Sixth Week in Ordinary Time
Luke 9:46–50

Children occasionally appear in the Gospel story, and whenever they do appear they are always portrayed in a positive light. In today's gospel reading, Jesus places a little child by his side, as a way of teaching his disciples something important. They had been arguing about which of them was the greatest. It was a silly argument and Jesus wanted to nip it in the bud. He took a child and said that just as God was present in himself, so he is present in someone as vulnerable and fragile as a little child. If his disciples really want to be great, they must welcome the most vulnerable and frail members of the community, such as children, as if they were welcoming Jesus himself. Elsewhere in the gospels, Jesus says that he is present in the sick, the hungry, the thirsty, the stranger, the imprisoned. Jesus seems to be saying that he is most present in our lives when we are at our most frail and vulnerable, when we are at our weakest. Whenever people serve us when we are in great need, they are serving Jesus himself in a very personal way. Sometimes, when we are at our weakest, our most frail, we feel that we have very little to offer. We might even think of ourselves as a burden on others. However, in the gospels Jesus assures us that in those very moments of greatest weakness he is most powerfully present to others through us. Our very weakness, our incapacity, gives others the opportunity to meet the Lord in a special way. Those who welcome us, who serve us, when we are at our lowest, are serving Jesus in a very personal way, and serving God who sent Jesus to us.

28 September, Tuesday, Twenty-Sixth Week in Ordinary Time
Luke 9:51–56

When our good intentions, our worthwhile initiatives, meet with indifference or even hostility from others, it can be very discouraging and we can be tempted to lash out verbally in response. In that sense, the reaction of the disciples in today's gospel reading is very human. As Jesus headed south from Galilee to Jerusalem, he sent his disciples into a Samaritan village to prepare the way for him. However, the Samaritans would not receive this Jew heading for Jerusalem. The disciples lash out verbally, asking Jesus if they should beseech God to destroy this village. Jesus did not appreciate his disciples' angry outburst and rebuked them. Instead, he accepted the Samaritans' rejection of him and went on to another village. Jesus was not prepared to add to the animosity between Jews and Samaritans by responding to the Samaritans as they had to him. In Luke's second volume, the Acts of the Apostles, the risen Lord would again reach out to the Samaritans, this time through the preaching and ministry of Philip. On this occasion, the Samaritans respond enthusiastically to Jesus and his Gospel. Jesus was prepared to wait on people; he did not take an initial rejection as their last word. Jesus is prepared to wait on us all. He keeps seeking us out in his love, even when our first or even second response to him is less than promising. He also looks to us to wait on each other, rather than returning insult for insult, injury for injury, as the disciples wanted to do. Jesus shows us that how people relate to us need not determine how we relate to them. Rather, we are called to relate to others as the Lord relates to us.

29 September, Wednesday, Saints Michael, Gabriel and Raphael
John 1:47–51

The three archangels whose feast we celebrate today have always been honoured within the Christian tradition. Michael is mentioned in the Book of Revelation as the archangel who defeated Satan and his forces and cast them out of heaven and has been venerated as protector of Christians in general and of soldiers in particular. Gabriel brought the good news to Mary that she was to be the mother of God's Son, and has been venerated as the patron of those involved in the world of communications. Raphael features prominently in the Book of Tobit, guiding Tobias, Tobit's son, to his future wife, Raguel, and healing the blindness of Tobit himself, and has been venerated as the patron of nurses, physicians and the blind. All three were God's messengers, engaged in the doing of God's work. Each of them points beyond themselves to God's greatest messenger, who completed God's work on the cross, Jesus of Nazareth. In today's gospel reading, Jesus says to Nathanael, 'You will see heaven laid open and, above the Son of Man, the angels of God ascending and descending'. These words of Jesus echo the dream of Jacob in the Book of Genesis in which he saw a ladder connecting heaven and earth and the angels of God ascending and descending on it. Jacob woke up and realised that the place where he had slept was a kind of meeting place between heaven and earth. So, he called the place 'Bethel', which means 'House of God'. In the gospel reading, Jesus is saying that he is the meeting point of heaven and earth, the place where God meets with us in a way that far surpasses how the angels brought God to people. It is Jesus who shows us the face of God.

When we look upon him, we are getting a glimpse of heaven. On this feast, in thanking God for the archangels Michael, Gabriel and Raphael, we thank God even more for the one to whom they point and who says to us, 'Whoever sees me, see the Father'.

30 September, Thursday, Twenty-Sixth Week in Ordinary Time
Luke 10:1–12

When Jesus sends out the seventy-two in the gospel reading, he makes clear to them that, whereas they will be welcomed by some towns, they will most certainly not be made welcome by other towns. However, regardless of how they are received, their message is to be the same, 'The kingdom of God is very near to you'. The reign of God in Jesus is equally present to those who reject it as it is to those who welcome it. We are being reminded that we do not make God present, nor, indeed, can we drive God away. God is present to us, through his Son, now risen Lord, whether we want God or not, whether we are aware of God or not. God is changeless in that God cannot but be present to us, even though as human beings we can change, regarding how present we are to God. Because the kingdom of God is always very near to us, because God's loving and just rule is powerfully present to us at all times, our calling is to keep opening ourselves to God's presence, to allow God to be Emmanuel, God-with-us. God has done all God can do for us; it falls to us to welcome what God has done for us. It has pleased God to give us the gift of the kingdom, the gift of his loving presence. God wants us to receive this gift and then to live out of the fullness and richness of this gift. God has drawn near to us through his Son and God desires us to draw near to him, to be in communion with him. The question that hangs in the air for is, 'Do we want to be in communion with God and with his Son, and to live out of that communion every day of our lives?'

1 October, Friday, Twenty-Sixth Week in Ordinary Time
Luke 10:13–16

We live in a culture that greatly values success. Sometimes our worth can be judged by how successful we are at something. Today's gospel reading suggests that Jesus did not always experience success. Rather, he, who was so accepting of others, was often rejected by others. In the gospel reading, he refers to three Galilean towns who rejected him, Chorazin, Bethsaida and Capernaum. He reminds these towns that there are consequences for rejecting him: 'Alas for you … '. Jesus mentioned all of this in the context of sending his disciples out on mission. He was preparing them for the experience of rejection that will inevitably be their lot as messengers of a rejected Lord. Jesus goes on to say in that reading that rejection of his messengers is rejection of himself, 'Anyone who rejects you, rejects me'. As people of faith we will sometimes experience rejection. Our faith, the Gospel we try to proclaim by our lives, will not always be well received by others. Sometimes those who matter most to us will not receive or value our faith and all it entails. Such rejection can be painful, as it was for Jesus, as it was for those he sent out. Yet, God worked powerfully through Jesus' most extreme experience of rejection, his death on a cross. Human rejection of the Gospel never has the last word. God can be powerfully at work for the spread of the Gospel through such painful experiences in ways that we are not always fully aware of at the time. All the Lord asks of us is that we be faithful in our witness, regardless of how it is received.

2 October, Saturday, The Guardian Angels
Matthew 18:1–5, 10

Today we celebrate the feast of the guardian angels. In the Scriptures, the angels seem to have a number of roles. One of their roles is that of messenger. God is portrayed as communicating with people through angels. For us as Christians, the story in the gospels that comes to mind to highlight that particular role is the annunciation to Mary. The angel Gabriel declares to Mary that she is to be the mother of God's Son. Another role that angels have in the Scriptures is that of protector or guardian, and it is that role that is emphasised by today's feast. In the temptation of Jesus according to Mark, angles serve Jesus after Satan had tempted him over forty days. They help to restore him after his gruelling ordeal. They express God's protection of him in the midst of his struggle. In today's first reading, the Lord promises to send an angel to guard his people and bring them safely to the place he has prepared for them. The guardian angels speak to us of God the protector, God as one who watches over us to keep us safe from harm. It is that aspect of God's relationship with us that we invoke when we pray, 'Deliver us from evil and lead us not into temptation'. Today's feast assures us that, even though evil may touch our lives in one shape or form, God will ultimately deliver us from all evil if we are open to him, if we have the openness of the child towards him that Jesus speaks about in today's gospel reading. God will bring us safely to the place he has prepared for us, if we turn towards him in our need.

4 October, Monday, Twenty-Seventh Week in Ordinary Time
Luke 10:25–37

There are two striking stories in today's readings. The first reading was the beginning of the story of Jonah, the reluctant prophet. The Lord wanted him to preach the Lord's message to the people of Nineveh, who were Israel's enemies. Jonah wanted nothing to do with this mission and fled as far as he could from the Lord. However, the Lord would not let him go and pursued him. Jonah would, in the end, be obliged to preach the gospel of God's love to the enemies of Israel, bringing God's life-giving message to them. If, in the first reading, Jonah flees from the Lord's call to minister to his enemies, in the gospel reading, someone responds generously to the Lord's call to minister to the enemy. A Samaritan travelling from Jerusalem to Jericho came upon a Jew who was half-dead by the roadside. He did not run from him, as the priest and Levite had done, even though Jews and Samaritans were traditional enemies of each other. If Jonah is the reluctant messenger of God to the enemy, the Samaritan is the willing messenger of God to the enemy. He heard the Lord call out to him in and through the enemy, the stranger, the other. The Lord can be calling us to serve the most unlikely of people, those we would normally distance ourselves from. There can be something of the reluctance of Jonah in all of us in response to that call. The gospel reading calls on us to have something of the spontaneous generosity of spirit of the Samaritan. As Jesus says in commenting on the story, 'Go and do likewise'.

5 October, Tuesday, Twenty-Seventh Week in Ordinary Time
Luke 10:38–42

Saint John Henry Newman had a wonderful reputation as a preacher. In one of his sermons he comments on the passage we have just heard. In the story of Mary and Martha, he sees something of the struggle we are all engaged in, between anxiety for many things versus rest in the one thing necessary (even as we do *many things*). He says that while Jesus does not discount Martha's careful service, he won't permit her to imagine that serving him is a matter of multiplying projects and services. Love of God and neighbour, he says, certainly must include these, but preceding both is the heart that first says: *I love God, because he has first loved me; and I love my neighbour whom I can see for the sake of the One I cannot see.* I think Newman is saying that there is something more fundamental than the doing of many things, even if it is for the Lord, and that is our loving relationship with the Lord. Like Mary sitting at the Lord's feet listening to him speaking, we need to open ourselves to the Lord's personal love for us, for me, and we respond to his gift of love by loving him in return. Then out of that loving relationship with the Lord flows our active service of him. If our relationship with the Lord is what grounds us, 'resting in the one thing necessary', as Newman says, then our service of the Lord will be shaped by love rather than driven by anxiety or even, perhaps, resentment of others. Newman reflects on Mary's love for Jesus, 'sitting at the Lord's feet and listening to his teaching', and he asks the question, 'Is our heart in *that* place, or is it tossed about in a whirlwind of activity?' It is a question that is worth our while pondering.

6 October, Wednesday, Twenty-Seventh Week in Ordinary Time
Luke 11:1–4

Prayer can take many different forms for all of us. Sometimes our prayer is quite informal. We talk to the Lord as if to a friend, expressing spontaneously to him what is in our heart. The first reading portrays Jonah praying in this way. He was angry that the pagan people of Nineveh, the traditional enemies of Israel, had come to experience God as a God of tenderness and compassion, slow to anger and rich in graciousness, and he let God know this in no uncertain terms, 'Ah! Lord, is not this just as I said would happen when I was still at home?' He continues on in this vein, giving out to God. It is a very valid form of prayer and the Psalms are full of it. There are other times when we are glad to be given a prayer to pray rather than having to pray spontaneously ourselves. We look for guidance in how to pray, which is what we find the disciples doing in today's gospel reading: 'Lord, teach us to pray, just as John taught his disciples'. Jesus did not always find his disciples such willing pupils, but on this occasion their question revealed a great openness of heart to what Jesus had to teach them. In response to their request, Jesus gave them a prayer to say, which is itself a teaching on how to pray. Jesus begins by teaching that all prayer involves a surrender to God's purpose for our lives and the life of the world. We pray not to promote our own kingdom but to open ourselves to the coming of God's kingdom. This was the prayer of Jesus in Gethsemane, 'not my will but yours be done'. In prayer we are also to ask on behalf of ourselves. However, we are to ask for what we need and not just want we want. What do we need, according to Jesus? We need the daily sustenance that only he can provide; we need forgiveness for our sins and a willingness to pass on the forgiveness we receive to others; we need the Lord's sustaining presence when our faith and the values that flow from it are being put to the test. Here indeed is a prayer that is a true teaching on how to pray.

7 October, Thursday, Our Lady of the Rosary
Luke 1:26–38

Saint John Henry Newman was an Anglican before he became a Roman Catholic. He gave the following advice about the Rosary to a recent convert to the Catholic faith whom he directed, and it probably reflects Newman's own way of praying the Rosary: 'Before each mystery, set before you a picture of it, and fix your mind upon that picture, (e.g. the Annunciation, the Agony, etc.) while you say the Our Father and the 10 Hail Marys, not thinking of the words, only saying them correctly. Let the exercise be hardly more than a meditation. Perhaps this will overcome any sense of tedium.' He understood the Rosary as a meditation on the great mysteries of the life of Jesus and Mary. Speaking to a group of boys in Oscott College on one occasion, he said, 'Now the great power of the Rosary lies in this, that it makes the Creed into a prayer; of course, the Creed is in some sense a prayer and a great act of homage to God; but the Rosary gives us the great truths of his [the Lord's] life and death to meditate upon, and brings them nearer to our hearts. And so we contemplate all the great mysteries of his life and his birth in the manger; and so too the mysteries of his suffering and his glorified life.' He went on to say, 'the special virtue of the Rosary lies in the special way in which it looks at these mysteries; for with all our thoughts of him [the Lord] are mingled thoughts of his mother, and in the relations between mother and son we have set before us the Holy Family, the home in which God lived'. Newman shows us the essence of the Rosary. It is a vocal prayer, which is often prayed out loud, but it is more fundamentally a contemplative prayer. It puts before us the great mysteries of our Lord and our Lady for our meditation and contemplation. In that sense, the Rosary is in keeping with Mary's own way of praying. The Gospel of Luke says of Mary in relation to the words of her son, 'His mother treasured all these things in her heart'. When we pray the Rosary we treasure in our hearts the great truths of our Lord's life, death and resurrection and of his relationship with his mother.

8 October, Friday, Twenty-Seventh Week in Ordinary Time
Luke 11:15–26
It can be tempting for individuals or groups to demonise others, referring to them even as 'Satan'. Even the good can sometimes be demonised. Indeed, according to today's gospel reading, Jesus himself was demonised. His opponents claimed that the power behind his healing ministry was the power of Beelzebul or Satan. Their preoccupation with Satan prevented them from seeing what Jesus calls 'the finger of God' in his ministry. Jesus declares to them that it is not the kingdom of Satan but the kingdom of God that has overtaken them. Jesus speaks of himself as the 'stronger man'

who attacks and defeats the 'strong man', namely, Satan. Jesus is reminding all of us that the power of God is stronger than the power of evil. We cannot deny the existence of evil; we are all too well aware of it. Jesus teaches us to pray, 'Deliver us from evil'. We need to name evil for what it is. Yet, as followers of 'the stronger man', Jesus, we must not allow the presence of evil to make us despondent or to immobilise us. The Spirit of God, the Holy Spirit, whom Jesus released into the world, is stronger than the spirit of evil. I always found that statement of Saint Paul very encouraging: 'Where sin increased, grace abounded all the more'. That is true of our own personal lives and of the life of our world. The kingdom of God is always overtaking us, even when the darkness of evil and sin seems to be triumphing.

9 October, Saturday, Twenty-Seventh Week in Ordinary Time
Luke 11:27–28

When we think of a beatitude, we usually understand it as something that Jesus addresses to others. We are very familiar with the Beatitudes at the start of the Sermon on the Mount in the Gospel of Matthew, which begin, 'Blessed are the poor in spirit, for theirs is the kingdom of heaven'. However, in today's gospel reading, a beatitude is not spoken by Jesus but addressed to him. A woman in the crowd praises Jesus by proclaiming a beatitude over his mother, 'Blessed is the womb that bore you and the breasts that you sucked.' This is not the first beatitude that embraces Mary in this Gospel of Luke. At the very beginning of Luke's Gospel, when Jesus was still in Mary's womb, Elizabeth pronounces Mary blessed: 'Blessed is she who believed that there would be a fulfilment of what was spoken to her by the Lord.' Within our own Roman Catholic tradition, we have always declared Mary blessed. We have honoured her in our liturgy, in our prayers and in our art. In today's gospel reading,

Jesus does not reject the beatitude that the nameless woman in the crowd pronounced over Mary. However, he broadens the beatitude to embrace all who, like Mary, hear the word of God and keep it. Jesus' own beatitude embraces all of us, in so far as we learn from Mary to surrender to God's word, allowing God's word to shape our lives. To hear and keep the word of God is to hear and keep the word of Jesus, because he is the Word of God who became flesh and dwelt among us. We spend our lives listening attentively to the Lord's words to us and trying to live out his words in our day-to-day living.

11 October, Monday, Twenty-Eighth Week in Ordinary Time
Luke 11:29–32

In the gospel reading, people ask Jesus for a sign. They wanted a more powerful sign than he had given them so far, in order to take him seriously and believe in him. We can all have a tendency to look for signs from the Lord. We are always looking for great clarity and certitude when it comes to our relationship with the Lord. If only he would give us a clear sign, then we would know what to do. Yet, in response to the people's request for a sign, Jesus tells them that God has already given them a sign. Jesus himself is the sign, someone who is greater than the great wise man Solomon and greater than the prophet Jonah. Jesus is saying the same to us today. God has given us the gift of his Son. He is the sign, the sacrament, of God. He makes God present to us in a way no one else who lived on earth has ever done. There is nothing greater that God can give us. In giving us Jesus, God has given us all we need for our journey through life. In his gospel, the evangelist John says of Jesus, 'from his fullness, we have all received'. There is no fuller sign that God can give us than the life, death and resurrection of Jesus, and the sending of the Spirit. There is a fullness, a richness, there that we can never exhaust in this life. We are always receiving from the Lord's fullness. No matter how much we have received in the past, there is always more to be received into the future, and more again in eternity. The Lord who is present to us in all his fullness is always inviting us to draw life from him anew. We need no other sign than him.

12 October, Tuesday, Twenty-Eighth Week in Ordinary Time
Luke 11:37–41

We have become more aware in recent times of the damage we are doing to the environment. Pope Francis has written a wonderful encyclical on care for our common home. The Scriptures often celebrate the created world as a revelation of God. A glimpse of God can be caught in the natural world that God has created. A little booklet, *Seeing God in a Leaf*, has been written by an Irish Jesuit. That understanding of creation is present both in today's first reading and in the psalm. The responsorial psalm declares that the heavens proclaim the glory of God and the firmament shows forth the work of God's hands. According to today's first reading from Paul's letter to the Romans, 'ever since God created he world, his everlasting power and deity ... have been there to see in the things he has made'. There is an understanding of the world here that invites us to look deeper than the surface of created things, seeing beyond creation to the Creator. Many poets have had that contemplative view of nature. I am fond of the poem of the Irish poet Joseph Mary Plunkett which begins, 'I see his blood upon the rose, and in the stars the glory of his eyes'. In the gospel reading, Jesus challenges his host to see deeper, in a different sense. The Pharisee who invited Jesus to his table was preoccupied with the fact that Jesus did not observe traditional Jewish washings before eating. Jesus declares that beyond such external ritual cleanliness lies the deeper form of cleanliness of mind and heart. What is within is more important than externals. The heart is where God wants to reside and that is what we need to get right. As Jesus says in one of the Beatitudes, 'Blessed are the pure in heart, for they shall see God'.

13 October, Wednesday, Twenty-Eighth Week in Ordinary Time
Luke 11:42–46

In today's gospel Jesus is the guest at the table of one of the Pharisees. In the course of the meal he is addressed by a lawyer, someone who would have been considered an expert in the Jewish Law and in the interpretation of that law. As Jesus had earlier criticised the Pharisees, he now criticises the lawyers for loading unendurable burdens onto people. Having done so, they make no effort to help people carry those burdens. Jesus is clearly contrasting the teaching of the lawyers with his own teaching. He has come to proclaim good news, not to burden people and then leave them to their own devices. He spoke of himself as the bridegroom and his followers as the wedding guests; his ministry is a time of celebration, a time to rejoice that the lost were being found. He came to proclaim the year of the Lord's favour, when good news would be preached to the poor and release to captives. If our faith becomes a burden, and nothing else, we have somehow managed to lose its essence. The Lord's call can be demanding, but it is demanding in the way that love can be demanding. The Lord's path can be difficult, because of what it asks of us, but along that path we are promised a joy and a peace that the world cannot give because it is the fruit of his sustaining presence with us.

14 October, Thursday, Twenty-Eighth Week in Ordinary Time
Luke 11:47–54

The lawyers that Jesus critiques in today's gospel reading were the experts in the Jewish Law; they were more akin to modern-day theologians than to modern lawyers. He accuses them of taking away 'the key of knowledge'. Their study of God's law should have given them a key to allow people to come to know God more fully. Instead, they show themselves hostile to Jesus, the one person who knows God fully and who can reveal God fully to others. Not only have they not believed in Jesus as God's unique messenger themselves, but they have put obstacles in the way of other people believing in Jesus. In that sense, in the words of Jesus, 'they have not gone in themselves and prevented others going in who wanted to'. They have used their key to lock the door, who is Jesus. Jesus was always critical of those who were an obstacle to others coming to believe in him. People of status, like the lawyers, could use their influence to prevent people from coming to Jesus. If we find ourselves with a key of knowledge, with some access to the knowledge of God, we need to use that key to open doors to God for others. We are all called to come to know the Lord with our heart and our mind so that we can reveal him to others and lead them to him.

15 October, Friday, Twenty-Eighth Week in Ordinary Time
Luke 12:1–7

The conclusion of today's gospel reading has that very striking image of God as one who cares for the details of creation. Not one sparrow is forgotten in God's sight. The conclusion Jesus draws for his listeners is that how much more, therefore, is God going to be concerned about the details of our lives, because we are each worth more than hundreds of sparrows. It can be tempting to think that God does not concern himself with the details of our lives. Yet, in a way that is beyond our comprehension, he is concerned with the concrete issues of our lives, our hopes and fears, our joys and sorrows, our struggles and failures. In the way that Jesus taught, in the many stories he told, it is clear that he paid attention to the detail of the lives of his contemporaries. He was attuned to what was going on in people's lives and he invited people to share the details of their lives with him. Jesus reveals a God who wants to be involved in the concrete circumstances of our lives. That is why we can, with confidence, reveal ourselves to the Lord in prayer, knowing that the Lord will receive us as we are in our unique, concrete situation.

16 October, Saturday, Twenty-Eighth Week in Ordinary Time
Luke 12:9–12

We are familiar with the three great virtues of faith, hope and love. Of the three, the one that we tend to focus less on is, perhaps, hope. We strive to be people of faith, and we know that our faith in God is to find expression in the love of others. Yet our faith is also to be a hopeful faith. We believe in a God of love, so we are hopeful about the future, including our eternal future. In the first reading, Abraham is presented as a person of hope, a man of hopeful faith: 'Though it seemed Abraham's hope could not be fulfilled, he hoped and he believed'. God made a promise to Abraham, which at the time, seemed unlikely to be fulfilled, yet Abraham believed in God's promise to him and remained hopeful that God would fulfil his promise to him. We are called to be people of hopeful faith, like Abraham. Jesus makes many promises to us throughout all of the four gospels. We find one such promise in today's gospel reading. He promises that if we declare ourselves for him before others, if we witness publicly to our faith in him, then he will declare himself for us before the angels in heaven. Elsewhere, he promises us that if we turn to him in trusting faith, he will bring us to the banquet of eternal life. He makes many other promises to us, a lot of them relating to life beyond this earthly life. Like Abraham, we are called to trust his promises, and, so, to have a hopeful faith. To keep our faith hopeful, Jesus has given us the gift of the Holy Spirit. That is another promise Jesus makes in today's gospel reading: 'The Holy

Spirit will teach you what you must say'; and it is a promise for this present life. The Holy Spirit keeps us hopeful, because the Holy Spirit is the 'first fruit' of eternal life, in the words of Saint Paul.

18 October, Monday, Saint Luke, evangelist

Luke 10:1–9

Luke is the only evangelist to have written a work in two parts, the Gospel of Luke and the Acts of the Apostles. Having told the story of the life, death and resurrection of Jesus, he went on to tell the story of the early Church, in particular the story of Saint Paul and his great missionary journeys. This two-volume work begins in the city of Jerusalem with the priest Zechariah, the father of John the Baptist, at his duties in the Temple, and it ends in Rome with Paul under house arrest, yet preaching the Gospel to all who came to visit him. Luke understood that the Gospel, the Church, began in Jerusalem, but by the time he came to write it had reached the city of Rome. From Jerusalem to Rome is a wonderful sweep. Both cities have been the two primary places of Christian pilgrimage from the earliest days of the Church until today. Luke was very aware that the story of the early Church was the continuation of the story of Jesus, and what linked the two stories for him was the Holy Spirit. The same Holy Spirit who came down upon Jesus at his baptism and shaped his life and ministry came down upon the followers of Jesus, the Church, at Pentecost and shaped the life and ministry of the Church. We are part of that story of the Church today and in so far as we are open to the Holy Spirit, our story will continue the story of Jesus. The risen Jesus wants to continue his life and ministry in us, the church, through the Holy Spirit. In the very way Luke has written his two-volume work, he is telling us that the Church has no meaning apart from Jesus, and, in a sense, Jesus has no meaning apart from the Church. As Jesus sent out the seventy-two in the gospel reading, he keeps sending us out as labourers in God's harvest, empowering us with the Holy Spirit as he sends us out. The work Jesus did in Galilee, Samaria and Judea, he continues to do in and through all of us who are the Spirit-filled community of his disciples. This is our calling and our privilege.

19 October, Tuesday, Twenty-Ninth Week in Ordinary Time
Luke 12:35–38
Very often the stories Jesus tells and the images he uses fly in the face of the conventions of the time. A striking example would be the portrayal of the father in the parable of the prodigal son, showing unconditional love to a very undeserving son. Another example is the portrayal of the vineyard owner in the parable of the workers in the vineyard, giving a day's wages to those workers who worked only an hour. We have another of those unconventional images in today's gospel reading. A wealthy man returns from a wedding feast to find his servants alert and ready to open the door to him; he then proceeds to relate to them as they would normally relate to him, sitting them down at table and waiting on them. This certainly flies in the face of the master-slave relationship at the time. We are reminded of what Jesus does in the Gospel of John in the setting of the Last Supper, washing the feet of his disciples, behaving towards them as their servant, even though he was their Lord. Jesus is showing us in all these ways that he, and God whom he makes present, does not relate to us according to normal human conventions. God's ways are not our ways. God is not a more powerful version of some human reality. God relates to us out of the abundance of his love for us, a love that is greater than any human love. Paul expresses this conviction in his own distinctive way in the first reading: 'However great the number of sins committed, grace was even greater'. That is what it means to say, in the words of today's psalm, 'the Lord is great'; 'God is great'.

20 October, Wednesday, Twenty-Ninth Week in Ordinary Time
Luke 12:39–48

In the gospel reading, the reason one servant starts abusing his trust by beating up other servants, eating, drinking, getting drunk and making a general nuisance of himself, is that 'my master is taking his time coming'. He was prepared to behave responsibly for as long as he felt his master was likely to turn up sooner rather than later. However, as soon as he began to realise that his master's absence could go on indefinitely, he let go of all self-restraint. He could be responsible for a short period but not for the long haul. The gospel reading is reminding us that being a faithful disciple of the Lord is for the long haul. We are to be standing ready, regardless of when the Lord comes. You often hear the expression, 'it's a marathon, not a sprint, so pace yourself'. The life of faith, the following of the Lord's way, is a marathon. It begins at baptism and takes us through childhood, adolescence, adulthood, old age. Our faith will express itself differently at all these stages of our earthly lives. At every one of those stages, we need to be at our employment, in the language of the gospel reading. We need to be busy about our Father's affairs, to quote the child Jesus in the Temple or, in the somewhat martial language of Paul in the first reading, we need to 'make every part of your body into a weapon fighting on the side of God'. We won't run this marathon, this long-haul race, without the Lord's help but, as Paul reminds us in our first reading, 'we are living by grace'. The Lord provides for us every step of the way.

21 October, Thursday, Twenty-Ninth Week in Ordinary Time
Luke 12:49–53

It is strange to hear Jesus say in today's gospel reading that he did not come to bring peace but rather division. However, the Gospel as a whole suggests that we have to understand Jesus to mean that he did not come with the explicit intention of causing division but, rather, that division was the consequence of his coming. As Simeon prophesied to Mary in the Temple of Jerusalem, her child was destined 'for the falling and rising of many in Israel'. Some would accept him and rise, others would reject him and fall. Early in our gospel reading, Jesus had said that he came to bring a fire to earth, the fire of the Holy Spirit. That spiritual fire would be welcomed by some as a life-giving power and vehemently rejected by others as too explosive and dangerous. If Jesus created divisions, so, Jesus implies, his followers who allow themselves to be led by his Spirit will also create divisions, even within their own family. Some of the great saints did not always bring harmony everywhere they went. They were often perceived as bothersome and troublesome by many. John Henry Newman, who was canonised in recent years, was no different in that regard. His unflinching search for the truth led to many people opposing him both within the Anglican communion and later within the Roman Catholic Church. The gospel reading is reminding us that if we are committed followers of the Lord, if we are earnestly seeking to be led by his Spirit, we won't always succeed in bringing everyone with us, and we may find ourselves sharing the distress of Jesus that he refers to in today's gospel reading: 'How great is my distress till it is over'. At such times, we need to place our trust in the Lord, in the words of today's psalm.

22 October, Friday, Twenty-Ninth Week in Ordinary Time
Luke 12:54–59

In the gospel reading, Jesus criticises his contemporaries because they are not reading the signs of the times. The great sign of their times was the presence of Jesus. He was present among them as someone greater than Solomon and greater than Jonah, yet they did not really recognise the significance of his presence. They were not taking that great sign of the times seriously enough. They could interpret the signs of the sky, which enabled them to forecast the weather, but could not interpret the signs of the times. We often speak about the importance of reading the signs of the times today. Not all of the signs that mark our time are very encouraging. The increase in crime, the rising disrespect for life, the pollution of our natural environment, are all signs that worry us. Yet, the Lord's presence remains as much a sign of the times today as it was two thousand years ago in places where Jesus lived and worked. We can continue to say with Saint Paul in today's first reading, 'Thanks be to God through Jesus Christ our Lord'. The Spirit of the Lord is moving in our times, if we have eyes to see and ears to hear. As one example, in the face of the growing pollution of our environment, the Spirit is moving huge numbers of people to take action to protect our environment. That is one of the more positive signs of the times. As followers of a risen Lord who continues to pour out his Spirit among us, we need to keep naming all those positive signs of the times, all the ways the Lord is moving among us today, even in places and situations that seem devoid of hope.

23 October, Saturday, Twenty-Ninth Week in Ordinary Time
Luke 13:1–9
In the first reading, Saint Paul makes a very consoling statement, 'the Spirit of God has made his home in you'. We don't often think of ourselves as the home of the Holy Spirit. We can be much more aware of our failings. Yet, in virtue of our baptism and the Lord's continued investment in us, we are all homes of the Holy Spirit, or, as Saint Paul puts it in another one of his letters, temples of the Holy Spirit. God has poured the Spirit of his Son, the Spirit of Christ, into our hearts. That continuing initiative of God towards us does not leave us complacent, but it means that we can be always hopeful in

our own regard. There is no telling what good the Spirit can do in our lives, if we give him half a chance. The man who looked after the vineyard in the parable of today's gospel reading had a hopeful attitude towards the barren fig tree. His hopeful attitude stands in contrast to the dismissive attitude of the vineyard owner: 'Cut it down'. As far as he was concerned, it was a waste of good space. Jesus would have recognised himself much more in the man who worked in the vineyard than in the vineyard owner. He was always hopeful in other people's regard. Even when his own disciples kept getting him wrong and letting him down, he never lost hope or faith in them. The Lord who has given us his own Spirit never loses hope or faith in us. As a result, when it comes to our relationship with the Lord, we have no reason to lose hope or faith in ourselves. The Lord keeps investing in us, as the man in the parable kept investing in what seemed like a hopeless fig tree. All the Lord asks is that we keep responding to his ongoing investment in us, never losing heart but always setting our face to go where the Lord is leading us.

25 October, Monday, Thirtieth Week in Ordinary Time
Luke 13:10–17

The Invictus Games are an international adaptive multi-sport event, created by Prince Harry, in which wounded, injured or sick armed services personnel and their associated veterans take part in sports, including wheelchair basketball, sitting volleyball and indoor rowing. Former mine warfare specialist Paul Guest was playing in a doubles wheelchair tennis match in Sydney alongside his playing partner at the last games. He had been seriously injured in the course of his work in 1987, leaving him with neck and spine injuries, and he has suffered since then with post-traumatic stress disorder. While he was playing the tennis match, a helicopter flew overheard and the sound of it left him distressed and in a state of panic. His Dutch playing partner, who was also in a wheelchair, went over to him and hugged him and helped him to recover his composure. The pair went on to win the tennis match narrowly. It was a very emotional moment for all who were watching the match. One man's compassionate touch brought healing and calm to another man. I was reminded of that incident by today's gospel reading. Jesus touched a woman who had been crippled end enfeebled for eighteen years, laying his hands on her. His touch brought her healing and in response she glorified God. Here was a wonderful moment to celebrate, just as the people watching that tennis match celebrated what unfolded before them. However, in the gospel story, the leader of the synagogue, far from celebrating, became indignant at both Jesus and the woman, because the healing took place on the sabbath. He missed the significance of the moment. We can all play a part in making such significant moments happen. We can all be present to people in ways that bring them healing and peace. When that happens, it is right and good to celebrate and give praise to God.

26 October, Tuesday, Thirtieth Week in Ordinary Time
Luke 13:18–21

Both of the parables in today's gospel reading contrast small beginnings with powerful results. The tiny mustard seed becomes a tree, providing shelter for the birds of the air. The small amount of yeast leavens a large batch of flour, providing bread for humans. There is also a contrast between what is hidden and what is visible. The seed sown in the ground does its work invisibly and becomes visible only when the plant begins to push through the soil. The yeast works invisibly in the flour and its impact becomes visible only when the batch of dough rises. Jesus declares that these sets of contrasts can be compared to the kingdom of God. In what sense? Jesus seems to be saying that the kingdom of God comes to pass through actions that seem very insignificant at the time and may not be visible to others. There is an important message there for the times in which we live as Church. In the past, the size and visibility of the community of faith, the Church, was evident to all. Today the presence of the Church is smaller and seems almost invisible to many. Jesus is reminding us that God can work powerfully through what seems small and invisible. Our calling is to sow the seed and become the leaven, in accordance with our gifts and energy levels, and to trust that the Lord will work through us in ways that will surprise us.

27 October, Wednesday, Thirtieth Week in Ordinary Time
Luke 13:22–30

In today's gospel reading, Jesus is asked a question: 'Will there be only a few saved?' He doesn't really answer that question directly. Instead, he uses the question as an opportunity to issue a challenging call to those gathered about him: 'Try your best to enter by the narrow door'. In this way he seems to be suggesting that speculating about how many will be saved is not helpful. Rather than engage in such idle speculation, we should strive to enter by the narrow door. It is easy to pass through a wide door. However, if we are to pass through a very narrow door, we need to be focused, we need to pay attention and zoom in on the door, as it were. By means of this image, Jesus is suggesting that taking and staying on the path that leads to life involves struggle and effort. There is a striving involved. However, it is not an anxious striving, because the Lord is drawing us through that door. The Lord is striving on our behalf. It is his wish that, in the words of the gospel reading, people from east and west, from north and south, would get through that door and take their places at the feast in the kingdom of God. The Lord's drawing us to himself is always prior to our efforts to go through the narrow door.

28 October, Thursday, Saints Simon and Jude, apostles
Luke 6:12–19

Today we celebrate the feast of two of the twelve apostles, Simon and Jude. They are both mentioned in the list of the twelve in today's gospel reading, 'Simon called the Zealot, Judas son of James'. We know very little about them. However, what we do know is that they answered the call of Jesus to belong to that group of twelve who were to share in Jesus' life and mission in a special way. The twelve had privileged access to Jesus and they had a special share in his ministry both before and after his death and resurrection. The feast of these two members of the twelve reminds us that Jesus calls each one of us to share in his ministry in today's world, each of us in our own distinctive way. No matter where we are on our life journey, whether we are healthy or sick, whether we are young or old, we all receive a call from the Lord to share in his life, to be in communion with him, and then to go forth in his name, bringing his loving presence to those we meet. It is a wonderful calling and it can give a truly meaningful shape to our lives. There are times in our lives when we might feel that we cannot do much for the Lord. Our energy levels may be failing, our health may be deteriorating, or the demands on us from others may be great. However, there is something that we can all do and that is pray. We share in the Lord's work by our prayer, just as Jesus shared in God his Father's work by his prayer. At the very beginning of our gospel reading, we heard that 'Jesus went out into the hills to pray; and he spent the whole night in prayer to God'. Jesus gave a huge amount of time to prayer, because he knew that when he was praying he was doing God's work as much as when he was busy serving people. His choice of the twelve came out of his prayer. Indeed, everything he did flowed from his prayer. His prayerful communion with God was at the core of his life. Prayer needs to be at the core of our lives as well, if the

Lord is to continue to do his work through us. One of the primary ways that we respond to the Lord's call is by spending time with the Lord in prayer. That is something we can all do, whether our mobility is restricted or whether we are fully mobile. Whenever we open ourselves to the Lord in prayer, the Spirit will work through us in ways that will surprise us.

29 October, Friday, Thirtieth Week in Ordinary Time
Luke 14:1–6

It can be a great distress to us when people who are significant for us do not share our faith. Parents, in particular, can be very upset when the faith that means so much to them seems to mean so little to their children. They wonder if there is more they could have done to pass on the faith to their children. Yet, while distress is understandable, self-blame serves no purpose in that situation. It is striking that Saint Paul was faced with the same kind of distress, as is clear from today's first reading. He was very troubled that the majority of his own people did not come to share his faith in Jesus. We can hear his distress in that reading, 'My sorrow is so great, my mental anguish so endless, I would willingly be condemned and be cut off from Christ if I could help my brothers of Israel, my own flesh and blood'. His own flesh and blood did not come to share his faith in Jesus as risen Lord and he was deeply troubled by this. Gifted preacher that he was, he was helpless before the refusal of his own flesh and blood to believe the Gospel. In the gospel reading, Jesus too is helpless before the experts in the Jewish Law who refused to recognise that God was working through him in a life-giving way. Rather than recognising Jesus as God's blessing to people, they saw him as a breaker of God's Law. Yet, in spite of Jesus' disappointment with some of his contemporaries, he continued to witness to God's powerful presence through his day-to-day ministry. It was likewise with Paul. In spite of his deep sorrow at the failure of his flesh and blood to share his faith, he continued to be faithful to the call that he had from the risen Lord to proclaim the Gospel. We too need to be faithful to our own calling to treasure the gift of faith we have received and to bear witness to it, even when that faith is not shared by those who are significant for us. At the end of the day, we can only really take responsibility for our own faith. If we remain faithful to the Lord, he will often work through us to touch the lives of others in ways that we will surprise us.

30 October, Saturday, Thirtieth Week in Ordinary Time
Luke 14:1, 7–11

In the culture of Jesus' time, the seeking and gaining of honour tended to be a high priority for people. Being publicly honoured meant everything, whereas the worst fate imaginable was to be publicly shamed. To be honoured was to be recognised by others as significant. People of wealth had easier access to honour. They could use their wealth to gain honour. They might pay for the erection of some building, such as a library or public baths, or the laying of a pavement, and they would expect to be honoured in return, perhaps by having their name carved on the construction for all to see. Jesus is often depicted in the gospels as seeking to cut across this honour-seeking culture. In today's gospel reading he speaks a parable that is aimed at those among his guests who go out of their way to pick the places of honour at the meal to which they had been invited. The most honourable place would have been at the right hand of the wealthy host. Jesus' message in that parable is that the only honour worth having is the honour we receive from God, and God's criteria for honouring people are very different to those of the culture. Jesus declares that it is those who humble themselves whom God exalts or honours. Saint Paul said of Jesus that he emptied himself, taking the form of a servant, and that he humbled himself and became obedient unto death, even death on a cross, the most shameful of deaths, and, therefore, God then exalted or honoured him, giving him a name that is above all names, the name 'Lord'. All who follow in Jesus' way of self-emptying, humbling service of others will be honoured by God. Jesus' life, death and resurrection shows us that the only honour that matters is the honour received from God, and it also shows the path that leads to such divine honouring. Jesus is saying to us that honour is not something we are to seek. Rather we seek to serve others in the same self-emptying way that Jesus did, confident that God will honour us for such a life in eternity.

1 November, Monday, Feast of All Saints
Matthew 5:1–12
A teacher once asked her pupils what a saint was and one of them, thinking of the stained-glass windows in her church, said that a saint was someone who lets the light in. Out of the mouth of children can come great wisdom. Saints let the light of Christ's presence shine through their lives. Just as there are many colours in a stained-glass window, so there are many ways of reflecting Christ. Each of us reflects the light of the Lord's presence in a way that is unique. Grace always builds on nature and, whereas we share a common human nature, each of us has a uniquely personal nature. The particular way that the light of the Lord's loving presence shines through any one of us will be distinctive.

The Beatitudes in today's gospel reading are a little bit like a stained-glass window. Jesus is giving us a portrait of a saint. The different beatitudes could be understood as like the different pieces of coloured glass that make up a stained-glass window. In one sense, Jesus is giving us a self-portrait. He is uniquely the person that is portrayed in those Beatitudes, yet he was also showing us the kind of person that he calls us to be, and can empower us to be through his Spirit. Sometimes when you look at a stained-glass figure you can find yourself drawn to some particular element in it. In a similar way, we might find ourselves drawn to one particular beatitude. Whereas the Beatitudes as a whole portray the follower of Jesus, each individual beatitude is itself a way of following the Lord. Some ways of following the Lord will come more naturally to us than others. We might find ourselves drawn to some of the Beatitudes more than to others. If we give expression in our lives to any one of the Beatitudes, it can easily lead to the living out of all the others. Perhaps you might ask yourself, 'To which of the beatitudes do I feel especially drawn?' Goodness, holiness, comes in different hues, just as there are different colours in a stained-glass window. The beatitude, 'Blessed are those who mourn', for example, refers to those who mourn over the presence of sin, the absence of goodness, in their own lives and in the lives of others; they mourn that the kingdom of heaven is not yet a reality on earth. Such people will hunger and thirst for what is right. They will be merciful, showing merciful love to those who cry out for it; they will be peacemakers, working to reconcile those who are divided. Some people might be drawn to the beatitude, 'Blessed are the pure in heart'. The pure in heart are those whose hearts are given over to God before all else. They seek what God wants in all things. Such people will invariably be poor in spirit; they will recognise their complete dependence on God for everything. They will tend to be gentle, in the sense of not arrogantly insisting on their own way but always seeking God's way. One beatitude always leads to others, and, eventually, they all lead into each other.

Jesus is saying that the people who live out of these attitudes and values are truly blessed. They will know the Lord's joy in this life and in eternity. Jesus is putting before us in the Beatitudes a way of life that is worth our while striving for. We won't always attain it. We will fall short from time to time; we will stumble. All the Lord expects is that, having asked his forgiveness, we keep journeying on. I like the saying, 'every saint has a past, and every sinner a future'. The Lord calls all of us to be saints, even though he knows we are sinners. Saint Paul in his letters refers to all the baptised as saints. He addresses his letters to the saints of God in a particular city, all the members of the Church. We are already saints, in the sense that the Holy Spirit has been poured into our lives from the moment of our baptism. Through the Spirit, we have come to share in Jesus' own relationship with God, calling God, 'Abba, Father'. That is why the second reading calls on us to 'think of the love that the Father has lavished on us by letting us be called children of God', and it goes on, 'we are already the children of God'. God has already done and continues to do a good work, a holy work, in our lives. Our calling is to keep opening ourselves to what God is doing in our lives, by walking the path of the Beatitudes. At the end of our earthly journey, we will come to that eternal moment when, in the words of the second reading, 'we shall become like God, because we shall see him as he really is'. Then, we will finally be holy as God is holy, loving as God is loving, and we will join that 'huge number, impossible to count', referred to in the first reading. I came across a statement recently that I found thought-provoking. 'To be a saint means to live in such a way that one's life would not make sense if God did not exist'.

2 November, Tuesday, Commemoration of All the Faithful Departed
Mark 15:33–39; 16:1–6)
Today is a day when we remember all our loved ones who have died. We all have people we want to remember and pray for today. Our praying for the dead is one of the ways that we give expression

to our communion with our loved ones who have died. We believe in the communion of saints, that deep spiritual bond between those who have reached the end of their earthly pilgrimage and ourselves who are still on that pilgrimage. In the gospel reading, a group of women who had followed Jesus in Galilee and had come up to Jerusalem from Galilee with him, were in communion with Jesus as he was dying. They were looking on from a distance as he hung from the cross. Once he died, they must have thought that their communion with him was broken for ever. Yet when they went to the tomb to anoint his body on that first Easter morning, they heard the wonderful news that Jesus who had been crucified was now risen. Their communion with Jesus and his with them had not been broken by death after all. He would continue to relate to them, and they could continue to relate to him, in a new and different way. Because of Jesus' death and resurrection we believe that beyond death, our loved ones are being drawn into the risen life of Jesus; for them, life has changed not ended, and our relationship with them has changed, not ended. Because of our communion with the Lord in this life, and their new communion with the Lord in the next life, we and they remain in communion, in an even deeper communion, even though it is not visible. Every year, the church gives us this day, 2 November, to express in a prayerful way our communion with those we were close to in this life who have died. We pause this day to give thanks for their lives, to pray for them, and to ask them to pray for us.

3 November, Wednesday, Thirty-First Week in Ordinary Time
Luke 14:25–33

The language at the beginning of today's gospel reading about the need to hate family members so as to become a follower of Jesus seems very strange to our ears. It is a Semitic idiom of expressing preference, whereby if someone prefers one thing or one person over another, they are said to love the one and hate the other. The Jesus who said, 'love your enemies', is not asking us to hate our own flesh and blood. Yet, he is calling for a level of allegiance to himself that takes priority over even the most cherished of human allegiances. He is to be the primary love in our lives. That doesn't mean that we will love others less, including the members of our family. Rather, if the Lord is the first love in our lives, then our natural loves will be enhanced; we will be empowered to love others in the way the Lord loves them. When we love the Lord with all our heart, soul, mind and strength, we will be caught up into the Lord's love for others. The more we give ourselves to the Lord, the freer we are to give ourselves to others in the way the Lord gives himself to them. Jesus is aware that he is asking a lot of us, which is why the parable he speaks calls on us to think seriously about our response to his call, just as a builder has to think everything through before he starts to build and a king has to think carefully before he goes to war, especially if he has the smaller force. Yet, elsewhere in the gospels, Jesus assures us that if we respond to his call, all embracing as it is, we will receive from him far more than we give him.

4 November, Thursday, Thirty-First Week in Ordinary Time
Luke 15:1–10
When Jesus first spoke the two parables in today's gospel reading, his hearers might have thought that the behaviour of the shepherd and the woman was a bit excessive. Why would a shepherd leave ninety-nine sheep on their own in the wilderness to go out looking for one who got lost and then, having found it, have a celebratory meal with friends and neighbours. It seems a bit over the top. Likewise, why would a woman make such a fuss over one of her ten drachmas that was lost somewhere in her small house? It was

bound to turn up sooner or later. Then when she found it, she had a celebration with her friends and neighbours. People would be likely to say that it was again a little over the top. People were probably always losing and finding things in their one-roomed dwellings. In many of the parables Jesus speaks, people seem to go beyond what would be considered the norm. Perhaps this is the point of those parables. Jesus is saying that God is not like us. God, and Jesus who reveals God, is passionate about seeking and finding the lost to a degree that seems excessive to us. Herein lies the good news, the Gospel. The Lord never gives up on us. He seeks us out until he finds us. He pursues us until we take notice of him. He leaves no stone unturned to call us into that relationship with himself that will bring us life to the full. If the Lord doesn't find us, it won't be for any lack of effort on his part. We, of course, have our part to play. We need to allow ourselves to be found. At some point, in the words of the first reading, we need 'to live for the Lord'. Yet, if we do so, the parables assure us that the Lord will be there anxiously searching for us and always delighted to find us.

5 November, Friday, Thirty-First Week in Ordinary Time
Luke 16:1–8

The parable we have just heard is one of the most puzzling of all the parables that Jesus spoke. The main character in the story is a steward who is dishonest and wasteful, as a result of which he is dismissed from his post. After his dismissal he takes decisive action to safeguard his future as best he can. Calling together his master's creditors, he reduces what they owe, probably by cancelling the cut that he would have got for himself. In other words, he forfeited money he would have received to ensure that he received something more valuable, the good will and hospitality of his master's creditors. In a moment of crisis he realised that being in communion with others is more important than money and, on that basis, he took decisive action. Jesus spoke this parable because the children of light, his followers, have something to learn from this somewhat shady character. It took a moment of personal crisis for this steward to realise that human relationships have a higher value than acquiring money through whatever means. We can all get our priorities a bit skewed from time to time. Sometimes a moment of crisis in our own lives can help us to look again at our priorities so as to bring them more into line with what the Lord desires for us. The steward learned that at the end of the day people are more important than possessions, and that is a lesson we all need to keep relearning.

6 November, Saturday, All the Saints of Ireland

Luke 6:20–26

According to the Second Vatican Council's decree on the church, *Lumen Gentium*, 'So it is that the union of the wayfarers with the brothers and sisters who sleep in the peace of Christ is in no way interrupted, but on the contrary, according to the constant faith of the Church, this union is reinforced by an exchange of spiritual goods' (*LG* 49). In the Creed, we profess our faith in 'the communion of saints', that deep spiritual bond between the 'wayfarers', those of us who are still on our pilgrim way, and those who are now with the Lord. The Council speaks of 'an exchange of spiritual goods' between believers still on earth and those believers who are now seeing the Lord face to face. In that sense, all the saints of Ireland are not simply figures of the past that we can look back to for inspiration. They are also figures of the present who can guide us today on our pilgrim way. The Letter to the Hebrews speaks of us being 'surrounded by so great a cloud of witnesses' and assures us that this great cloud of witnesses helps us to 'run with perseverance the race that is set before us'. Today's feast invites us to look to the saints of Ireland as our spiritual companions on our pilgrim way. Very few of this great 'cloud of witnesses' have been officially canonised by the Church. Most are saints by acclamation of the local Church. Also included are those whose lives of sanctity and goodness were known only to their family, friends and parish community. There is a local dimension to this feast. We are encouraged to think of those men and women from our local area whose loving way of life was an inspiration to other believers. They were all people of the Beatitudes. They may have been poor in worldly terms but were rich in the sight of God. Their lives may have been marked by hunger, sadness and various trials and tribulations, but they were at peace in themselves, 'satisfied', and they exuded a deep sense of joy, a sharing in the Lord's own joy. They show us what really matters in life and inspire us to want to belong in their company.

8 November, Monday, Thirty-Second Week in Ordinary Time
Luke 17:1–6
The first part of today's gospel reading has to do with how we relate to each other, and the final part with how we relate to God. In the first part, Jesus initially warns against becoming an obstacle to others on their journey of faith. We are not to undermine the faith of others by giving scandal. We are very interdependent when it comes to our faith journey. We either build each other up in faith or we do the opposite. Saint Paul often called on the members of the early Church to build each other up in faith. We have some responsibility not just for the material well-being of others, but also for their spiritual well-being. Inevitably, we will not always live in ways that build up the faith of others. Jesus is a realist, and in the gospel reading he recognises that we will often wrong each other. When that happens we must stand ready to forgive others the wrong they have done us

if they express sorrow and ask pardon. Sometimes we are the ones who will ask pardon of someone; at other times we will be asked to forgive someone who asks pardon of us. Jesus outlines a way of relating to others here that is ultimately rooted in our relationship with the Lord, in our faith. Here is a way of life that flows from our faith, and that is why we need to make our own the prayer of the apostles in the gospel reading: 'Increase our faith'. Yet the reply of Jesus to this prayer reminds us that we should never underestimate the faith we have. The Lord can work powerfully through faith that is only the size of a mustard seed. Even our little faith can be the wellspring of that loving way of relating to each other that Jesus outlines in the gospel reading.

9 November, Tuesday, The Dedication of the Lateran Basilica
John 2:13–22

The Lateran Basilica is one of the four great basilicas of Rome. The original basilica was erected by the Emperor Constantine, the first Christian emperor. It is the cathedral church of Rome and, so, is the church of the bishop of Rome, the pope. For that reason, it has come to be known as the mother church of Christendom. Before the time of Constantine there were no public buildings called churches. Christians met in ordinary spaces, such as people's homes. Writing to the church in Corinth about thirty years after the death and resurrection of Jesus, Paul says to them, in the words of today's first reading, 'You are God's building ... God's temple'. For Paul, it was the Christian community, rather than any physical building, that was the place of God's presence in the world. In the gospel reading, Jesus points to himself as the Temple of God. He, more than any human being, is the place of God's presence in the world. As individuals and as a community we look to the Lord to help us to be the place of God's presence in the world, to be church, in that sense. We gather in a building we call a church, to open ourselves to the presence of the Lord, so that we can become more fully the Church of God, the body of Christ, in our world. Even when we cannot gather in a building called a church, we remain what the first letter of Peter calls 'living stones' in a 'spiritual house' whose cornerstone is the Lord.

10 November, Wednesday, Thirty-Second Week in Ordinary Time
Luke 17:11–19

The onset of Covid-19 last year made social distancing a reality for all of us. In the time of Jesus, social distancing was always a reality for lepers, which is why in today's gospel reading the lepers who came to meet Jesus 'stood some way off and called to him'. Although they were socially distant from each other, Jesus and the lepers were emotionally and spiritually close. The prayer of the lepers was heartfelt, 'Jesus! Master! Take pity on us', and Jesus' response was immediate, 'Go and show yourselves to the priests'. Having been healed along the way, there was now no need for any social distance between themselves and Jesus. However, only one of the ten lepers, a Samaritan, 'turned back', praising God, and then threw himself at the feet of Jesus, thanking him. While the other nine kept going, delighted with their healing, he alone turned back to the source of his healing, to God and to Jesus through whom God had worked. His turning back distinguished him from his companions. It wasn't just a physical movement of turning around and facing in the opposite direction but a spiritual movement of turning towards God present in Jesus. We all need to find those moments of 'turning back' in our lives, when we stop to consider the ultimate source of all the blessings that have come our way. For the Samaritan, his healing was an experience of God and not just a piece of good fortune. He recognised God at work in his life. He inspires us to be attentive to the ways that the Lord is touching our lives in the course of our day. He praised God and thanked Jesus. The prayer of praise and thanksgiving is a natural response to that deeper seeing which recognises the Lord at work beneath the surface of life.

11 November, Thursday, Thirty-Second Week in Ordinary Time
Luke 17:20–25
The teaching Jesus gives in the gospels is often in response to the questions that people ask, as is shown by today's gospel reading. The Pharisees ask Jesus when the kingdom of God was to come. They want to know when God will come in power to claim his people and, indeed, the earth, as his own. The reply of Jesus might have given his questioners food for thought: 'The kingdom of God is among you'. Jesus is saying to them, 'Don't just look to the future, look to the present'. We can all be tempted either to live in the past or to live in the future. Jesus calls on us to pay attention to the present and, especially, to the signs of God's powerful activity in the present. God was powerfully working through Jesus, if only the Pharisees had eyes to see. God's will was being done, God's kingdom was coming, in and through all that Jesus was saying and doing. The same Jesus, now risen Lord, is working among us today, through his Spirit, the Holy Spirit. Whenever the Holy Spirit moves people to share in Jesus' work in some way, there the kingdom of God is among us. The first reading says that Wisdom 'passes into holy souls, and makes them friends of God'. We can substitute 'the Lord' or 'the Spirit' for 'Wisdom'. The Spirit of the Lord is always at work within us and among us, moving us to make the Lord's work a reality in our own time and place. That is true even of the times in which we live that can be so discouraging to people of faith. Jesus' words remain true: 'The kingdom of God is among you'. We need the eyes to see the ways God's kingdom is among us and, also, the

openness to the Lord's Spirit prompting us to make the presence of God's kingdom even more of a reality among us.

12 November, Friday, Thirty-Second Week in Ordinary Time
Luke 17:26–37

In the gospel reading Jesus mentions the kind of human activity that was the stuff of life at the time and remains so today – 'eating and drinking, marrying wives and husbands, buying and selling, planting and building'. We could easily add a whole host of other activities that are of the essence of living, such as, reading and writing, travelling and shopping, and so on. All of these activities are good in themselves. However, in the gospel reading, Jesus is warning about becoming so absorbed by these activities that we lose sight of the daily coming of the Son of Man, God's daily visitation. We are not being asked to step away from all those activities but to remain present to God in the midst of them. We are being invited to be alert to the deeper dimension of our experiences and activities, to the Lord who calls out to us in all that we do and engage in. The first reading from the Book of Wisdom makes a similar point. The author recognises the grandeur and beauty of God's creation, God's creatures, yet the author is also aware that if we become too absorbed by the grandeur and beauty of God's good creation, we will fail to attend to the Author of all this grandeur and beauty, the Creator. We are to see beyond God's good creation to the Creator God and to his Word, Jesus, through whom he created all things. Both readings call on us to be attentive to the divine depth to everything. We could call this a contemplative approach to the whole of life. It is one we can spend our whole lives growing into.

13 November, Saturday, Thirty-Second Week in Ordinary Time
Luke 18:1–8

Jesus was aware that there was always a temptation for people of faith to lose heart, especially when they found themselves faced with hostility. According to today's gospel reading, Jesus' parable of the widow and the judge was about the need to pray continually and never lose heart. It portrays a widow who refuses to lose heart even when repeatedly faced with an unjust judge who refused to defend her rights, as he was obliged to do. There was every reason for her to lose heart. The judge was a powerful man and she was a powerless woman. Yet, she persevered with her plea for justice and eventually wore down the unjust judge. Jesus sees in the dogged perseverance of this widow the kind of faith that his followers need to have. That is why in his comment on the parable, Jesus asks the question, 'When the Son of Man comes, will he find any faith on earth?' Will he find the kind of persevering faith that the widow displayed or will he find instead that people of faith have lost heart in the face of evil and injustice? The introduction to the parable suggests that it is continual prayer that gives rise to persevering faith, a faith that never loses heart: 'Jesus told his disciples a parable about the need to pray continually and never lose heart'. We give expression to our faith in calm, trusting, constant prayer, but such prayer also keeps our faith strong, especially in the face of hostility, injustice and evil. In prayer we open ourselves to receive the strength that the Lord gives which allows us to face what we could not otherwise face if left to our own resources. As Saint Paul says in his letter to the Philippians, 'I can do all things in him who strengthens me'.

15 November, Monday, Thirty-Third Week in Ordinary Time
Luke 18:35–43

Several times in the gospels we find people of persistent, persevering faith. We have one such example in today's gospel reading, the blind man of Jericho. Once he heard that Jesus of Nazareth was passing through Jericho, he had a strong desire to get Jesus' attention, crying out in his need, 'Jesus, Son of David, have pity on me'. His prayer for help immediately met with resistance. The people who walked in front of Jesus gave out to him and told him to be quiet. Yet this man had the kind of faith that was prepared to break through barriers that others put in his way. He may have been physically blind but he could see Jesus with the eyes of his heart, and he recognised him as God's messenger. The people's hostile response to the man's first prayer only made him pray all the louder. It was then he discovered that Jesus was not like the people who were rebuking him. Jesus stopped his walk when he heard the blind beggar and addressed him in a very personal and respectful way, 'What do you want me to do for you?' Jesus must have known what the man wanted but he gave him the opportunity to express what he wanted for himself: 'Let me see again'. The man's persistent faith created an opening for Jesus to heal him. Having been healed, he gave further expression to his faith by following after Jesus while praising God. Here is one of the minor gospel characters who can be a real inspiration to us. He displays for us the kind of faith we all need today, a faith that is ready to break through barriers that others place in our way. His story also shows us that such persevering faith will be recognised and generously responded to by the Lord.

16 November, Tuesday, Thirty-Third Week in Ordinary Time
Luke 19:1–10

There is a quality to this gospel story that most of us find quite engaging. Zacchaeus is a believable kind of character. There is something about how he is portrayed that finds an echo in our heart. At one level he had a lot going for him. He had a good steady job, which left him reasonably well off and probably with a decent house by the standards of the time, yet there was some unease in him. He recognised that he was not the person he could be and that he fell short of what he sensed was God's will for his life. At different times in our lives, we can all feel that same unease. At one level, things can be going quite well for us, but at another deeper level we sense that all is not as it could be. That place of dis-ease, of unease, can be unsettling but it can also open us up to God's purpose for our lives. Our unease can be the catalyst for action. That was the case with Zacchaeus. His unease led him to do something unconventional for a person of his social standing, to climb a sycamore tree so as to catch a glimpse of Jesus. That step, that literal going out on limb, turned out to be transformative for Zacchaeus. The Lord powerfully entered through the opening that this step created, and Zacchaeus' life was changed forever. His story shows us that the Lord can work powerfully in and through our unease, if we acknowledge it and allow it to propel us in the direction of the Lord who is always seeking us.

17 November, Wednesday, Thirty-Third Week in Ordinary Time

Luke 19:11–28

Jesus spoke the parable we have just heard to counteract the expectation of some people that the full coming of God's kingdom was imminent. They were preoccupied about the future. The parable Jesus speaks direct their attention to the present. The parable speaks of a man of noble birth who went to a far country and who would eventually return as king. However, the preoccupation for his servants was not to be the day of his return but how they could use the resources he had given them in the here and now. Too great a concern about the future can distract us from the present. What matters is the generous and courageous use of the gifts and resources that the Lord has given us for the service of others here and now. This is the approach to life the Lord is encouraging. The servant who put his pound away safely out of fear is the antithesis of this approach to life. In our use of our gifts and resources we may fail and make mistakes, but the parable suggests that failure is preferable to fearful inactivity. In the gospels the opposite of a trusting faith is fear. The first letter of Saint John declares that perfect love casts out fear. When we come to experience the Lord's perfect love in our lives we will have the trusting faith to set out into the deep, knowing that even if we start to sink the Lord is there to support us.

18 November, Thursday, Thirty-Third Week in Ordinary Time
Luke 19:41–44

Luke tends to play down the emotions of Jesus in his gospel. Yet, in today's gospel reading he portrays Jesus weeping over the city of Jerusalem. He weeps because he knows that the city, at least those who rule there, will not recognise him as the visitor from God who brings God's peace. Jesus will be put to death in the city as God's rejected prophet, God's rejected Son. Jesus is helpless before this ill-fated decision that the city will make. All he can do is weep. Earlier in Luke's Gospel Jesus had said of Jerusalem that he had desired to gather her children as a hen gathers her brood under her wings, but they were not willing. There is a sense in which the Lord remains helpless before human unwillingness to respond to his longing for us. There is only so much he can do to enter into a loving relationship with us; at some point he will need our willingness, our openness. He needs our free response, yet the good news of the Gospel is that he remains faithful to us; he waits patiently for our response. Even if it comes at the eleventh hour, he welcomes it. His tears do not make him bitter or close his heart to us; his tears are always tears of love, a faithful love that endures in the face of human resistance.

19 November, Friday, Thirty-Third Week in Ordinary Time

Luke 19:45–48

Religious buildings can be very significant for people. Parishioners have a great love for our parish church. A lot of work is being done at the moment to conserve and restore the fabric. The most important religious building for the Jews in the time of Jesus, and before his time, was the Temple in Jerusalem. It had been profaned by the pagan rulers of Judea about 150 years before the coming of Christ. Today's first reading is the story of the Temple's joyful rededication after the people of Israel regained control of it from the pagans. In the gospel reading, Jesus recognises the value of the Temple, declaring it to be a house of prayer. Perhaps that is a good description of our own parish church, a 'house of prayer'. However, Jesus could see that the focus of the Temple was no longer prayer but various commercial activities, so he drove out of the Temple all who were selling. There is a little warning there to us also. We must be careful that prayer ,and not some commercial activity, remains the focus of our own church building, no matter how well intentioned. This building is about the work of prayer, the prayer of the liturgy, the Eucharist and other sacraments, the prayer of the Church, the praying of the Rosary, the private prayers of people who come into the church, often expressed through the lighting of candles. When we are entering this church, we are entering a house of prayer and the focal point of that house is the presence of the Lord in the Eucharist calling us to prayer. In this place, we open ourselves to the Lord in prayer so as to be better able to bring the Lord to those we meet when we leave this house of prayer.

20 November, Saturday, Thirty-Third Week in Ordinary Time
Luke 20:27–40

In the gospel reading Jesus speaks of 'the children of this world' who, after death, become 'children of the resurrection'. In response to his critics, the Sadducees, who had no real belief in life beyond this earthly life, Jesus speaks of the transformed life that awaits those who die believing in him. What distinguishes the children of the resurrection from the children of this world, he says, is that the children of the resurrection can no longer die. Jesus is speaking of a life in which there is no death. Such a life is clearly of a very different order from the life we now live. Jesus also says that the children of the resurrection are sons of God, sons and daughters of God. As Saint Paul reminds us more than once in his letters, we are already sons and daughters of God in this life, because of the Holy Spirit that we received at baptism. We already share in Jesus' own relationship with God, as the Spirit makes us cry out, 'Abba, Father'. We already have an intimate relationship with God. Yet Jesus is saying that as children of the resurrection, in that life in which there is no death, our relationship with God will be even more intimate, deeper and closer than it could ever be in this life. The closer we come to God in this life, the closer we come to each other. There is always a communal dimension to our relationship with God. That must be true of the life of the resurrection as well. As we become sons and daughters of God in an even more intimate sense, as our relationship with God deepens beyond death, so our relationship with others will also deepen, both with those who are already children of the resurrection and with those who are still children of this world. Our deeper communion with God will create a deeper communion with others, a communion which, according to Jesus in our gospel reading, transcends even the most intimate of human communions in this life, such as the communion of husband and wife in marriage.

22 November, Monday, Thirty-Fourth Week in Ordinary Time

Luke 21:1–4

A number of phrases and images from the Bible have made their way into the English language, such as Job's comforters, salt of the earth and the wisdom of Solomon. Today's gospel reading has given rise to the expression 'the widow's mite'. We understand the meaning of the expression when it is used, don't we? We recognise that what seems like a small contribution, is in reality worth a great deal, because of the generosity of spirit that lies behind it. The widow's contribution to the Temple treasury was tiny. The 'two copper coins' that she put into the treasury were the smallest coins then in circulation. They might be equivalent to our one cent coins. She seems to have given very little, almost nothing, in comparison to the contributions of the well-to-do. Yet, Jesus recognises that, in reality, she was being more generous than anyone else, because the little she gave was 'all she had to live on'. In giving these two small coins, she was giving her all. Jesus understood that the quantity of her giving, which was meagre, bore no relationship to the quality of her giving, which was exemplary. The widow was a type of Jesus himself because, like her, he gave his all. We tend to measure generosity in quantitative terms. We often fail to see the quality of people's generosity if quantity, output, measurable result, is missing. There can be times in our lives when we have very little to give, and not just in monetary terms. Our human resources can be at rock bottom. Yet, at such times, we can be more generous than we might have been when our human resources were at their height, if we give generously from the little we have.

23 November, Tuesday, Thirty-Fourth Week in Ordinary Time

Luke 21:5–11

According to the interpretation of Daniel's dream in today's first reading, a succession of kingdoms will all come to an end eventually. However, these earthly kingdoms will be replaced by God's kingdom, which will never be destroyed but will last for ever. In their day, the various earthly kingdoms looked as if they might last forever. Yet, as each kingdom replaced its predecessor, that kingdom in turn was replaced by another, until the coming of God's kingdom which will not give way to any other kingdom. The message of Daniel's vision is that everything of this world, even what seems destined to last, will pass away, but the reign of God will never pass away. In the gospel reading, the disciples of Jesus are full of admiration for the wonderful Temple in Jerusalem that Herod built, which was considered at the time to be one of the seven wonders of the world. It must have seemed that it was destined to last forever. However, in response to the disciples' admiration of the Temple, Jesus says to them, 'Everything will be destroyed'. Not even the most hallowed religious structure for the people of Israel will last. Indeed, forty years after the death of Jesus, the Temple was destroyed by the Romans. We can sometimes think that the way things are is how they are destined to be. However, it is only God who is the same yesterday, today and for ever. Everything human changes and often changes radically, including the Church. The realisation that the Lord remains the same in the midst of all the change helps us to live with change and, with his help, to manage it well.

24 November, Wednesday, Thirty-Fourth Week in Ordinary Time
Luke 21:12–19

In today's gospel reading, Jesus paints a very dark picture of the future for his disciples. He speaks of persecution, betrayal, hatred and even death. That was the reality for many of the earliest Christians. We only have to think of the persecution of the church in Rome by Nero in the year 64 arising from the great fire in the city that year. Yet Jesus inserts a great light into the midst of that dark picture. He promises to give his disciples the resources they need to withstand the hostility they will experience. As a result, not a hair of their heads will be lost. That same promise is made to all of us. When our following of the Lord, our response to the Lord's call, brings us into difficult and threatening territory, the Lord will always be there with us. In the darkness of the struggle, he will always be our light. He will always provide the resources we need to remain faithful or, in the language of the gospel reading, to endure. Faithfulness, endurance, is what the Lord asks of us, and it is his resourceful faithfulness to us in difficult times that will make our faithfulness and endurance possible.

25 November, Thursday, Thirty-Fourth Week in Ordinary Time
Luke 21:20–28

Jesus paints a very distressing picture of the future in today's gospel reading. He looks ahead to the destruction of Jerusalem by the Romans, resulting in its inhabitants being killed or taken into captivity. In those dark days for the holy city, nature itself will seem to share the anguish of the city and its inhabitants, with disconcerting signs in the sun and the moon and the stars. Jesus seems to be using a very dark palette to paint this scene. Yet, a light emerges against the dark backdrop. Jesus declares that at that very moment when people are dying of fear, the Son of Man will come with great power and glory. His power is not a destructive power, like the power of Rome, but a liberating power, a power that frees people from all that threatens to destroy them: 'Stand erect, hold your heads high, because your liberation is near at hand'. Jesus does not play down the dark, destructive forces that threaten God's people, but he insists that these dark forces will not ultimately win out. There is a greater force at work among us, God's force or power, present through his risen Son, the force of a love that liberates and makes whole. We are all called to be channels of that liberating force of God. We can allow ourselves to be paralysed by the dark forces that stalk the land, or we can hold our heads high in confident hope, in the assurance that the Lord of all is in our midst and trusting, in the words of Saint Paul, that his power working among us can do immeasurably more than all we can ask or imagine.

26 November, Friday, Thirty-Fourth Week in Ordinary Time
Luke 21:29–33

We live in a world of rapid change. We have had great changes in society and in the Church in recent decades. Many people find change disconcerting and unsettling. In the midst of change we need some constants. We find change easier to manage if at least some things remain the same. If we are to come to terms with change, especially very significant change, we need some element of stability. In the gospel reading, Jesus speaks about change, not just change on a small scale, but change on a cosmic scale, hugely significant change. He makes reference to heaven and earth passing away; it is hard to imagine a more radical experience of change than the change Jesus refers to. Yet, having spoken of such radical change, he immediately refers to something that will never change. 'My words,' he says, 'will never pass away'. In the midst of all our changes the word of the Lord remains a constant, because the Lord himself remains a constant. In the midst of disconcerting change we know that the Lord abides; when everything else is moving, he remains steady, and our connection with him, our relationship to him, and his to us, will help to keep us steady when all else seems unsteady.

27 November, Saturday, Thirty-Fourth Week in Ordinary Time
Luke 21:34–36

The response to today's responsorial psalm is 'Marana tha! Come, Lord Jesus!', which is the great Advent prayer. We are on the cusp of Advent, which begins this evening. Advent is a quiet, prayerful season. Today's gospel reading captures the mood of Advent, even though it is the last gospel reading of Ordinary Time. 'Stay awake, praying at all times'. That call to prayerful watchfulness is very much the call of Advent. The reference to 'praying at all times' suggests that we are to be in a permanent state of prayerful attentiveness. Even when we are not praying in any focused way, we are to have a prayerful spirit, one that is attentive to the Lord's coming and presence. The gospel reading warns us against allowing ourselves to be distracted and absorbed by the pleasures and cares of life. Advent is a time for recovering our prayerful spirit, our prayerful attentiveness to the Lord's presence in our lives. We are to 'stay awake' to the Lord's presence at the heart of this earthly city, praying at all times. Such prayer, such worship, is not just an activity for the time that we spend in church. As Paul says in his letter to the Romans, all of our life is to be an act of spiritual worship, in which we offer ourselves to God and God's purpose for our lives and our world. Paul declares this will involve not allowing ourselves to be conformed to the values of this world, or, as Jesus puts it in today's gospel reading, nor allowing our hearts to become coarsened by the pleasures and cares of this life.

If we can 'stay awake' in this rich sense, then something of God's kingdom will become a reality here on earth in and through our lives.